Fundamental Rights, Religion and Human Dignity

This collection examines theoretical and practical issues concerning the relationship between freedom of religion or belief and other fundamental rights, in the context of secular States, from the perspective of human dignity.

As the *Universal Declaration of Human Rights* made clear, human dignity constitutes the foundation of human rights, among which freedom of thought, conscience, and religion occupies a prominent place. As a consequence of the inter-cultural debate that is ongoing in contemporary Western societies, which are increasingly pluralistic, the concept of human dignity faces important challenges in terms of what it requires. The five chapters included in the first part of this book discuss some of these conceptual challenges, such as the implications of common good constitutionalism for the understanding of human dignity and the role of religious freedom from the perspective of Western experiences and legal thinkers. The chapters in Part II explore particular questions involving human dignity and the relationship between freedom of religion or belief and other human rights, for example, how to build bridges between religious freedom and other fundamental freedoms when people make conflicting legitimate choices. Taken together, the book offers an insightful range of perspectives on some contemporary challenges raised by the exercise of religious freedom in societies that claim to be based on respect for human dignity and human rights.

The volume will be a valuable resource for academics, researchers, and policy-makers working in the areas of Law and Religion, Human Rights Law, Constitutional Law, and International Relations.

Javier Martínez-Torrón is Professor of Law at Complutense University (Madrid), Vice-President of the Section of Canon Law and Church-State Relations of the Spanish Royal Academy of Jurisprudence and Legislation, Titular Member of the International Academy of Comparative Law, and Honorary Foreign Member of the National Academy of Law and Social Sciences of Cordoba, Argentina. He is also President of the International Consortium on Law and Religion Studies (ICLARS).

Li-ann Thio is Provost Chair Professor of Law at the National University of Singapore. She was a Nominated Member of the Singapore Parliament (2007–2009), and a member of the ICLARS Steering Committee from 2022. She teaches and has published widely in the fields of constitutional and administrative law, law and religion, human rights in Asia and public international law. She was formerly Chief Editor, Singapore Journal of Legal Studies, General Editor, Asian Yearbook of International Law and is currently Co-Series Editor of the Hart Constitutionalism in Asia series.

ICLARS Series on Law and Religion

The *ICLARS Series on Law and Religion* is a new series designed to provide a forum for the rapidly expanding field of research in law and religion. The series is published in association with the International Consortium for Law and Religion Studies, an international network of scholars and experts of law and religion founded in 2007 with the aim of providing a place where information, data, and opinions can easily be exchanged among members and made available to the broader scientific community. The series aims to become a primary source for students and scholars while presenting authors with a valuable means to reach a wide and growing readership.
Series Editors:
Silvio Ferrari, University of Milan, Italy, Russell Sandberg, Cardiff University, UK, Pieter Coertzen, University of Stellenbosch, South Africa, W. Cole Durham, Jr., Brigham Young University, USA, and Tahir Mahmood, Amity International University, India

Other titles in this series:

Religious Freedom and COVID-19: A European Perspective
A European Perspective
Edited by Jelle Creemers and Tatiana Kopaleishvili

Human Dignity, Religion and the Law
Pluralism and Reasonable Accommodation of Religious Practices
Edited by Mark Hill KC and María-José Valero-Estarellas

Freedom of Religion and Religious Diversity
State Accommodation of Religious Minorities
Edited by Md Jahid Hossain Bhuiyan and Ann Black

Fundamental Rights, Religion and Human Dignity
A Constitutional Journey
Edited by Javier Martínez-Torrón and Li-ann Thio

For more information about this series, please visit:
www.routledge.com/ICLARS-Series-on-Law-and-Religion/book-series/ICLARS

Fundamental Rights, Religion and Human Dignity

A Constitutional Journey

Edited by Javier Martínez-Torrón and Li-ann Thio

Routledge
Taylor & Francis Group
LONDON AND NEW YORK

First published 2025

by Routledge

4 Park Square, Milton Park, Abingdon, Oxon OX14 4RNand by Routledge

605 Third Avenue, New York, NY 10158

Routledge is an imprint of the Taylor & Francis Group, an informa business

British Library Cataloguing-in-Publication Data
A catalogue record for this book is available from the British Library

Library of Congress Cataloging-in-Publication Data
Names: Martínez-Torrón, Javier, editor. | Thio, Li-ann, editor.
Title: Fundamental rights, religion and human dignity: a constitutional journey / edited by Javier Martínez-Torrón and Li-ann Thio.
Description: Abingdon, Oxon [UK]; New York, NY: Routledge, 2024. | Series: ICLARS series on law and religion | Includes bibliographical references and index.
Identifiers: LCCN 2024032218 | ISBN 9781032847931 (hardback) | ISBN
9781032856421 (paperback) | ISBN 9781003519188 (ebook)
Subjects: LCSH: Freedom of religion. | Civil rights. | Constitutional law . | Repect for persons–Law and legislation. | Religion and law.
Classification: LCC K3258 .F87 2024 | DDC 342.08/52–dc23/eng/20240716
LC record available at https://lccn.loc.gov/2024032218

ISBN: 978-1-032-84793-1 (hbk)
ISBN: 978-1-032-85642-1 (pbk)
ISBN: 978-1-003-51918-8 (ebk)

DOI: 10.4324/9781003519188

Typeset in Galliard
by Deanta Global Publishing Services, Chennai, India

Contents

List of Contributors

Javier Martínez-Torrón:	Complutense University of Madrid, Spain
Li-ann Thio:	National University of Singapore
Leonard Francis Taylor:	Atlantic Technological University, Ireland
Hans-Martien ten Napel:	University of Leiden, The Netherlands
Lara Scaglia:	UNAM México
Piotr Szymaniec:	Angelus Silesius University, Poland
Brett G. Scharffs:	Brigham Young University, USA
François Venter:	North-West University, South Africa
Santiago Cañamares Arribas:	Complutense University of Madrid, Spain

Introduction

Contemporary Debates on Human Dignity and the Implications for Freedom of Religion – A Provisional Exploration

Javier Martínez-Torrón and Li-ann Thio

Human Dignity as the Backdrop of Debates on Human Rights

In the aftermath of the barbaric devastations of World War Two that 'outraged the conscience of mankind', the adoption of the *Universal Declaration of Human Rights* (UDHR) in 1948 as an authoritative normative baseline for structuring and legitimating domestic governments was a remarkable achievement. After exhaustive debate over some two years, the final product reflected a consensus among nations of disparate historical, political, cultural, and religious traditions. A secular document by intent,[1] the UDHR was a repudiation of the anti-humanitarian ideology that spawned the racist, genocidal war spearheaded by Nazi Germany, Fascist Italy, and Imperial Japan. It was a determined effort to move away from statist conceptions of state sovereignty, which grounded the legitimacy of a state in whether it was in control of the population of a territory, to recognising that the end of states and governments was to protect and secure the welfare of human beings, in recognition of their intrinsic, normative worth.

The drafters of the UDHR deployed the concept of human dignity as the foundational basis for human rights, as part of the 'faith' in fundamental human rights based on 'the dignity and worth of the human person'. The UDHR refers to dignity five times (twice in the preamble, arts 1, 22, and 23(3)), with the ideal of 'human dignity' carrying the weight of a self-evident axiomatic proposition. It is likely that the drafters took for granted that 'human dignity' would endure as the unifying legal, political, and intellectual basis for the just treatment of all human persons in all countries, as befitting an instrument of declared universal application. They may not have anticipated that many years later, human rights law, and indeed, its foundational principle

1 Johannes Morsink, *The Universal Declaration of Human Rights: Origins, Drafting and Intent* (University of Pennsylvania Press, 1999).

DOI: 10.4324/9781003519188-1

of human dignity, would be at the centre of passionate political and scholarly debates between people who held opposing views about what 'human' and 'dignity' mean in theory and practice. While a universal ideal, the content of what 'human dignity' entails is contested and indeterminate.

Certainly, the framers of the UDHR did not seek to articulate a precise concept of human dignity that could be universally accepted. They knew that such an attempt would be unrealistic and would undermine the very project of the Declaration. Their choice of human dignity, as the cornerstone of the normative architecture of the human rights project, was a pragmatic one. They chose 'human dignity' as a useful term, a vague instrumental notion, which would help to navigate a *via media*, to find an agreement between two apparently irreconcilable positions about human rights: those who hold that human rights are rooted in natural law, often understood from a religious perspective, and those who denied the existence of any transcendent or spiritual dimension in human beings. Indeed, as Charles Malik put it during the first meeting of the Human Rights Commission, the crucial point was not just a discrepancy about the nature of rights, but about the very meaning of 'human', the nature of the person: 'When we speak of human rights, we are raising the fundamental question, what is man? Is man merely a social being, like a bee or an ant? Is he merely an animal with biology governing his destiny? Is he just an economic being, a rational calculator of self-interest?'[2]

This instrumental approach towards human dignity and human rights sought to prioritise attending to the more urgent task at hand, which was to come up with a sensible declaration whose text could be accepted by all nations. The many philosophical questions would be deferred and left open for future deliberation. Indeed, the content of human dignity will draw substance from the political philosophy and socio-political matrix within which it operates as a basic value. The drafters were well aware of this, but they did not consider the UDHR to be the 'last word' on the topic, but rather, an important start to a continuing project. This practical bent is reflected in the often-quoted sentence by Jacques Maritain, a French philosopher and head of the French delegation to UNESCO, who helped promote acceptance of the UDHR: 'we agree on these rights providing we are not asked why'.[3]

The fact is that human dignity was an expression that was well-sounding and acceptable to everyone irrespective of their view on the nature of the human person and on the tension between the individual and society. Its

2 *The More Important Speeches and Interventions of Charles Malik, Taken from the Verbatim Records of the First Session of the Human Rights Commission*, 11–12 (Papers of Charles Habib Malik, Library of Congress, Manuscript Division). Cited by Mary Ann Glendon, *The Forum and the Tower* (Oxford University Press), p. 205.

3 Jacques Maritain, *The Man and the State* (The University of Chicago Press, 1951), p. 77. See also C.M.A. McCauliff, 'Cognition and Consensus in the Natural Law Tradition and in Neuroscience: Jacques Maritain and the Universal Declaration of Human Rights', *Villanova Law Review* 54 (2009), pp. 435–477.

relative ambiguity, its openness to various interpretations, was an advantage from the political perspective, which at that time was essential to getting the UDHR approved.

The notion of human dignity was not new, as it is a concept with rich antecedents. It has been present in various religions and was especially central in the Judeo-Christian tradition. The belief that men and women were created in the image and likeness of God (*imago Dei/tzelem Elohim*), and the understanding of God as the common father to all human beings, were substantial foundations for an egalitarian idea of universal brotherhood. In contrast, in the Ancient Near East, only the king and his offspring were made in the image of God, and they alone had this exalted status, which was the basis of their authority to rule. The Judeo-Christian tradition democratised this idea previously applicable to the king alone, pointing to the glory of all the human race.[4] Indeed, the Christian doctrine of personality, as Carl Friedrich noted, informed the 'faith in the worth of each human being', which was constitutionalist in its insistence 'upon the individual as the final value, the emphasis upon the transcendental importance of each man's soul', which created 'an insoluble conflict with any sort of absolutism'.[5]

Despite its historical distortions in practice, such an idea of universal brotherhood, that all human beings have a spiritual soul and share a common dignity as a consequence of being children of God, was deeply embedded in European culture and spread through the geographical expansion and the colonising activity of European nations since the late 15th century. This notion, even if imperfectly applied, was at the root of the doubts of the Spanish Crown about the right way of treating native Americans[6]; the egalitarian ideal of dignity also fuelled efforts in England for the abolition of slavery, led by the Evangelical Christian Member of Parliament, William Wilberforce, in the 19th century.

A secularised version of the intrinsic worth of human beings was inspirational for many of the Enlightenment philosophers; the vision of Immanuel Kant, for example, was that human beings, who possessed rationality, should only be treated as ends, not as a means to an end. The ideal of brotherhood was proclaimed by the French revolutionaries ('*liberté, égalité, fraternité*') even in the middle of the Reign of Terror. The essential equality of men, and its legal and political consequences, is affirmed in the Declaration of Independence of the United States as a non-negotiable premise for living in a society based

4 Yair Lorberbaum, Ch. 12, 'Human Dignity in the Jewish Tradition' in *The Cambridge Handbook of Human Dignity: Interdisciplinary Perspectives*, Marcus Duwell, Jens Braarvig, Roger Brownsword and Dietmar Mieth eds. (Cambridge University Press, 2014).

5 Carl J. Friedrich, *Limited Government: A Comparison* (New Jersey: Prentice-Hall, 1974), pp. 12–13.

6 See, for instance, *Great Christian Jurists in Spanish History*, Rafael Domingo and Javier Martínez-Torrón, eds (Cambridge University Press, 2018), especially chapters 4–11; Francisco de Vitoria, *Vitoria Political Writings: On the American Indians* (Cambridge University Press, 1991), Anthony Pagden and Jeremy Lawrance eds., pp. 231–292.

on the consent of the governed.[7] Men educated in the Judeo-Christian tradition could believe or not believe in God; they could be implacable and cruel to each other, but they knew that all human beings shared the same nature. This is probably the reason why even the most merciless tyrants have typically felt the need to provide a public and allegedly rational explanation for their terrible actions, even if this was only a cynical attempt at garnering legitimacy.

It would be naïve to think that, at the time when the UDHR was adopted, there was consensus about the meaning and foundation of human dignity and human rights. Quite the contrary, there were profound disagreements over the origins, nature, scope, and content of rights, fuelled by philosophies as diverse as Aquinian thought, Confucian humanism, and Soviet socialism. Nonetheless, both the concept of human dignity and human rights provided some measure of common ground between holders of differing ideological and political views, a common platform, a point of departure on which to begin a dialogue and perhaps cooperation. Political opponents were aware that the future of the entire international community, on how individuals and groups should be treated by states, necessitated having a conversation, which might be fraught with the tensions that arise from disagreement; however, good faith and respectful deliberation amongst all parties could, through negotiation, eventually lead to at least a partial agreement on the key elements of these ideas. The relevant states and other actors would have disputes, but in a plural world, none of them would think of arrogating to themselves the authority to unilaterally declare the 'true' interpretation of human dignity and human rights – or at least declaring it openly.

Unfortunately, since then, much has changed. What is noteworthy, particularly from the beginning of the 21st century, is that human rights have ceased to be a unifying vision of human flourishing and have instead become a form of divisive militant politics, used as a politicised tool to attack and delegitimise a competitor holding a rival viewpoint. Where there is no objective theory of human rights, human rights become subject to capture by subjective political agendas, confusing legal rights with political claims where these are cast as human rights as a matter of political strategy. Disagreements about whether a claim is a right or over the precise content of a recognised human right have often turned into claims of having the exclusive 'orthodox' or 'pure' understanding of their meaning, which justifies dispatching any divergent view as unacceptable without taking the effort to find common ground or engage in a proper discussion. The same has occurred with human dignity, whose ambiguity as a concept allows it to be treated as an empty container, to be filled with the preferred philosophy *du jour*. For example, it may be invoked to support

7 Thomas Jefferson wrote in the American Declaration of Independence (1776): 'We hold these truths to be self-evident, that all men are created equal, that they are endowed by their Creator with certain unalienable Rights, that among these are Life, Liberty and the pursuit of Happiness'.

wearing religious dress that covers the face like the burqa, as part of the right of religious freedom, or to oppose this, as an inegalitarian form of oppressing women. It may be invoked to either endorse or reject a right to abortion, depending on whether the accent is on the protection of the unborn child's or foetus's right to life or on the reproductive rights of the pregnant woman, and to support policies either against or in favour of euthanasia, depending on whether the emphasis is on the state's obligation to protect every human life as valuable or to recognise a supposed individual right to die with dignity and to choose the time and means of one's own death.

Even when it comes to established human rights like freedom of speech, burning flags or holy books as a form of expression would receive radically different treatment in the USA, Singapore, and China. Criticising government leaders or monarchs may be fair game in the USA and UK but would be a form of contemporary blasphemy under Thai *lèse-majesté* laws. Before one can know what a 'human right' is, we must know what a human being is – whether physical, psychological, or pneumatic. As for human dignity, what this composes turns on one's philosophy: one may see human dignity as a universal attribute of personhood in the abstract; one may also view human dignity as an aspect of social relationship, broadly related to an elevated status or rank within a hierarchically ordered society; as a personal attribute or accomplishment, which resonates with the Roman idea of *dignitas*.

The transformation of human dignity and human rights from unifying ideals to divisive forces, which reflects their legitimating power, stems from contests over what they constitute or require. In acknowledging that disagreements exist over what these ideals entail, the appropriate posture to adopt, if common ground is the objective, is not a dogmatic stance, as though one were the keeper of orthodoxy; rather, to accept that differing views warrant consideration and, where possible, accommodation. It is no easy task to secure both core universal ideals and legitimate differences in a plural world, perhaps mediated through a global margin of appreciation. Nonetheless, it remains a necessary task.

One of the consequences of this new (and in 1948 unforeseen) contestation over the key concepts in the UDHR has been a debate relating to human dignity as a foundational basis for human rights: is it a helpful concept and term in our contemporary setting?

At the risk of over-simplifying a complex phenomenon, we can identify two key opposing alternative approaches amongst scholars. Firstly, we may find those who are sceptical about the possibility of reaching a minimum consensus about its essential meaning, and who therefore consider human dignity a useless or redundant notion, unable to serve as a foundational concept for human rights; moreover, the term 'human dignity' would be open to manipulation, depending on the cultural and legal context where it is invoked. Secondly, there are scholars who, while not ignoring the considerable difficulties involved in reaching a minimum or working consensus on the precise meaning of human dignity, still think it is a valid notion that is worth exploring; they appreciate its utility and what it could contribute to the universal discourse on human flourishing and what constitutes good governance. This is because it may yet help build common ground for divergent views about human rights and provide ways to find practical solutions in cases where there is a conflict of rights between parties claiming that their respective right should be recognised as having primacy.[8]

This book aligns with the second position, and not because its authors ingenuously believe that someday we all will entirely share an identical understanding of human dignity, but because we are persuaded that it moves us to pose the right questions and to walk in the right direction. Like human rights, human dignity is, and will always be, a work in progress. It indicates the itinerary to follow; and, following the old mountaineers' motto, we could say that 'the journey is the destination'. We may come from diverse pathways, but we are embarking on a shared expedition. This begins with the acceptance of human dignity as a universal notion, which compels us to recognise that every human being has intrinsic value. Following from this, we are inspired to commit to trying to find balanced solutions to the existing tensions between the value of each person and the limitations on individual rights that are a consequence of living in society. In the words of English metaphysical poet, John Donne, 'No man is an island, entire of itself. Every man is a piece of the continent, a part of the main'. We are human beings and social beings, and there is dignity in recognising all facets of our existence.

This book intends to be a modest contribution to that work in progress. Its chapters were presented as papers at the Sixth Conference of ICLARS (International Consortium for Law and Religion Studies), held in Cordoba in September 2022, whose general topic was 'Human Dignity and Religious Diversity: Designing the Future of Inter-Cultural Societies'. The focal point of the book is the relationship between human dignity and religious freedom. This is, of course not a new theme, as demonstrated by the title of the Second Vatican Council's declaration on religious freedom, *Dignitatis Humanae* (1965), where the Catholic Church proclaimed the doctrine that protecting the religious freedom of every person is a necessary requirement of human

8 For an interesting presentation of the different positions on human dignity, see the interdisciplinary collection of essays *Understanding Human Dignity*, Christopher McCrudden, ed (Oxford University Press, 2013). In an attempt to find middle ground between opposing positions about human dignity, and with particular reference to the relation between human dignity and law, McCrudden argues that, despite the profound disagreements about its meaning and source, human dignity plays an important role in the development of human rights interpretation and adjudication, not by providing a substantive agreed content to human rights, but from a methodological perspective, 'providing a language in which judges can appear to justify how they deal with issues such as the weight of rights, the domestication and contextualization of rights, and the generation of new or more extensive rights' (see Christopher McCrudden, 'Human Dignity and Judicial Interpretation of Human Rights', *The European Journal of International Law* 19 (2008), pp. 655–724.

dignity, as all human beings have the right – and the moral duty – to seek the truth.

Religion, Human Dignity, and Contemporary Challenges of Constitutionalism

The book is divided into two parts. The first part deals with some of the most important themes concerning the conceptual challenges of human dignity and its relationship with religion from the perspective of constitutional theory.

The first chapter, written by Leonard Taylor, raises an important question: how do we avoid the situation where sovereign states are seen as the final arbiters and implementers who determine whether human rights are effectively protected and able to limit the arbitrariness of state power? Such a problematic situation is possibly caused – or at least exacerbated – by a proliferation of untenable claims or 'new rights', an overreach of rights that has conflated rights with interests, against the classical conception of recognised rights, to which states afforded strong protection. In the context of what he calls a 'tapestry (or cacophony) of conflicting approaches' to human rights, Taylor argues that the classical notions of natural law and common good – as the primary obligations of political authorities – may provide valuable contributions.

For Taylor, after the Renaissance, constitutionalism evolved towards a notion of the state as responsible for the public good and later the public interest, typically understood from an individualistic perspective – individual rights within public order. That was very different from the Roman and medieval idea of the ruler's duty to achieve the common good, which emphasised the virtues of the sovereign and, by extension, of all those endowed with political authority, including those who inhabited the religious sphere. As Taylor points out, 'in a world that often relies solely on a liberal understanding of religion and has provided a plurality of approaches to justice, the possibility of articulating the virtues and corresponding duties that appeal to the common good, seems remote'.

Following Habermas (after the 'disintegration of Christian natural law', human dignity is the key to making it possible for the 'egalitarian and universalistic substance of morality' to be 'imported into law'),[9] Taylor affirms the possibility of linking, in contemporary constitutionalism, the notion of the common good and human dignity. In the political context of plural understandings of justice – often universalistic and conflicting with each other – human dignity may be a mediating factor that could, at the same time, resuscitate the idea of virtues and corresponding duties in a world dominated by the commitment to human rights ideology. In this direction, he refers to Jacques

9 Jürgen Habermas, 'The Concept of Human Dignity and the Realistic Utopia of Human Rights', *Metaphilosophy* 41, no. 4 (2010), pp. 68–69; cited by Leonard Taylor in Chapter 5 of this book.

Maritain's personalist project of a common thought, a secular faith, articulated around the notion of human dignity and a 'moral Charter' for a society of free men. This could reach a balance between the extreme individualism characteristic of a society whose political skeleton is based solely on individual rights that are continuously expanding, and the totalitarian collectivism preached by Marxist philosophy that subordinates individual rights to state imperatives.

Taylor mentions that, after the UDHR, states were supposed to legally formulate duties corresponding to the rights recognised in the Declaration, but this has been a neglected task, possibly because of the increasing fragmentation in the perception of human rights all over the world. Religious freedom is a clear demonstration of this. According to Taylor, its conception has shifted from an emphasis on a communal dimension towards becoming progressively individualistic and subjected to various limitations by states and international institutions. These authorities seem to be more concerned about maintaining a façade of religious neutrality than about the contribution that religion and religious freedom – in its collective as well as its individual dimensions – can provide to the goal of the common good. This has led some scholars, like Mary Ann Glendon, to maintain that religious freedom is today, for some, a 'second class right'.[10]

Hans-Martien ten Napel, in Chapter 2, moves along similar lines, focusing on two particular books (by Vermeule and Loughlin, respectively),[11] with a more specific emphasis on religious freedom as a case study. He starts with the notion of the common good constitutionalism as centred on the state, which is tasked with securing the well-being of members of society. It is, therefore, a form of positive constitutionalism that opposes the original liberal constitutionalism, which was negative, given its focus on the idea of limited government. It constitutes an alternative to a model of liberal constitutionalism that has individual freedom and equality as its main guiding values. What Vermeule proposes is a return to a classical notion of government whose legitimacy derives from the pursuance of the common good, and not just from formal adherence to values such as liberty and equality, or from the maintenance of traditional liberal institutions. It should not be, however, a blind return to the past but rather an inquiry into classical political theory that tries to adapt classical ideas to current times and circumstances so that it is possible to overcome some of the functional and conceptual deficiencies of liberal constitutionalism, such as the valorisation of individual autonomy, weak sense of community, and an overtly 'neutral' state supposedly not committed to securing shared

10 Mary Ann Glendon, 'Religious Freedom – a Second-Class Right (Harold J. Berman Lecture)', *Emory Law Journal* 61 (2011–2012), p. 971; cited by Leonard Taylor in Chapter 5 of this book.

11 Adrian Vermeule, *Common Good Constitutionalism. Recovering the Classical Legal Tradition* (Polity Press, Cambridge, UK & Medford, MA, 2022); Martin Loughlin, *Against Constitutionalism* (Harvard University Press, 2022).

values and the common good. (These deficiencies, we might add, are increasingly evident, as the moral quality of politicians and the political culture of the people decline, in part due to the growing phenomena of populism and ultranationalism, in part due to the fractiousness of culture wars and tribalism along ideological lines, which spawns an intolerant form of illiberal 'liberalism' that seeks to impose its ideology through a remoralised state).[12]

Napel then turns to Loughlin's critique of constitutionalism as opposed to constitutional democracy. Constitutionalism is a part, and a valuable part, of constitutional democracy, which revolves around rights, at least in its traditional Western liberal conception. The problem, for Loughlin, is that constitutionalism has ended up threatening constitutional democracy by becoming an ideology, as well as by intruding into the private sphere of citizens and the relationships between them. Everything becomes constitutional in contemporary Western democracies; moreover, with the rise of 'cosmopolitan constitutionalism', the same attitude tends to spread to international institutions. This 'total constitution' also becomes an 'invisible constitution', composed no longer of a set of rules but a set or abstract principles whose authority does not derive from the constituent power of the people who adopted the text, and whose meaning evolves as social conditions change and is defined by a judicial body.

In Napel's view, one of the consequences of that new reality has been a 'rights revolution', an inflation of rights, a gradual blurring of the distinction between rights and interests, which has had an impact on the protection of religious freedom. In the European context, religious freedom is now often outweighed by new rights or interests, especially those linked to the sphere of individual privacy. For Napel, it is significant that a number of scholars have recently suggested that rights-fundamentalism be abandoned and that a richer discourse about ethics that includes the duty and virtues of right-holders should be recovered. In the area of religious freedom, this entails linking freedom of religion and conscience with each person's capability, and moral obligation, to seek the truth. At the same time, the idea of common good constitutionalism goes hand in hand with a clear and strong recognition of the collective dimension of religious freedom, which does not necessarily have to yield to other competing individual rights, as some recent constitutional and international case law seems to suggest.

Napel notes that some scholars fear that common good constitutionalism might have a negative impact on freedom of religion – if religion plays a more prominent role in the state's policies, the freedom of choice of citizens in this area might become restricted. He argues, however, that such a worry is unfounded. On the one hand, in Vermeulen's words, the notion of the

12 See Patrick Deenen, *Why Liberalism Failed* (Yale University Press, 2019); James Kalb, *The Tyranny of Liberalism: Understanding and Overcoming Administered Freedom, Inquisitorial Tolerance and Equality by Command* (Intercollegiate Studies Institute, 2nd ed., 2008).

common good implies 'the flourishing of a well-ordered political community', which in turn comprises respect for fundamental rights, including freedom of religion or belief. On the other hand, in the doctrine of the Roman Catholic Church, which has historically been one of the pillars of common good constitutionalism, the idea of respect for freedom of religion and conscience is firmly rooted, at least since the Second Vatican Council. Ultimately – Napel points out – in this as in other areas, it is essential to understand that for common good constitutionalism, the notion of the common good is inseparable from the protection of human rights.

In line with Taylor's and Napel's reflections on alternatives to a strictly individualistic version of contemporary constitutionalism and its relations with religion, Chapter 3 by Li-ann Thio provides different perspectives in the context of the practical legal solutions adopted in the particular society of Singapore, which she describes as 'the world's most religiously diverse polity', where the state takes an active role in building a harmonious society and a communal life based on a substantive vision of the Good and the good citizen. The case of Singapore is particularly interesting as a complementary view vis-à-vis the first two chapters of the book. While the notion of the common good developed in those chapters is based on philosophical, legal, and political ideas that grew up in a Christian environment, the idea of religious harmony present in the Singapore constitutional and legal order is one driven by a strong, pragmatic government with non-liberal, neo-Confucianist communitarian leanings considered to be broadly compatible with the diversity of religious views that exist in the island city-state. Within this complex society, where the main religious groups are the Buddhists, Christians, Muslims, Sikhs, and Taoists, ideas that relate to human dignity and to religion may be dissimilar, which may lead to clashes. The government actively intervenes to avoid inter-group tensions by emphasising shared values and common spaces, pursuant to relational constitutionalism that seeks the common good of maintaining good, durable relationships between the various groups. The government seeks to keep the peace as well as to ensure religious groups enjoy a reasonable degree of religious freedom to keep their faith, without imperilling religious harmony as an integral facet of public order.

Taking into account the diverse and sometimes ambiguous meanings of human dignity, Thio's departure point is the insufficiency – or perhaps the deficiency – of a constitutionalism based solely on the protection and promotion of individual autonomy, which leads to a proliferation of politicised rights-claims, and consequently to hyper-litigation. The government does not consider harmony in diversity to be 'the natural state of things', and what has evolved in building identity and mediating differences is a brand of relational constitutionalism that focuses on right relationships and not just a rights-orientation, which pivots around individualistic rights-based claims and adversarial legal processes. In it, the notion of a legal system that pursues a well-ordered society plays a crucial role, especially considering that public order is understood in a broad way that implicates the promotion of friendly relationships as well as securing the sustainability of social relations built on religious and racial harmony. The key point from a legal perspective – Thio maintains – is what can or should be the role of law in facilitating and promoting such harmony, which in the West is supposed to arise 'spontaneously' from the ethics of society rather than from legal institutions (a rather naïve supposition when one looks around in current Western societies).

As Thio explains briefly and clearly, the constitutional and legal system of Singapore tries to reconcile the state's religious impartiality, religious freedom, and a notion of public order that pivots around the idea of religious harmony – indeed, the main statute in this area carries the name of the Maintenance of Religious Harmony Act, first introduced in 1990 and amended in 2019. The emphasis is on the preventive function of law, not merely on punitive solutions, which materialises in measures such as restraining orders to avoid, for example, instances where excessive zeal in proselytising activities can hurt religious sensitivities and lead to a breach of social peace. However, as Thio points out, there are some ambiguities in the legal text and its application, such as how to ascertain whether 'religious feelings' are wounded.

Emphasis on harmony is also expressed in the use of non-judicial ways to resolve disharmonious situations; among them are rituals of reconciliation aimed at repairing relationships between people of different religions and beliefs, instead of solidifying social divides through sustained acrimony that a legalistic approach may engender. The so-called Community Remedial Initiative is part of this architecture and seeks to provide, on a voluntary basis, alternative means of resolving conflicts that are deemed to be more appropriate than classical judicial trials in cases of offences or insults to a religious group. The goal is to persuade both the offender and the offended to look for ways to mend a relationship in a manner that is beneficial and satisfactory for all people involved. This could be through the practice of apology and forgiveness, as well as by personal interaction, recognising the other person as a moral interlocutor, which seems more in accordance with respect for the human dignity of each of the parties. As Thio notes, instead of trusting a rigid judicial procedure based on individual claims and possible punitive measures, 'the focus is on the responsible exercise of rights as well as the right reaction in the aftermath of a disharmony incident, in living a commitment to conciliation and friendly relations'. Certainly – Thio notes – law cannot operate genuine moral transformation, but legal mechanisms like the Community Remedial Initiative in Singapore can facilitate positive personal interaction eventually leading to depolarisation, 'which is a prelude to reconciliation'. Of course, the promoters of this initiative are not naïve and are aware that it can be misused as just a staged insincere performance, but they prefer to give citizens the opportunity to restore communal relations, which serves the common good of solidarity.

Interestingly, there are significant points of confluence between the common good constitutionalism inspired by Christian natural law and the relational constitutionalism advocated by Thio, in which she recognises Confucian roots and can observe features similar to those of the Greek notion of *eiréné* and the Hebrew concept of *shalom.* In all those cases, we can identify an underlying idea of humanity and human dignity, where 'individuals are viewed not as atomistic, utility and autonomy maximizing agents, but whole and complex persons with feelings, psychological needs, emotions, rationality and conscience'. This is very different from the radical individualism that is today characteristic of most Western societies, where the legal universe has been virtually reduced to the state and (or sometimes versus) the individual citizen.

The fourth chapter, written by Lara Scaglia, keeps the focus on the need to open contemporary Western constitutionalism to dialogue with alternative understandings of the human dignity of individuals and their relationships with the community. This time, such alternative views have a diverse religious root, Islam. The departure point of Scaglia's chapter reviews the efforts of a number of Islamic countries, in recent times, to propose a notion of human dignity that could be acceptable both for Western countries and Muslim culture. She examines the historical tensions between the universalist and communalist interpretations of *karamah*, the Arabic term equivalent to dignity. The universalist notion is parallel to the Western idea of dignity as something that belongs to every human being, irrespective of their behaviour or their religious or moral choices. Conversely, the communalist version identifies *karamah* with honour, a social status that is based on the honourability of a person's behaviour, in accordance with the values of the community; such honourable behaviour should include making the right choice on religious matters, i.e., Islam.

Scaglia maintains that in modern Islamic thinking, there is a tendency to align with the universalistic notion of dignity, distinguishing it from honour. While the latter depends on the nobility or honourability of personal conduct, the former is God-given and implies the freedom to make choices on religious matters; therefore, it cannot be lost by disbelieving in Islam. According to Scaglia, it is possible to find, in this version of *karamah*, significant analogies with the Christian and Kantian concepts of human dignity.

On the other hand, Scaglia argues that while a communalist interpretation of dignity leads to a blurring of individuality, the recognition of the intrinsic worth and uniqueness of every human being may lead to the opposite, i.e., an exaltation of individual autonomy. This is why she refers to Hegel's emphasis on the idea that the notion of dignity cannot be detached from relationality; without relationships with others, it would be impossible to have a moral sense of oneself. Here, we can note some interesting connections with the relational constitutionalism advocated by Li-ann Thio.

The last chapter of the first part of the book, Chapter 5, written by Piotr Szymaniec, takes us back to the articulation of constitutionalism in the European continent, with particular reference to the understanding of human dignity in Central Europe. Its purpose is to analyse whether it is possible to discern a specific notion of human dignity in the constitutional systems of the countries of the Visegrad Group (Czechia, Hungary, Poland, Slovakia), and to what extent such notion — which is specifically mentioned in their respective constitutions – may have been influenced by German constitutionalism. The German *Grundgesetz* (Article 1) declares human dignity inviolable,[13] and the Federal Constitutional Court has interpreted that notion following the so-called 'object formula', according to which it would be unacceptable to treat a human person solely as an object of state power.

Szymaniec explains how this doctrine – proposed by the German scholar Günter Dürig, who was inspired by Kant's ethics – has influenced the jurisprudence of the Polish Constitutional Court in several cases, among them some concerning abortion (affirming the dignity of the foetus) and biomedical experimentation of a non-therapeutic nature without the participant's consent. Dürig's formula has also been used by Czechia's Constitutional Court, in cases involving the protection of the personal sphere of individuals, such as the autonomy of mentally ill persons and the right to adopt a child by persons not bound by marriage. Something similar has occurred in the Constitutional Court of the Slovak Republic, on issues regarding criminal law, limitations on social rights, conflicts between freedom of expression and the right to privacy, and abortion. In the case of abortion, a comparable approach was taken by the Constitutional Court of Hungary in 1998, which balanced the dignity of human foetal life against the woman's right to self-determination as part of her right to dignity. It concluded that the latter should be given priority in the first three months of pregnancy. In subsequent years, however, the current text of the Constitution of Hungary (Fundamental Law of 2011) changed this position by declaring the inviolability of human dignity and recognising the protection of the life of a human embryo from the moment of conception.[14] The Constitution has also declared the 'dignity of any community of a national, ethnic, racial or religious nature', which cannot be lawfully denied in the name of freedom of expression.[15]

Szymaniec concludes that Germany's Dürig's formula has influenced the theoretical notion of dignity in Polish, Hungarian, Czech, and Slovakian constitutionalism, but its practical consequences have been interpreted differently in those countries and in ways not necessarily moulded by their religious traditions. Thus, while in Poland it was used by the Constitutional Court to protect unborn human life, in Slovakia and Hungary, it was used in the opposite direction, i.e., to justify legal access to abortion.

13 *Grundgesetz für die Bundesrepublik Deutschland*, Artikel 1 (1): 'Die Würde des Menschen ist unantastbar. Sie zu achten und zu schützen ist Verpflichtung aller staatlichen Gewalt' (Human dignity is inviolable, and all state authorities have the obligation to respect and protect it).

14 The Fundamental Law of Hungary, Article II: 'Human dignity shall be inviolable. Every human being shall have the right to life and human dignity; the life of the foetus shall be protected from the moment of conception' [English translation of the Hungarian original, as provided in the web pages of the Hungarian Parliament: https://www.parlament.hu/documents/125505/138409/Fundamental+law/73811993-c377-428d-9808-ee03d6fb8178].

15 Cfr. ibid., Article IX (5).

Navigating the Tensions between Freedom of Religion and Other Fundamental Rights

In the second part of the book, four authors analyse in their respective chapters, some aspects of the relation and existing tensions between freedom of religion or belief and other fundamental rights, with various suggestions about how the notion of human dignity can help deal with those tensions.

In Chapter 6, Brett Scharffs begins by reminding us of something that is often forgotten in the sometimes heated contemporary debates about religion: the fact that religious freedom is at the origin of most of the fundamental rights that constitute the liberal notion of democracy that emerged in the late 18th century, including freedom of speech, freedom of the press, freedom of assembly, freedom of association, and the right to petition the government for grievances. This – Scharffs argues – explains why those rights are mentioned together in the First Amendment of the United States Constitution, together with religious freedom (significantly at the forefront), which suggests an early understanding of the connection between them.[16]

Notwithstanding that obvious historical connection, Scharffs notes that, in recent times, some voices have been raised, making claims against the 'speciality' or normative priority of religious freedom, or even proposing its exclusion from the list of human rights, as unnecessary. This fact emphasises the need for more careful attention to be paid to the specific quality and value of religious freedom and its relation with other fundamental freedoms.

For Scharffs, one of the most important legal and political challenges we have today is building bridges between religious freedom and other human rights. He suggests four ways to pursue that goal: empathy, familiarity, bonding over similarities, and focusing on something the other party cares about. In addition, he stresses the significance of tolerance as a legal concept, which is compatible with other deeper and higher notions, such as respect or love, which belong to the sphere of social and personal relationships and cannot be enforced by law (although, as Li-ann Thio explained with regard to Singapore, the law can design procedures that facilitate respect – at least externally – for the religion or worldview of other persons).

Scharffs refers to 'the generative power of human dignity', which is manifested, among other things, in its role as a dialogue facilitator. Even when people disagree about the precise meaning and legal consequences of human dignity, it helps keep alive the conversation about human rights in conflict and lowers the temperature; in his words, 'human dignity elevates rather than degrades our human rights discourse'. He also warns against an atomisation of the understanding of human rights, looking at them as isolated concepts,

16 This is the literal text of the First Amendment: 'Congress shall make no law respecting an establishment of religion, or prohibiting the free exercise thereof; or abridging the freedom of speech, or of the press; or the right of the people peaceably to assemble, and to petition the Government for a redress of grievances'.

which favours conflicts of rights instead of a harmony of rights that are a consequence of human dignity and contribute to making dignity influential in the realm of law and politics.

In Chapter 7, Javier Martínez-Torrón deals with some aspects of the relation between two classical fundamental rights of the utmost significance: freedom of expression and freedom of religion. These two freedoms are not necessarily in conflict. Just the opposite, in principle, they are supposed to reinforce each other. The right of religious people and leaders to speak about their doctrines in public, as well as in private, is protected both by religious freedom and by freedom of speech. Likewise, freedom of expression also contributes to guaranteeing the right not to be instrumental in the dissemination of a message that some people consider contrary to their beliefs, even if such dissemination is done through very modest channels, as demonstrated by the so-called 'gay cake cases' in Britain and the United States.[17] Freedom of religion or belief not only protects the rights of religious people but also the freedom of non-religious persons to express publicly their beliefs and opinions, even if they contradict the tenets of majority religions in a given country.

Public offences against religion by people exercising their freedom of expression have been a constant for a long time in Western societies and have given rise to frequent litigation in constitutional courts around the world as well as in international courts. Martínez-Torrón analyses some of the key issues in the existing tensions between these two fundamental rights, in the specific context of the case law of what is likely the most important international jurisdiction on human rights: the European Court of Strasbourg. Among those issues, he pays special attention to the issue of the propagation of false information and the manipulation of history as a means to disguise a message of hate speech. Martínez-Torrón maintains that the protection of religious feelings is not per se a part of the right to religious freedom; there does not exist a right not to be offended, and it would be a mistake to confuse dignity, which is objective, with the subjective feeling of offence. However, he emphasises the relation between respect for others and the value of public morals, which is mentioned by Article 10.2 of the *European Convention on Human Rights* as one of the legitimate aims that may justify limitations on freedom of expression.

He criticises, however, the European Court of Human Rights for not having been interested apparently, so far, in exploring such notion of public morals and the conditions under which it could be used legitimately as a restriction on free speech. He also criticises the ambiguity of some of the criteria used by the European Court in this complex area of the tensions between freedom of expression and freedom of religion, as well as the seemingly erratic way the

17 In the UK, *Lee v Ashers Baking Company Ltd and others*, [2018] UKSC 49. In the US, *Masterpiece Cakeshop v. Colorado Civil Rights Commission*, 584 U.S. ___ (2018). With different nuances, both cases, decided by the supreme courts of the respective countries, involved a baker's refusal, for religious reasons, to prepare custom cakes in support of same-sex marriage.

Court has applied them at times, especially in cases concerning hate speech as well as in cases involving insult against sacred persons or religious symbols.

In the end – Martínez-Torrón notes – conflicts of this kind will never cease to exist. And, as in many other areas concerning human rights, putting all the responsibility on the law and the courts is probably not the right approach. Legal instruments, like political decisions, can help achieve a higher level of social harmony (or they can make it more difficult); but this is ultimately a responsibility of society as such, which is partly represented and structured, but not replaced, by the state and its institutions. Law, and litigation, are not the only ways to fight attacks on social harmony and mutual respect. In his own words, 'the pernicious effects of excessive or abusive free speech could be often remedied with a spontaneous and vigorous social response more efficiently than with the use of legal instruments'.

The following chapter, Chapter 8, by François Venter, focuses on academic freedom – usually understood as an aspect or subset of freedom of expression – and its relation with religion and with state neutrality in religious matters, which is assumed by Western constitutionalism as one of the essential features of contemporary states. As Venter points out, the notion of neutrality is far from unanimous; is it disinterestedness, detachment, non-involvement, objectivity, or fair arbitration? How neutral is neutrality? Moreover, 'if the neutral state is required to arbitrate over religious disagreements, on which epistemic constitutional premises is it to be done, and how does this impact on the notion of academic freedom?'

After noting that the academic freedom of individuals and institutions entails protection against interference from the state, Venter reminds us that such freedom is not absolute. In autocratic states, limitations on academic freedom – and on other fundamental rights – are the consequence of subjection to certain interpretations of ideologies or religions (e.g., Islam or communism). But in liberal democracies that follow the idea of the state's religious neutrality, the ideological basis for limitations on academic freedom is more difficult to identify.

Part of the problem, according to Venter, originates from the different notions of state neutrality, as illustrated by the education cases in the US Supreme Court or by the Islamic headscarf cases in Europe. Ultimately – adds Venter – we must accept that neutrality is not a neutral word and implies some subjective choices. The same occurs in scholarship, and not only in the humanities and social sciences but also in the physical sciences, which necessarily depart from ontological and epistemic premises. Otherwise, we would be assuming a notion of neutrality that would include, in Venter's words, 'detachment, disinterest, non-engagement, uncaring blandness and disregard for one's personal convictions – an attitude incompatible with honest scientific investigation'.

On the other hand, argues Venter, if we equate religion with worldview or belief for legal purposes, it is difficult to accept that even liberal states can be completely neutral because their stance on religion is rooted in the worldview or *Weltanschauung* upon which their constitutions and laws are founded. For Venter, if we try to find a common element to all countries in the tradition of Western liberal constitutionalism, this would be 'the firm belief in the primacy of the free and equal human individual ... the optimal protection of the person and rights of every citizen to pursue one's conceptions of 'the good life' without, or with minimal external interference'. This dogma, according to Venter, constitutes the core of what he calls the 'liberal religion'. The consequence is that we often find restrictions on academic freedom justified on the grounds that some scholarship or teachings do not conform to the tenets of liberalism. This is why he proposes replacing the notion of neutrality – which is an illusion as it entails, even inadvertently, subjective choices on ethical issues – with the notion of objectivity, with the aim of finding solutions that take into account all relevant interests and not only those in agreement with the orthodox liberal view about the individual and his or her relations with the state and society.

The final chapter, Chapter 9 of the book, written by Santiago Cañamares, analyses a particularly sensitive area where the contrast between the supposed neutrality of the state can conflict with some religious worldviews: gender equality policies, with specific reference to the context of healthcare in United States law. Cañamares explains that traditional and well-established rules against discrimination on the ground of sex – existing in international law as well as in virtually every democratic legal system – were based on sex as a biological reality that was part of every person's identity. The problems began when the notion of sex, for the purposes of non-discrimination, was enlarged in recent times, by legislation or by the courts, to embrace sexual orientation as well and a self-defined gender identity against personal biological reality. Such conceptual metamorphosis in an area as important as the principle of equality – which in turn is based on the equal dignity of all human beings – is not inspired by a morally neutral approach. This is evident in that the doctrine of a number of religions considers that biological sex as an objective fact should be the point of reference, and not a self-defined, fluid view of sexual or gender identity based on subjective feelings or preferences.

These divergent views between religious doctrines and the law and policies of a state have an important impact on certain areas, such as education and healthcare. Cañamares focuses his analysis on the latter, examining the implications of the anti-discrimination and contraceptive mandates of 'Obamacare' for health institutions with a religious ethos, and their evolution in the light of judicial and legislative activity in the United States. An important turning point in that evolution was the decision of the US Supreme Court in *Bostock* (2020), which held that, for the purposes of the prohibition of discrimination in the Civil Rights Act, sex as a protected characteristic should be interpreted as including also sexual orientation and gender identity. The author emphasises the different legal treatment of religious freedom vis-à-vis the contraceptive mandate in comparison with the anti-discrimination mandate. While broad exemptions from complying with the contraceptive mandate – especially when abortion is involved – have been recognised as belonging to institutions with a religious ethos, the application of the anti-discrimination mandate has been rigid, with obvious negative practical consequences for the protection of the free exercise of religion protected by the First Amendment to the US Constitution.

Human Dignity, Religious Freedom, and the Spiritual Dimension of Human Beings

If we had to identify a *Leitmotiv* in the different chapters of this book, it would be the need to overcome a fundamentalist individualism in the interpretation of human rights by using the notion of human dignity to develop a broader and richer view of the human person in society, which involves reinforcing the role of freedom of religion or belief as an aspect both of spiritual autonomy and the distinct identities of religious communities.

Human dignity, notwithstanding the diverse and sometimes opposing understandings of this notion, is essential for forms of constitutionalism – such as those based on common good or social harmony – that aspire to constitute an alternative to the strict individualism that is spreading through most liberal democracies today. Accepting even the mere term of human dignity helps begin a conversation between conflicting ways of looking at the world, because it implies a recognition of all human beings as equals. Once this is adopted as a premise, the idea of a community where individuals are necessarily integrated comes naturally, and they can then begin then to be seen not just as right-bearers but as persons who also have duties – moral, not only legal – towards the society within which they live and find meaning. Taking the intrinsic human dignity of each person as the departure point entails breaking the asymmetry of a comprehension of individuals as endowed with human rights – which are *recognised* and not *given* by the state – but whose obligations derive exclusively from the state laws and who do not have intrinsic ethical duties towards the community.

When individuals are seen as autonomous islands whose only nexus between them is their obligation to abide by state law (where fundamental rights become embedded) and to contribute towards the financial maintenance of state institutions (they will take care of every social need from the womb to the tomb, with no reason for the individual to be concerned about the other), we end up being taxpayers and consumers instead of morally responsible persons and citizens. At first sight, this implicitly materialistic view of individuals may be beneficial to them, as governments tend to pamper them to obtain their support (and vote). But in reality, when the state establishes itself as the only 'true' representative of society, and natural communal structures are entirely replaced by artificial state structures and this is seen as desirable social progress, the isolated individual becomes more vulnerable, a pawn in the chess game played by wielders of political power. Without a solid societal backbone that recognises and fosters the moral responsibility of people, the state, as designated guardian of rights, can easily degenerate into a leviathan that exploits the weaknesses of lone individuals. There is also a poverty in human existence where relationships are treated as merely transactional, rather than covenantal.

Human dignity is inseparable from the acceptance of a moral dimension in human beings, which implies a recognition that persons are endowed with a spiritual side. Spirituality does not necessarily have to take the configuration of a religion – although it very often does in practice – but it involves the acknowledgement of something unexplainable, and to some extent unattainable, in human nature; something that has the force to overcome our predatory or survival instincts and makes us capable of seeking the truth, the good, and beauty; something that shows us we are capable of having respect, compassion, forgiveness, and love for others. This is precisely why freedom of religion or belief is so important, and so closely related to human dignity. It is the freedom that protects the effort of every person in the search for the meaning of life. It is directly connected with other fundamental rights, such as freedom of expression, freedom of association, the right to privacy, or the right to marriage; however, it cannot be subsumed under these rights, as religious freedom protects the faith and the conduct of persons in pursuit of their own destiny. Our religion or our beliefs define our identity – not only what we *do* but who we *are*. Hence, freedom of religion or belief protects our right to be ourselves, and it is often exercised in a way that makes people understand themselves to be in profound spiritual connection with other human beings.

Ultimately, the redundancy of religious freedom can only be affirmed when the spiritual and moral dimension of the person is rejected, or at least when it is maintained that secular law has nothing to do with it and must ignore it as much as possible.[18] The guarantee of the right to freedom of religion or belief entails many challenges – and the different chapters of this book mention some of them. It would be most unfortunate to treat this fundamental freedom as irrelevant or, even inadvertently, as a second-class freedom, a 'Cinderella' among human rights. It would be to deny or diminish the condition of our shared humanity as *homo religiosus*, that human existence is inherently religious, that this religiosity does not per se refer to creedal belief or institutional allegiances, but to 'our existential drive towards transcendence, freedom and meaning-making',[19] which we share, regardless of our different religious backgrounds or convictions.

18 On the relevance of spirituality for law, see Rafael Domingo, 'Why Spirituality Matters for Law: An Explanation', *Oxford Journal of Law and Religion* 8 (2019), pp. 326–349, also, by the same author, *Law and Religion in a Secular Age* (Washington DC: The Catholic University of America Press, 2023).

19 Todd Dubose, 'Homo Religiosus', in DA Leeming, eds, *Encyclopedia of Psychology and Religion* (Boston MA: Springer, 2014), pp 827–830.

Part I

Human Dignity, Religion, and Constitutionalism

A Necessary Dialogue

1 Human Dignity and Common Good Constitutionalism

Leonard Francis Taylor

Introduction

Situating elements of classical legal thought with the development of human rights in the 20th century has eluded the project of human rights and left it weaker struggling as a 'secular faith' and separated from the classical tradition's concern for the *jus gentium*. Human rights as a political project shaped by liberal concerns in the 20th century, has struggled with the indeterminacy of the legal arguments presented by the cause and remains challenged by the structural bias of the institutions created to sustain the human rights project.[1] However, human rights do have roots that extend into the classical legal tradition and are also bound to a tradition concerned with human dignity, with virtues, and with duties. This chapter proposes to develop how these ideas can orientate human rights to the common good through recognition and provide stability and further coherence to the project again. It is argued that in this process the place of religious freedom and belief is better secured.

The Current Debate within Human Rights

With the conclusion of the Cold War the appeal of belonging to the international community underpinned by human rights law took shape most profoundly with an assembly at the World Conference on Human Rights, held by the United Nations in Vienna, Austria.[2] There was resistance at that time, with a debate over Asian values versus human rights values occurring, and the debate about the relationship of Islam to human rights.[3] One direction from

1 Martti Koskenniemi, 'The Politics of International Law – 20 Years Later', *European Journal of International Law* 20, no. 1 (2009); 'The Politics of International Law', *European Journal of International Law* 1 (1990).
2 United Nations, 'World Conference on Human Rights: Vienna Declaration and Programme of Action', *International Legal Materials* 32, no. 6 (1993).
3 Michael E. Goodhart, 'Origins and Universality in the Human Rights Debates: Cultural Essentialism and the Challenge of Globalization', *Human Rights Quarterly* 25, no. 4 (2003); Ann Elizabeth Mayer, *Islam and Human Rights: Tradition and Politics*, 4th ed. (Boulder, Colo.: Westview Press, 2007).

DOI: 10.4324/9781003519188-3

the Vienna Declaration and Programme of Action (1993) that has not aged well was the assumption that 'the universal nature of these rights and freedoms is beyond question'.[4] Such disputes questioned the secularising of human rights during the period, and remain pertinent to the response of classical legal scholarship.[5] Human dignity represented a cornerstone of the Vienna Declaration, and the preamble stated, that 'all human rights derive from the dignity and worth inherent in the human person, and that the human person is the central subject of human rights and fundamental freedom'.[6] It fell upon the duty of states, 'regardless of their political, economic and cultural systems, to promote and protect all human rights and fundamental freedoms'.[7] The argument that states must in some respect disregard their own particularities and duties in pursuit of this newly ordered project constituted a transformation of the post-Cold War system.

In the thirty years that have passed, we have witnessed a gradual process of de-globalisation with the return to a balance of powers reminiscent of the 19th century international order, and in tandem a deep questioning of the assumptions that a secular and liberal reading of the human rights ideal had entailed.[8] The growth of non-Western powers has coincided with the growth of non-compliance globally, or at least brings the place of human dignity and corresponding weight of fundamental freedoms and rights into focus, with the role of human rights becoming marginalised to national interests globally. In fact, nothing has been more bewildering over the last decade than the fragmentation of the human rights project in light of new competing forces but not so more than from within the project itself. Structural fault lines have come from the fundamental belief that human rights would act as a secular overlapping consensus among increasingly secularising governments and nations.[9]

Human rights institutions were gradually strengthened as the Cold War concluded, with human rights treaty bodies growing in confidence and

4 United Nations, 'World Conference on Human Rights: Vienna Declaration and Programme of Action', 1.

5 Daniel Malachuk, 'Human Rights and a Post-Secular Religion of Humanity', *Journal of Human Rights* 9, no. 2 (2010). See further, Stephen Mulhall, Adam Swift (1997) *Liberals and Communitarians*, Oxford.

6 United Nations, 'World Conference on Human Rights: Vienna Declaration and Programme of Action'.

7 Ibid. 5.

8 See Hurst Hannum, *Rescuing Human Rights: A Radically Moderate Approach* (Cambridge University Press, 2019) 3. There are of course other factors, including the 2008 Global Financial Crash that shattered confidence in global financial regulation. The migrant crisis of 2015 similarly highlighted deep economic and cultural inequalities within Western states and spurred the rise of further populist and nationalist movements in Europe.

9 This concept of an overlapping consensus is common in the lexicon of human rights, for example, drawing on the work of Rawls and Habermas. See John Rawls, *Political Liberalism* (Columbia University Press, 1996) and Jürgen Habermas, *Between Naturalism and Religion: Philosophical Essays*, trans. Ciaran Cronin (Cambridge: Polity Press, 2008).

significance through their reports and observations about the state of human rights around the world. However, even as that is the case, as Sikkink reports, 'pessimism about human rights progress is widespread'.[10] Seventy years after the adaptation of the *Universal Declaration of Human Rights*, Hannum observed that 'instead, human rights are on the verge of becoming a victim of their own success'.[11] Hannum further summarises some of the critics that are lining up and who have reflected on the 'limits',[12] 'twilight',[13] or 'end-times'[14] of human rights, and question the human rights project's very survival. The more generous write about human rights being at a 'crossroads' or 'in crisis', and write that now is the time for asking 'hard questions', examining 'critical perspectives', or imagining varying kinds of human rights 'futures', with many of them pessimistic.[15] This is no longer an academic exercise, in 2015 the UN High Commissioner for Human Rights, Zeid Ra'ad Al Hussein, addressed the Human Rights Council offering a frank and difficult portrait of human rights today.[16] He expressed the view, that with, 'alarming regularity, human rights are disregarded, and violated, sometimes to a shocking degree. States claim exceptional circumstances. They pick and choose between rights'.[17]

Various generations of human rights, from civil and political to social rights, and more recently. solidarity and environmental rights, have led to a concern for the proliferation of untenable claims.[18] Human rights remain a complex modern phenomenon that has become easily articulated but more difficult to rationally defend. For example, Habermas proposes that the 'concept of human rights is a product of an improbable synthesis of these two elements'.[19] Firstly, we have the place of subjective conscience within human rights theory, that in Habermas' view is followed by the 'disintegration of Christian natural law, [and] it followed the justification of morality as anchored in the individual conscience', and 'which in Kant withdraws entirely into the transcendental

10 Kathryn Sikkink, *Evidence for Hope: Making Human Rights Work in the 21st Century*, Kindle ed., Human Rights and Crimes against Humanity (Princeton University Press, 2017) 7.

11 Hannum, *Rescuing Human Rights: A Radically Moderate Approach*. 3.

12 Wiktor Osiatynski, *Human Rights and Their Limits* (Cambridge University Press, 2009).

13 Eric A. Posner, *The Twilight of Human Rights Law* (Oxford University Press, 2014).

14 Stephen Hopgood, *The Endtimes of Human Rights* (Cornell University Press, 2013).

15 See for instance, Conor Gearty, Can Human Rights Survive? (Cambridge University Press, 2006). See also Stephen Hopgood, Jack L. Snyder, and Leslie Vinjamuri, *Human Rights Futures* (Cambridge UK; New York: Cambridge University Press, 2017).

16 Hannum, *Rescuing Human Rights: A Radically Moderate Approach*. 7.

17 Ibid. 7.

18 See, for example, Karel Vasak, 'A 30-Year Struggle; the Sustained Efforts to Give Force of Law to the Universal Declaration of Human Rights', *The UNESCO Courier* (1977). Vasak proposed that the international community was then embarking upon a third generation of human rights, which may be called 'rights of solidarity'.

19 Jürgen Habermas, 'The Concept of Human Dignity and the Realistic Utopia of Human Rights', *Metaphilosophy* 41, no. 4 (2010). 69.

domain'.[20] Furthermore, he argues a second element in human rights is 'the coercive, positive, enacted law that served absolutist rulers or the traditional assemblies of estates as an instrument for constructing the institutions of the modern state and a market society'.[21] More interestingly, he indicated that progress in the evaluation of human dignity is the true achievement of the human rights project, proposing, 'the origin of human rights in the moral notion of human dignity explains the explosive political force of a concrete utopia'.[22] Therefore Habermas concludes,

> [H]uman dignity forms the 'portal' through which the egalitarian and universalistic substance of morality is imported into law. The idea of human dignity is the conceptual hinge that connects the morality of equal respect for everyone with positive law and democratic law-making in such a way that their interplay could give rise to a political order founded upon human rights. To be sure, the classical human rights declarations when they speak of 'inborn' or 'inalienable' rights, of 'inherent' or 'natural' rights, or of '*droits inaliénables et sacrés*' betray their religious and metaphysical origins: 'We hold these truths to be self-evident, that all men are endowed … with certain unalienable rights.' In the secular state, however, such predicates function primarily as place-holders; they remind us of the mode of a generally acceptable justification whose epistemic dimension is beyond state control.[23]

Gewirth has similarly acknowledged how human dignity is the basis of rights and proposes that 'human rights are based upon or derivative from human dignity'.[24] Furthermore, he proposed, it is 'because humans have dignity that they have human rights'.[25] He also observed that 'Thomas Jefferson held it to be "self-evident" that all humans equally have certain rights'.[26] However, therein lies the contradiction in the theorising on the substance of human rights, often relying on a thin conception of a human right that lies somewhere between a self-evident truth and one that would rely on an idea of human dignity to give a more substantive account to negative and positive liberties associated with human rights.

20 Ibid. 69.
21 Ibid. 69.
22 Ibid.
23 Ibid. 68
24 Alan Gewirth, 'Human Dignity as the Basis of Rights', in *The Constitution of Rights: Human Dignity and American Values*, ed. Michael J. Meyer and William A. Parent (Ithaca, NY: Cornell University Press, 2019).
25 Ibid.
26 Alan Gewirth, 'The Epistemology of Human Rights', *Social Philosophy and Policy* 12, no. 1(2) (1984). See also 'Why There Are Human Rights', *Social Theory and Practice* 11, no. 2 (Summer 1985).

Recently, Tasioulas has raised a concern over the conceptual overreach of rights claims to the detriment of core obligations that human rights bring.[27] One argument that has sought to support human rights is derived from a belief that 'the values that ground human rights are somehow importantly distinctive in character'.[28] In his view, human rights, 'even more than the rule of law, have come to play the role of "universal secular religion", purporting to offer a comprehensive ethical framework'.[29] This overreach of the human rights project that set out to establish basic legal standards and is preoccupied with individualistic concerns, cannot engage with considerations such as non-rights-based values, such as kindness, loyalty, and mercy or communitarian concerns of solidarity and the common good.[30] The latter are properly upstream from legal rights and should remain so as values born primarily by families, cultures and nations, or cosmopolitan institutions such as religion and guaranteed as such. However, the modern conceptual overreach of rights has inflated rights with interests, purporting to be an elicitor to every human ill, whereas more traditionally rights are laden with duty-bearing responsibilities. Every human concern that may have once called upon the exercise of the virtues to remedy the concern or direct our human interest, is embedded in the promise of rights. The classical and more conservative view of rights had been established 'as *robust* entitlements to certain modes of treatment'.[31] In the identification of rights, there was a sense that each right had the presumption of being 'inalienable and imprescriptible rights, antecedent and superior to all positive law'.[32] Again to Tasioulas, this classical understanding of rights 'generate strong protections because they impose duties on others, and it's seldom justified to override a duty outside of emergency situations'.[33] Indeed, this reasoning is a clear recalling of the natural law tradition that enumerated a higher law of fundamental rights that could guarantee obligations for duty bearers. This tallies well with Vermeule's proposal of 'human rights without progressivism' that sustains a classical conception of rights in the common good.[34] This argument arises from a recognition that rights so conceived in the

27 John Tasioulas, 'The Inflation of Concepts. Human Rights, Health, the Rule of Law – Why Are These Concepts Inflated to the Status of Totalising, Secular Religions?', (29 January 2021), https://aeon.co/essays/conceptual-overreach-threatens-the-quality-of-public-reason.

28 Ibid.

29 Ibid. See further James Griffin, *On Human Rights*, Kindle ed. (Oxford: Oxford University Press, 2008)

30 Tasioulas, 'The Inflation of Concepts. Human Rights, Health, the Rule of Law – Why Are These Concepts Inflated to the Status of Totalising, Secular Religions?'

31 Ibid.

32 Irish Constitution (1937) Art 41.1.1.

33 Tasioulas, 'The Inflation of Concepts. Human Rights, Health, the Rule of Law – Why Are These Concepts Inflated to the Status of Totalising, Secular Religions?'

34 Adrian Vermeule, *Common Good Constitutionalism*, EPUB ed. (Medford: Polity Press, 2022) 216.

Universal Declaration of Human Rights (1948), and codified in international treaties two decades later had retained a concern for the common good.[35] The erosion of those core assumptions, and the hollowing out of natural law groundings, so evident during those early stages of codification of international rights, has altered the course of human rights.

The debate over origins, foundations, and substance of human rights does little to distract from the normative reality that human rights are formally recognised in international treaty law and substantiated by the agreement of sovereign states. Formally speaking, the political power of sovereign governments remains the last arbiter of the effectiveness of human rights law, even as human rights law's purpose is to coerce state compliance. In this respect, we can find remnants of state obligations that flow back to the origins of international law, which set limits of the exercise of sovereign power.[36] By focusing on sovereignty, duties, and the common good that draw on a classical articulation of the natural law it may be possible to offer further coherence to modern human rights. From the outset human rights have developed as an acceptable grounding for the place of the dignity of the individual within the civil state, the protection of individual and group liberties and claims, and the prohibition of acts contrary to fundamental rights. However, in this very brief and preliminary summary of the context and problems the human rights project faces as a cosmopolitan order, it is worthwhile to consider the contribution of the common good and the classical tradition of natural law theory of duties and the common good in this tapestry (or cacophony) of conflicting approaches. By evaluating the complementary role of duties in relation to the development of rights, we can identify a richer and more complete narrative on the history of the contribution of human rights and human dignity to contemporary law.

The Duty of the Sovereign and the Common Good

Studies of the history of human rights have given rise to a greater understanding of the classical legal tradition's contribution to our understanding of rights.[37] This has revealed both a continuity in the minds of some between natural law and natural rights and a definitive break in that tradition in the early Modern and post-Enlightenment period.[38] Undoubtedly, there are significant

35 Mary Ann Glendon and Seth D. Kaplan, 'Renewing Human Rights', (2019), https://www.firstthings.com/article/2019/02/renewing-human-rights.

36 See for example, Draft Declaration on Rights and Duties of States (1949), General Assembly Resolution 375 (IV) of 6 December 1949.

37 See generally, Leonard Francis Taylor, *Catholic Cosmopolitanism and Human Rights* (Cambridge: Cambridge University Press, 2020), see also John Witte, *God's Joust, God's Justice: Law and Religion in the Western Tradition* (Grand Rapids, Mich.; Cambridge: Eerdmans, 2006).

38 Richard Tuck, *Natural Rights Theories: Their Origin and Development* (Cambridge: Cambridge University Press, 1979). Brian Tierney, *The Idea of Natural Rights: Studies on Natural Rights, Natural Law, and Church Law, 1150–1625*, Emory University Studies in Law and

differences between what had been a natural law understanding of rights, and those natural rights of the 17th century that proposed a subjective, individual, right.[39] More recently, Vermeule has correctly observed that our law has 'all but lost the memory of its own origins and formative influences in the classical legal tradition – particularly the *ius commune*, the classical European synthesis of Roman law, canon law, and local civil law'.[40] In acknowledging the role of duties, he proposes, 'the master principle of our public law should be the classical principle that all officials have a duty, and corresponding authority, to promote the common good'.[41] There is a good basis to emphasise the role of duties in the exercise of government to promote the common good.

Cicero was the first author who defined the public thing as the thing common to all, the thing of the people, a notion that eventually would turn into the common good or the public good: *res publica*, *res populi*.[42] In Zoller's view, the *res publica* 'is what ties the people together; it forms the *raison d'e^tre* of their will to live together, in short, to form a society'.[43] Zoller writes, that by 'investing the medieval kings with a general duty to rule over their estates and people for the common good, the Church changed the nature of government'.[44] In the work of Saint Thomas Aquinas, *On the Governance of Rulers*, he proposes that the *res publica* takes on this new purpose and duty to govern souls.[45] Aquinas offers his study on the nature of public office and the functions and duties associated with the office of the sovereign.[46] The analogy of the beehive is proposed by Aquinas in this work, to reveal that the sovereign who rules do so not by instinct but by reason over subjects, and is as a soul to the body. This analogy is followed many centuries later by Pope Leo XIII who proposed there are two powers working in collaboration because God 'has given the charge of the human race to two powers, the ecclesiastical and the civil, the one being set over divine, and the other over human, things'.[47]

Religion (Atlanta, Ga.: Scholars Press, 1997). Annabel Brett, *Liberty, Right and Nature: Individual Rights in Later Scholastic Thought* (Cambridge University Press, 2003).

39 Dan Edelstein, *On the Spirit of Rights* (Chicago: University of Chicago Press, 2019) 9.

40 Vermeule, *Common Good Constitutionalism.*

41 Ibid.

42 Élisabeth Zoller, *Introduction to Public Law: A Comparative Study*, Brill Nijhoff E-Books Collections: Human Rights and Humanitarian Law (Leiden: Martinus Nijhoff Publishers, 2008) 4.

43 Ibid. 4.

44 Ibid. 10.

45 Ibid. 10. See further, Thomas Aquinas, 'On the Governance of Rulers (De Regimine Principum)', (New York: Sheed, 1938).

46 Aquinas, 'On the Governance of Rulers (De Regimine Principum)' 20. See further Charles F. Briggs, *Giles of Rome's De Regimine Principum: Reading and Writing Politics at Court and University, C.1275–C.1525, Cambridge Studies in Palaeography and Codicology* (Cambridge: Cambridge University Press, 1999).

47 Pope Leo XIII, 'Encyclical Letter Immortale Dei. On the Christian Constitution of States', *Acta Sanctae Sedis* 18 (1 November, 1885) § 13.

The church and state are necessary for each other, and there 'exist between these two powers a certain orderly connection, which may be compared to the union of the soul and body in man'.[48]

This structure of the relationship between public duties and a concern for the common good and good governance present in both religion and the rule of the sovereign changed thorough history, and 'with the Renaissance, the management of the *res publica* was organized according to political and moral standards different from those implied by the notion of common good'.[49] Furthermore, Zoller writes,

> [T]he old notion of common good waned with the rise of individualism. Common sense limited the former 'common good' to a 'public good,' necessarily implying a 'private good'—and the old notion was diluted even further with the shift from the 'public good' to the 'public interest'.[50]

One of the challenges that remains is to identify a coherent political theory for the use of sovereign power in the Middle Ages because this period did not excel in providing systematic accounts of political authority or its uses and abuses.[51] Nevertheless, various disputes over the extent of the power of the prince over his domain, including the lives and property within their territory, was something both discussed and theorised.[52] One assumption from the medieval period had been that sovereign power was circumvented by natural and divine law, which implied that any act of the King that contravened the natural and divine law became void. The significance of this body of law remains, in a quest to discover the nature of sovereign duties and the limits of sovereign power, where there still existed a concern for the common good. [53]

A useful pathway to this endeavour is the literary tradition from the ancient to the early modern periods that proposes the obligations and duties of sovereigns called the *specula principum* (mirror of princes).[54] This tradition gained

48 Ibid. § 14.

49 Zoller, *Introduction to Public Law: A Comparative Study.* 11. See further, James. Hankins, *Political Meritocracy in Renaissance Italy: The Virtuous Republic of Francesco Patrizi of Siena* (Harvard: Harvard University Press, 2023).

50 Zoller, *Introduction to Public Law: A Comparative Study.* 11.

51 Harold J. Berman, *Law and Revolution: The Formation of the Western Legal Tradition* (Harvard University Press, 1983).

52 Kenneth Pennington, *The Prince and the Law, 1200–1600: Sovereignty and Rights in the Western Legal Tradition* (University of California Press, 1993) 203. See also 'The Canonists and Pluralism in the Thirteenth Century', *Speculum* 51, no. 1 (1976).

53 Pennington, *The Prince and the Law, 1200–1600: Sovereignty and Rights in the Western Legal Tradition.* 205.

54 Nicolai Rubinstein, 'Political Ideas in Sienese Art: The Frescoes by Ambrogio Lorenzetti and Taddeo Di Bartolo in the Palazzo Pubblico', *Journal of the Warburg and Courtauld Institutes* 21, no. 3/4 (1958).

that title in the course of the 12th and 13th centuries.[55] Those works span from Cicero's, *De Officiis* (44 BC) to Erasmus' *Institutio principis Christiani* (1516). By the mid-13th century there existed a revival of treatises on the art of government, that gave rise to 'an embryonic political science, based on the classical moralists of Cicero and Seneca and buttressed by the example of biblical, ancient and early Christian history'.[56] According to Catto, the genre of the '*mirror of princes*' began to take form 'wherever stable government subsisted'.[57] In this view, those works were contributions to the formulation of the idea of social order.[58] However, Blythe remarks that his literary tradition 'concentrated on the generic Christian virtues necessary for a good ruler and had little analysis of politics'.[59] Nevertheless, there are few corresponding works that can be currently identified in post-Enlightenment concern for the governance of civil states that might convey how public duties (and virtues more broadly) are associated with sovereignty, which are in turn orientated towards the common good. Curiously, this genre of writing all but disappeared by the early modern period, to be replaced with more expansive treatises on government and constitutionalism. The period of transformation reflected the era when the concept of sovereignty itself had gone through significant change.[60] The duties associated with the good government and administration of ruling sovereigns became concerned with the functions of an elected corpus of representatives of the general commonweal and their exercise of power.[61] Sovereignty invested in the populace, as occurred with the early modern theory of the civil state, implied creating new strategies concerning public duties of the state towards those they served, which in turn shaped relations to religion. However, the underlying virtues that were part of a broader intellectual structure had, we could speculate, been subsumed, with the possibility that the civil state became uninterested in the 'ends' of society, and greater emphasis on the 'neutrality' of the state towards the common good. Unsurprisingly,

55 Ronald W. Truman, *Spanish Treatises on Government, Society, and Religion in the Time of Philipp II: The 'De Regimine Principum' And Associated Traditions*, Volume 95 of Brill's Studies in Intellectual History/ Brill's Studies in Intellectual History (Leiden, Netherlands: Brill, 1999) 12.

56 Jeremy Catto, 'Ideas and Experience in the Political Thought of Aquinas', *Past & Present* 71, no. 1 (1976) 7.

57 Ibid. 7.

58 Ibid. 8.

59 Ptolemy of Lucca, *On the Government of Rulers: De Regimine Principum*, trans. James M. Blythe (Philadelphia: University of Pennsylvania Press, 2010) 5.

60 Eric H. Kantorowicz, *The King's Two Bodies: A Study in Mediaeval Political Theology*, (Princenton: Princeton University Press, 1997).

61 John Locke (translation by Jonathan Bennett), Second Treatise of Government, (Hertford College, Oxford: www.earlymoderntexts.com, 2008).

the conception of individual rights belonged to this process of democratising the relationship of the public to the broader concerns and ends of the state.[62]

This evolution of legal thought on the ends of the state had sought to replace an older historical understanding of classical law that existed prior to the early modern period and became peripheral to its concerns. Detailing the place of duties during this process of change will take significantly more work as this is a history that has not been clearly developed with our modern preoccupation with human rights. What could be said even from this preliminary study is that the period following the Enlightenment contributed to a transformation in our understanding of sovereignty that demoted or replaced the place of duty and the common good in the role of the right and order of the civil state. Furthermore, it may be proposed, that the role of sovereign duties upheld by medieval theories of governance was part of a broader articulation of political virtues in government, evident in the *specula principum* tradition, and envisaged as corresponding with the dignity of royal power. How those conceptions of duty, virtues and dignity became translated into concepts associated with civic power makes for a worthwhile investigation in the history of ideas, and into the history of human rights. The relationship between sovereignty and religion becomes a constituent part of that narrative.

Human Dignity between Rights and Duties in the Modern State

One further consideration is how rights and duties are intertwined, and if we can offer a reflection on the content of the moral and legal duties of the sovereign state, which might, in turn, serve the common good. However, that task is complicated by our advancement into the modern era. One complaint that is offered towards the work of John Finnis for example, is that this particularist appeals to ground justice and thereby the virtues have become undone with the advance of the early modern period.[63] While there is merit in reconstructing a classical account of justice as Finnis does, to reveal how the virtues and corresponding duties fragmented in a post-Christian culture, this view may remain particularist and unresponsive to the modern era that has expanded both the *scope* and *tasks* of justice.[64] Those spheres of justice became in O'Neill's view, highly attenuated towards concerns that are cosmopolitan in nature, as states differentiated from the Church, and the state from society, and society from the economy.[65] Today we think of the sphere of justice as one that consists of a multiplicity of viewpoints, which have given rise to

62 Jeremy Waldron, 'Dignity, Rank, and Rights', in *The Tanner Lectures on Human Values* (University of California, Berkeley: University of California, 2009).

63 Onora O'Neill, *Towards Justice and Virtue: A Constructive Account of Practical Reasoning* (Cambridge: Cambridge University Press, 1996) 26.

64 Ibid. 27.

65 Ibid. See further, Will Kymlicka, *Politics in the Vernacular: Nationalism, Multiculturalism, and Citizenship* (Oxford, UK: OUP, 2001).

numerous achievements including work on human rights, democracy and constitutionalism.[66] In a world that often relies solely on a liberal understanding of religion and has provided a plurality of approaches to justice, the possibility of articulating the virtues and corresponding duties that appeal to the common good, seems remote. However, the 20th century turn to human dignity as a resource common to various universalist conceptions of justice has been translated into the various institutional arrangements that came into focus when those competing claims took shape. Therefore, human dignity may become a further mediating resource to situate virtues and corresponding duties, in a world dominated by commitment to modern human rights. Furthermore, this concern for human dignity may advance a project in line with the classical legal tradition and orientated towards the common good.[67]

In one sense, the return to the classical legal tradition is a necessary and timely continuation of the work of Maritain who contributed to the process of developing a 'common thought' for modern democracies.[68] In his view, his political project did not 'belong to the order of religious creed and eternal life, but to temporal or secular'.[69] Most importantly, Maritain emphasised this '*faith* in question is a *civic* or *secular* faith, not a religious one'.[70] This proposal provided 'a definite advance within the scholastic natural law tradition'.[71] Maritain had gone further than the 16th century scholastic Suárez and had 'argued that civil society was a natural society', and 'in his more extensive claim that the adult citizen in our advanced Western societies has not fulfilled his obligation as a member of civil society by simply designating the authoritative legislator for his society'.[72] In this way, Maritain had begun the process of restoration of the common good to the theory of the civil state in a secularising society that had reinterpreted sovereignty and the place of religion. In many respects, Maritain was influenced by French republican thought but he grounds democratic ideas in the more substantive and classical tradition of law. Maritain therefore argues:

> Take for example the word 'democracy' as the progeny of Jean-Jacques Rousseau understood it, and our plan for civilisation would surely be opposed to that kind of democracy, for it is not through abstract freedom, an impersonal freedom, but through concrete and positive freedoms incarnate in social institutions and social bodies that the interior

66 O'Neill, *Towards Justice and Virtue: A Constructive Account of Practical Reasoning*. 28.
67 Vermeule, *Common Good Constitutionalism*.
68 Jacques Maritain, *Man and the State* (Washington, D.C.: Catholic University of America Press, (1951) 1998). 110.
69 Ibid. 110.
70 Ibid. 110 [emphasis included].
71 Gerald A. McCool, 'Maritain's Defense of Democracy', *Thought* 54, no. 213 (1979) 138.
72 Ibid. See further Maritain, *Man and the State*. 9–12.

> freedom of the person demands to be expressed on the external and social plane.[73]

Maritain reinterpreted French republican thought but only to show that 'one of the essential values included in the very ambiguous world 'democracy' is saved in this plan'.[74] That essential value was the dignity of the person, and the associated personal liberties, which Maritain emphasises against the depersonalised theory found in Enlightenment political philosophy. This was in his view a polity that had left just the individual and the state without mediating arrangements or societies to clarify our duties towards the common good. In his view only progress towards a 'new Christendom' could salvage the dignity of the person from within the various political forms found in the early 20th century, including future approaches to democracy. Importantly, Maritain had further looked at human dignity as problematic because it was liable to be the site of 'the clash between incompatible political philosophies', a theme that surfaced during the authorship of the Universal Declaration of Human Rights. His work sought to rebuild the relationship between the classical legal tradition and that which underpinned the civil state since the Enlightenment.

Furthermore, Maritain proposed the outline for a 'moral Charter' or a 'fundamental compact' for 'a society of free men' that contained the foundations of the core duties that were part of the common good.[75] Maritain extensively lists his moral Charter, which is worth recalling here, as he provides an example of the kind of social order conceivable when a classical and natural law foundation are once again proposed:

> [R]ights and liberties of the human person, political rights and liberties, social rights and social liberties, corresponding responsibilities; rights and duties of persons who are part of a family society, and liberties and obligations of the latter toward the body politic; mutual rights and duties of groups and the State; government of the people, by the people, and for the people; functions of authority in a political and social democracy, moral obligation, binding in conscience, regarding just laws as we as the Constitution which guarantees the people's liberties; exclusion of the resort to political coups (*coups d'état*) in a society that is truly free and ruled by laws whose change and evolution depend of the popular majority; human equality, justice between persons and the body politic, justice between the body politic and persons, civil friendship and an ideal of fraternity, religious freedom, mutual tolerance and mutual respect between various spiritual communities and schools of thought,

73 Jacques Maritain, *Integral Humanism; Temporal and Spiritual Problems of a New Christendom* (Notre Dame University of Notre Dame Press, (1936) 1973) 202.

74 Ibid. 201.

75 Maritain, *Man and the State*. 112.

> civic self-devotion and love of the motherland, reverence for its history and heritage, and understanding of the various traditions that combine to create its unity; obligations of each person towards the common good of the body politics and obligations of each nation towards the common good of civilised society, and the necessity of becoming aware of the unity of the world and of the existence of a community of peoples.[76]

Maritain's thought comes surprisingly close to the ideal found in French republican thought on the need for the state to educate citizens in civic virtue, and suggests, the 'conclusion is obvious. The goal aimed at by the educational system and the State is unity – unity in the common adherence to the democratic character'.[77] This 'moral Charter' or his 'fundamental compact' parallels the Universal Declaration of Human Rights which lists human rights principles, a document he contributed to through his initial philosophical contributions, and also reflect the content of the later papal document *Pacem in Terris*.[78] However lengthy and utopian Maritain's list of fundamental moral values are, they gave substance to the theory of a '*secular democratic faith*' as an adjustment in political thought moving towards a pluralist democracy. More optimistically, Maritain imagined the rejection of class conflict where the civil state had embraced these moral ends. There would arise 'a vitally Christian temporal regime would then teach respect for the human person in the individual and in the people, difficult as it would still be'.[79] In Maritain's view, the essential value of human dignity could be found in the rejection of two political distortions, firstly of Enlightenment individualism, and secondly a focus on 'the people' in Marxism. Two decades later Maritain wrote 'it is no more necessary to be a follower of Rousseau to recognise the rights of the individual than it is to be a Marxist to recognise the economic and social rights'.[80]

Jacques Maritain remains relevant to this debate because his writing provided an early contribution to the conceptual and philosophical architecture of our modern understanding of the common good in the secular civil state. Though his Personalist theory has received criticism within Integralist circles, his concern for the dignity of the human person as a foundation for a social philosophy that could inform human rights, remains a contemporary ideal.[81] Maritain's theory of the person sought to navigate between two temptations

76 Ibid. 112.
77 Ibid. 112.
78 UNESCO, 'Human Rights: Comments and Interpretations (with Introduction by Jacques Maritain)', (Paris: UNESCO, 25 July 1949). See also Pope John XXIII, 'Pacem in Terris', *Acta Apostolicae Sedis* 55 (1963) §8–30. See further Leonard Francis Taylor, *Catholic Cosmopolitanism and Human Rights* (Cambridge: Cambridge University Press, 2020) 205.
79 Maritain, *Man and the State*. 112.
80 Ibid. 105.
81 Jacques Maritain, *The Person and the Common Good* (Notre Dame, IN: University of Notre Dame Press, 1966).

as he saw it, that of the totalitarian state and that of the sovereignty and liberty of the individual.[82] Both 19th century liberal individualism and the then development of authoritarian states or exclusively communal conceptions of society to the further detriment of human dignity led to his further reflections on the person and the common good.[83] In this manner, we find in Maritain a detailed study of Thomistic personalism that sought to avoid those excesses. An emphasis on the common good becomes the natural end to which the dignity of the person is ordered, distinct from private goods that are nevertheless unsubordinated to that end. The complexity of this argument finds its justification in the liberty and dignity of the person, who in this classical thesis articulated by Aquinas, is reconciled by a unified vision belonging to both the person and their place in a divinely ordered world.[84] The argument presented by Maritain is at once both concerned with metaphysics, which gives the modern mind pause for thought, and practical ethics that might concern itself with the life of the city.[85] Those transcendent goods that include a concern for contemplation and the beatific vision, are in Martian's view common to every human person and constitute aspects of their dignity. By force of application of the norms associated with the right ordering of the *polis*, we find the various virtues that belong to each person bind each to the 'goods that are common among friends'.[86]

Human Dignity and Duties

We have seen that human dignity in the view of Habermas was the conceptual hinge that could provide a foundation for human rights. However, he argued that 'inalienable' rights, of 'inherent' or 'natural' rights, are merely placeholders for that which may be outside state control.[87] Conversely, Maritain had argued for the significance of human dignity but had viewed the rights and liberties of the human person in the context of the common good.[88] The post-Cold War intellectual environment fragmented our understanding of human rights, from one that viewed those rights in the context of human dignity and the common good, to an environment where human dignity remained but the context had been significantly changed. We may view the gradual re-evaluation of religious freedom, an observation Glendon made over a decade

82 Ibid. 11.
83 Ibid. 12.
84 Ibid. 20.
85 Ibid. 28. See more broadly Malcom Schofield, *The Stoic Idea of the City* (Chicago: University of Chicago Press, 1999).
86 Maritain, *The Person and the Common Good*. 21.
87 Habermas, 'The Concept of Human Dignity and the Realistic Utopia of Human Rights', 68.
88 Maritain, *Man and the State*. 112.

ago, as part of this change in our understanding of basic liberties.[89] In the era of Maritain, and the period of the drafting of the *Universal Declaration of Human Rights*, human liberties were still considered by many as belonging to ordinances of reason ordered to the common good.[90] The freedoms of the Declaration included substantive accounts of the 'inherent dignity and of equal and inalienable rights of members of the human family' and inferred a concern for duties towards the common good.[91]

The Universal Declaration of Human Rights also provided us with the first modern articulation of freedom of religion and the Declaration remains a 'significant landmark in the protection of international human rights'.[92] The Declaration developed out of a response to the atrocities of World War II and gives particular emphasis to Freedom of Religion because of the multiple attacks on religious communities during that war.[93] In Morsink's view, the states who authored the Declaration had corresponding duties in mind when they drafted the proposal.[94] They had acknowledged that while the Declaration would be limited to the formulation of overarching principles related to human rights, there was the presumption that corresponding duties should be formulated in a future legal instrument.[95] Obligations rested on states to provide the correlative duties to the rights established in the Declaration, as expressed in the two international covenants adopted in 1966 and came into force in 1976.[96] While it was not believed necessary to articulate the duties there was a sense that the exercise of sovereignty would require responding to the rights set out in the

89 Mary Ann Glendon, 'Religious Freedom – a Second-Class Right (Harold J. Berman Lecture)', *Emory Law Journal* 61 (2011–2012) 971–990.

90 Claudia Dangond Gibsone, 'The Influence of the Declaration of Bogotá on the Universal Declaration of Human Rights', in *Intercultural Dialogue and Human Rights*, ed. Luigi Bonanate, Roberto Papini, and William Sweet, Cultural Heritage and Contemporary Change. Culture and Values (Washington, D.C.: The Council for Research in Values and Philosophy, 2011). See also Mary Ann Glendon, 'The Forgotten Crucible: The Latin American Influence on the Universal Human Rights Idea', *Harvard Human Rights Journal* 16, no. Spring (2003).

91 See Article 29 that details 'everyone has duties to the community in which alone the free and full development of his personality is possible', in *Universal Declaration of Human Rights*, GA Res 217A (III), UN Doc A/810 (10 December 1948). For commentary on Article 29, see Torkel Opsahl and Vojin Dimitrijevic, 'Articles 29 and Articles 30', in *The Universal Declaration of Human Rights: A Common Standard of Achievement*, ed. Guðmundur S. Alfreðsson and Asbjørn Eide (Netherlands: Martinus Nijhoff Publishers, 1999) 633. See also Johannes Morsink, *Inherent Human Rights: Philosophical Roots of the Universal Declaration* (Pennsylvania: University of Pennsylvania, 2009) 40–46.

92 *Universal Declaration of Human Rights*, (10 December 1948). See Peter Cumper, 'Religion, Belief and International Human Rights in the Twenty-First Century', in S. Joseph and A. McBeth, *Research Handbook on International Human Rights Law* (Edward Elgar, 2010) 469.

93 Johannes Morsink, *The Universal Declaration of Human Rights: Origins, Drafting, and Intent* (Philadelphia: Univ of Pennsylvania Press, 1999) 36–91.

94 Morsink, *Inherent Human Rights: Philosophical Roots of the Universal Declaration*. 41.

95 Ibid. 41.

96 Ibid. 41.

Declaration with an additional concern for the common good. Interestingly, the state could still concern itself with the virtues of good government historically associated with the common good, and so well expressed in the medieval and early modern period. However, the state could not concern itself completely with the corresponding duties similarly grounded in human dignity where this might demand an authoritative articulation of the common good. It was not a satisfactory compromise and continues to lead to various forms of discord over the content of rights and human liberty. Freedom of religion, as an expression of various rights and duties, is uniquely caught in the intersection of those concerns. Rights and duties associated with religious freedom as fundamental claims associated with human dignity, are often interpreted solely as individual concerns directed to individual autonomy. However, in the classical legal tradition, those self-same religious claims can also be interpreted in the light of duties that are responses to the demands of the common good. The content of those claims that are viewed as 'inalienable' rights, of 'inherent' or 'natural' rights become contested in relation to the duties of states. The self-evident nature of those rights is often more clearly evident through the lens of moral duties but became mired in controversy in the confusion of the conceptual overreach of rights claims to the detriment of core obligations belonging to core rights.

Conclusion

This chapter has sought to contribute some of the research necessary to argue that concern for duties and the common good related to the exercise of sovereignty and government are frequently absent from our conversation on human rights, and thereby we lose an interpretive framework previously located in the classical legal tradition. This initial argument proposes that the classical tradition that embraces natural law jurisprudence can elevate the role of duties and the common good and thereby support fundamental rights in a challenging period for the human rights project.

2 Common Good Constitutionalism and Religious Freedom

Hans-Martien ten Napel

Introduction

The spring of 2022 witnessed the publication of a somewhat less conventional book on constitutionalism: Harvard Professor of Constitutional Law Adrian Vermeule's *Common Good Constitutionalism.*[1] The reason why the book is somewhat less conventional follows from its subtitle: *Recovering the Classical Legal Tradition.* Anyone in this day and age who makes a case for revitalizing the classical legal tradition automatically falls outside the mainstream by doing so. By the classical legal tradition, Vermeule means the 'ius commune', that is, the Roman-canon law as it and customary law have shaped Europe and England since the 11th century and formed the basis for American law.

In addition to Vermeule's book, another noteworthy book on constitutionalism, or rather, against constitutionalism, was published in the spring of the same year. Indeed, that is the title of Professor of Public Law at the London School of Economics and Political Science Martin Loughlin's new book, *Against Constitutionalism.*[2] In what follows, I will discuss both in connection with each other, thereby (hopefully) shedding more light on the potential usefulness and relevance of Vermeule's book for constitutionalism and religious freedom in a European context in particular.

The reason for zooming in on religious freedom is that this right can be considered vital to constitutional democracy. For the classical variant of constitutional democracy that Loughlin identifies, this is, in a sense, self-evident. After all, it was more or less 'invented' 250 years ago to optimize the experience of religious freedom.

Even in the contemporary, more liberal variant of constitutional democracy, however, religious freedom is still theoretically important. After all, because the government legislates morality less, or at least differently than in the classical variant, it is even more critical that a constitutional and democratic

1 Adrian Vermeule, *Common Good Constitutionalism. Recovering the Classical Legal Tradition* (Cambridge, UK & Medford, MA: Polity Press, 2022).
2 Martin Loughlin, *Against Constitutionalism* (Cambridge, MA: Harvard University Press, 2022).

DOI: 10.4324/9781003519188-4

ethos among the population continues to be nurtured from within the society itself. As I have argued elsewhere,[3] building on work by German jurist Ernst-Wolfgang Böckenförde, among others, freedom of religion can contribute to this.

The aim of looking at the European context is, as said, to examine the usefulness and relevance of the book *Common Good Constitutionalism* outside the United States on which it focuses. This is done on the express assumption that such usefulness and relevance exist, as it is the birthplace of the classical legal tradition. Much of Loughlin's critique of constitutionalism also applies to Europe in particular.

The concern is regularly expressed that returning to common good constitutionalism will exert a restrictive influence on religious freedom above all else. Hence, it may make sense to examine the current state of liberal religious freedom conversely. Since the picture emerging from this quick scan could be brighter, the following section asks what can be done to improve it.

In consecutive sections, the chapter will address three questions: what does Loughlin have against constitutionalism? Second, how does religious freedom fare under this constitutionalism? Third, what potential contribution can common good constitutionalism make to overcoming the problems with constitutionalism in general and those with religious freedom in particular? This third question superfluously already shows that those problems exist.

I will begin, however, by setting out what Vermeule understands by common good constitutionalism. The chapter concludes with some preliminary conclusions. Most importantly, adapting political and theological thought to modernity still needs to be completed. The prevailing view, especially regarding constitutionalism, is that this would be the case. Therefore, what happened more than 250 years ago belongs definitively to the past. To the credit of Vermeule's book, he punctures this myth.

That the effort to restore the classical legal tradition certainly also raises questions is inevitable. Vermeule rightly argues that it is necessary to 'translate' classical notions to current times and circumstances. '[L]ooking backward so that we may go forward', the author calls it. Or: *reculer pour mieux sauter* (p. 5).[4] It is the conviction from which this chapter is written that there is no escaping this for those who care about constitutional democracy. Religious freedom, moreover, constitutes an essential but also complex case study in this regard.

3 Hans-Martien ten Napel, *Constitutionalism, Democracy, and Religious Freedom. To Be Fully Human* (New York & London: Routledge, 2017).

4 Vermeule, *Common Good Constitutionalism*, p. 5.

What Is Common Good Constitutionalism?

In his book *The Principles of Constitutionalism* (2018), Oxford Professor of Constitutional Law and Theory Nicholas Barber distinguishes between negative and positive constitutionalism. Negative constitutionalism, according to him, is much the prevailing view. In it, constitutionalism is equivalent to 'limited government'. He, however, adheres to positive constitutionalism, which he calls a 'richer, more attractive' variant of the doctrine. Moreover, this variant has ancient papers, for already 'Aristotle drew the defining purpose of the state broadly: it exists to advance the well-being of its members'.[5]

Such a classical conception of constitutionalism, which, after Adrian Vermeule's book, can also be referred to as common good constitutionalism, represents an alternative to liberal constitutionalism. Originally, liberal constitutionalism equalled negative constitutionalism. It has since become positive, with liberty and equality as its guiding values.

Common good constitutionalism differs from contemporary liberal constitutionalism in that instead of freedom and equality, as its name implies, it focuses on promoting the common good. In this regard, the common good can be described, in Vermeule's words, as 'the flourishing of a well-ordered political community'.[6] That forms a sharp contrast to the contemporary liberal pursuit of, in practice, individual autonomy. As evidenced by earlier work,[7] Barber emphatically sees the state, following Aristotle, as a 'social group'. That gives citizens an essential role in the realization of the common good. It is no coincidence that he also identifies civil society and subsidiarity as principles of constitutionalism, alongside sovereignty, separation of powers, the 'rule of law', and democracy. Vermeule could not agree more.[8]

It is possible to view common good constitutionalism as a form of so-called post-liberalism. Philosopher Kevin Vallier distinguishes between liberalism, post-liberalism, and religious anti-liberalism. In doing so, he defines post-liberals as people who 'reject liberal values, though most accept liberal institutions such as constitutional democracy'.[9] Vallier adds, 'They are not yet enemies of liberal order. They're merely on the fence'.[10] His book is about religious anti-liberalism, mainly Catholic integralism. Anti-liberals 'seek to alter or abolish liberal orders, and they oppose all liberal political and ethical theories'. Catholic integralists, for example, believe'that governments must

5 N.W. Barber, *The Principles of Constitutionalism* (Oxford: Oxford University Press, 2018), p. 5.

6 Vermeule, *Common Good Constitutionalism*, p. 7.

7 N.W. Barber, *The Constitutional State* (Oxford: Oxford University Press, 2010).

8 Cf. Adrian Vermeule in his review of Barber's book: 'Echoes of the *Ius Commune*', 66 *The American Journal of Jurisprudence* 1 (2021): 85–96.

9 Kevin Vallier, *All the Kingdoms of the World: On Radical Religious Alternatives to Liberalism* (Oxford: Oxford University Press, 2023), p. 6.

10 Ibid.

secure the earthly and heavenly common good'.[11] Although Vallier deals extensively with Vermeule in his book, such integralism is absent in *Common Good Constitutionalism*.[12]

Post-liberalism, on the other hand, explicitly limits itself to the earthly common good. In light of the distinctions made by Vallier, the critical question, according to him, concerns the relationship between institutional and social liberalism. Specifically, does institutional liberalism sooner or later inevitably lead to social liberalism, or is it possible to continue to adhere to the former without receiving the latter in the process?[13]

Because of the complexity of the answer to this question, some may be tempted to leave things as they are. However, it is essential to remember that according to the classical legal tradition, to which common good constitutionalism harks back, rulers possess natural authority only as long as they act 'through reasoned ordinances conducive to the common good, to public rather than private interest'.[14]

Specifically, compliance with the principles of constitutionalism distinguished by Barber is a necessary but not a sufficient condition for political legitimacy. After all, these principles are not ends in themselves but are means to serve a higher goal. As he and Vermeule see it, the state's higher purpose is to promote the 'well-being of its members' or the 'common good'.

One of the merits of post-liberalism is thus that it recalls an old insight into political legitimacy. Many do see the problem of the apparent current crisis of authority in Western political orders but seek the solution in institutional reform proposals. In doing so, they consciously or unconsciously beat around the bush. However difficult, there is no escaping a substantive debate on the common good as described above, both at the state level and within the communities that make up the state.

That is not just about replacing the values of freedom and equality central to contemporary liberal constitutionalism with advancing the well-being of all citizens. It is also about the continued existence of many 'pieces of institutional liberalism', which, as Vallier admits in a somewhat contradictory way, 'predate social liberalism by centuries – in some cases, by millennia'.[15] For this reason, Vermeule avoids a term like 'institutional liberalism' and wishes to recover the classical legal tradition instead.

11 Ibid., p. 5.
12 Vermeule, *Common Good Constitutionalism*, p. 29.
13 Vallier, *All the Kingdoms of the World*, p. 268.
14 Vermeule, *Common Good Constitutionalism*, p. 19.
15 Vallier, *All the Kingdoms of the World*, p. 268.

What Does Loughlin Have against Constitutionalism?

Not only Vermeule but also Loughlin has written a masterful book. It is so haunting that, at times, it takes one's breath away. That's unusual for a book about constitutionalism. How is that possible?

Central to the book is the thesis that a distinction must be made between constitutionalism and constitutional democracy. The latter has, to a certain extent, ancient roots. The former emerged only at the time of the American Founding 250 years ago. In Europe, it gained a foothold much later, after World War II. By now, however, it has become a global ideology.

I will explain the difference briefly, in my own words. Constitutionalism is a part of constitutional democracy. In addition, as the term suggests, the latter has a democratic component. The difference between the two elements can be indicated, for example, by the terms private and public autonomy.[16] Public or collective autonomy concerns democracy. Private or individual autonomy revolves around rights.

In principle, rights are a valuable part of constitutional democracy. However, when those rights start to be written down in constitutions, as happened for the first time 250 years ago in the US, and those constitutions are declared supreme law, constitutionalism threatens to hijack constitutional democracy. More and more, the constitution or reason itself is deemed to reflect the will of the people rather than the democratic majority's decision or will. In other words, constitutionalism begins to turn into an ideology.

On top of that, for the constitution to indeed have the status of supreme law, the judiciary is needed to effectuate that principle. Indeed, when that judiciary, in carrying out its duties, takes the liberty to interpret the constitution according to the views of the moment, a 'juristocracy' emerges.[17] Ran Hirschl has shown that this trend is now global, in line with what might be expected based on Loughlin's book.[18] Hirschl's term 'new constitutionalism' is also appropriate to describe the metamorphosis from the constitutional elements in classical constitutional democracy.

That is still not all. In the process, the constitution has come to regulate the relationship between the state and citizens and increasingly between citizens themselves. Now, in a general sense, this is a desirable trend. After all, few would dispute that citizens, apart from governments, can suffer adverse consequences from decisions made by large tech or other companies, for example. Loughlin rightly points out, however, that in the name of constitutionalism, there is increasing intrusion into the utterly private sphere of citizens and their connections. There is no area of life left that is not, at least

16 Loughlin, *Against Constitutionalism*, p. 23.

17 Ibid., Chapter 9.

18 Ran Hirschl, *Towards Juristocracy. The Origins and Consequences of the New Constitutionalism*. Cambridge, MA: Harvard University Press, 2004.

theoretically, governed or can begin to be governed by 'constitutional' norms. The constitution thus acquires a comprehensive character. It becomes a 'total constitution'.[19]

Moreover, escaping this constitution is also no longer possible. With the rise of 'cosmopolitan constitutionalism',[20] national institutions and societies are governed by it, as well as international organizations and partnerships. Organizations like the European Union have come to serve, in part, the effectuation of this constitutionalism.

I hope that with this, I have conveyed something of the haunting character of Loughlin's book, although he has written it all down much more penetratingly. Its central message is that a cage, as it were, has been erected over democracy. Loughlin believes that, at their best moments, so-called 'populists' are intuitively aware of this and turn against it.[21]

Loughlin does so himself. In this way, he believes, constitutionalism has threatened classical constitutional democracy. That exists by the grace of a fragile balance between its two components, constitutionalism and democracy. The tension between the two is inherent in this form of government and will never go away. The danger of constitutionalism turning into an ideology is that it did eliminate that tension by merging democracy with constitutionalism. Constitutionalism then becomes synonymous with democracy, giving birth to the 'new constitutionalism' as Hirschl baptized it.

Before setting out the potential contribution common good constitutionalism can make to eliminating the problems for religious freedom caused by this new constitutionalism, it is necessary to first deal with how this fundamental right fares under the constitutionalism described so compellingly by Loughlin.

How Does Religious Freedom Fare under This Constitutionalism?

The Institutional Dimension

Loughlin does not say anything specific about this, but it can be inferred from his general argument. By itself, religious freedom is also a 'right'. As such, it is part of the 'constitutional legality' required for all state and other actions, as Loughlin describes it:

> In this totalizing era, a new species of law is emerging that advances the 'invisible constitution' as the overarching edifice of legality. This is constitutional legality, a type of super-legality that is depersonalized,

19 Loughlin, *Against Constitutionalism*, p. 130. Cf. Matthias Kumm, 'Who is Afraid of the Total Constitution? Constitutional Rights as Principles and the Constitutionalization of Private Law', 7 *German Law Journal* 4 (2006): 341–369. Kumm speaks of 'a commitment to complete constitutional justice'. (p. 369).

20 Loughlin, *Against Constitutionalism*, Chapter 13.

21 Ibid., p. 199–200.

> abstract, and ahistorical. It begins to emerge as the constitution, having acquired the status of 'higher law' with the judiciary its authoritative interpreter, becomes the expression of a society's fundamental principles. In the total constitution, all public authority emanates from and is conditioned by the written constitution; there can be no sovereign beyond it. But it is no longer just a system of rules; it is a set of abstract principles, an 'invisible constitution' that articulates the values of social order. And, crucially, the constitution no longer derives its authority from the constituent power of the people who adopted the text; once that historical link is broken, the constitution is treated as an order of values that evolves as social conditions change.[22]

However, as Loughlin describes, a 'rights revolution' has occurred.[23] As a result, rights first proliferated and have since been subject to inflation. Religious freedom thus faces competition from a still-increasing number of other rights. It is certainly possible that in a concrete case, the former may outweigh the latter. However, this is by no means a foregone conclusion.

After all, everything depends on how the balancing by a particular court turns out. Besides balancing rights against each other, the principle of proportionality plays an important role.[24] However, this seems more precise than it is. This gives judicial decisions a high 'Delphic Oracle' content. This also concerns how the difference between rights and interests has largely disappeared, so the latter can also stand in the way of realizing religious freedom.

The above impression, inspired by Loughlin's book, corresponds to the picture we can observe in practice. For example, it isn't easy to discern a common thread in the European Court of Human Rights case law in religious matters.[25] This is perhaps somewhat clearer in the Court of Justice of the EU case. That is because economic interests are undeniably considered, which brings its own problems. As John Witte, Jr and Andrea Pin have recently argued, this, in combination, leads to a not-very-rosy picture. They raise the troubling question of whether the Council of Europe and the EU, founded against the backdrop of the horrors of World War II, are not themselves working hard to worsen the situation around the fundamental right of religious freedom.[26]

22 Ibid., p. 161.
23 Ibid., p. 130
24 Ibid., p. 149.
25 Carolyn Evans, *Freedom of Religion Under the European Convention on Human Rights* (Oxford: Oxford University Press, 2001).
26 John Witte, Jr. and Andrea Pin, 'Faith in Strasbourg and Luxembourg? The Fresh Rise of Religious Freedom Litigation in the Pan-European Courts', 70 *Emory Law Journal* 3 (2021): 587–661.

Partly as a result, a Christian relief organization like Aid to the Church in Need, in its recent reports, citing the Pope, speaks of 'polite persecution'.[27] There is harsh persecution in large parts of the world that defies description. Nevertheless, partly due to the developments outlined in the constitutional field, there can also be talk of persecution in European countries, among others. There, for example, the protection of freedom of conscience decreases as new sexual and other morals become more strongly reflected in the legislation and case law.

Of course, institutional developments, such as those described by Loughlin, can only partially explain this shift. There is also a substantive factor at play. Moreover, this substantive factor partly explains the rise of constitutionalism as an ideology and the subsequent developments in the institutional sphere. It is to this substantial factor that we now turn.

The Substantial Factor at Play

As stated in the introduction, concerns about its implications for religious freedom are frequently raised in academic and other debates about common good constitutionalism.[28] While I do not wish to avoid discussing this issue, this thus risks obscuring an already existing problem. That problem reads, in short, that in the contemporary liberal state, it has become increasingly difficult to realize the 'natural' right of religious freedom.

Before elaborating on this point, it is worth noting that considering religious freedom as a 'natural right' is not uncontroversial. Moral theologian Nigel Biggar, for example, has recently profoundly problematized the existence of natural rights. Thus, his book *What's Wrong With Rights?*:

> [C]oncludes that much contemporary rights-talk obscures the importance of fostering civic virtue, corrodes military effectiveness, subverts the democratic legitimacy of law, proliferates publicly onerous rights, and undermines their authority and credibility. The solution to these problems lies in the abandonment of rights-fundamentalism and the recovery of a richer public discourse about ethics, one that includes talk about the duty and virtue of rights-holders.[29]

Such criticism is similar to the criticism voiced by adherents to the classical legal tradition central to common good constitutionalism. According to this tradition, 'natural right' is paramount, and 'natural rights' are derivative.

27 See, e.g., https://media-strapi-prod.acninternational.org/Executive_Summary_2023_EN_web_version_97f51e2efb.pdf, p. 11.

28 E.g., Andrea Picciotti-Bayer, 'How Would Religious Freedom Fare With Common-Good Constitutionalists?', *National Catholic Register*, 9 April 2021.

29 Nigel Biggar, *What's Wrong with Rights* (Oxford: Oxford University Press, 2020), flap text.

According to legal philosopher Javier Hervada, 'a natural right is any good that is owed to man by virtue of human nature'.[30] Speaking of natural rights as an independent concept, separate from a natural law context, is incompatible with this.

As Vincent Phillip Muñoz shows in his latest book, the American Founders established such a relationship with natural law at least.[31] Yet even at that time, the order seems to be reversed. Rights in the classical legal tradition are a derivative of natural law, but 250 years ago, natural law was, at most, a backdrop against which natural rights were to be interpreted. Rights thinking thus constitutes a factor in the transition to modern thinking, as it took shape in the constitutional field during the Founding.

It follows from the preceding that the Founders' view of religious freedom as a natural right can, with some justification, be characterized as 'liberal', as legal scholar Michael Stokes Paulsen does.[32] On the one hand, this view holds to the idea that religious truth exists. Therefore, religion also remains a good worth promoting and facilitating in the state. After all, if religious truth exists, it comes down to citizens being able to pursue that truth. This constitutes a classical element in the liberal view of religious freedom. To this was added a modern element, in that henceforth, it was up to citizens to determine what would count as religious truth in their cases.

Although, despite the use of the term 'natural right', it was not an ambition of the Founders to establish such a right universally, its formulation in the US Constitution did help inspire the later 1948 *United Nations Universal Declaration of Human Rights* and the subsequent *European Convention on Human Rights* (1950). As we will see later, religious freedom was also endorsed, e.g., during the Second Vatican Council. Indeed, both these developments also raise reservations around Paulsen's characterization of the view of religious freedom as a natural right as liberal. However, something remains to be said for claiming the term 'liberal' back from its current users.

Whatever the truth of this, religious freedom now encounters limits. The theory of the 'priority of God' developed by Paulsen in this context holds that the right has a severe chance of being realized only if the idea that religious truth exists continues to be adhered to. This notion, however, has been increasingly wearing thin in Western and, in particular, European countries since the cultural revolution of the 1960s. Until recently, the second element of the liberal vision of religious freedom, namely that everyone should enjoy

30 Javier Hervada, *Critical Introduction to Natural Right* (Montreal: Wilson & LaFleur, 2nd English edition, 2020), p. 62.

31 Vincent Phillip Muñoz, *Religious Liberty and the American Founding: Natural Rights and the Original Meanings of the First Amendment Religion Clauses* (Chicago: University of Chicago Press, 2022).

32 Michael Stokes Paulsen, 'The Priority of God: A Theory of Religious Liberty', 39 *Pepperdine Law Review* 5 (2013): 1159–1222.

the freedom to profess and practise his or her religion, was still adhered to. This element has now also come under increasing pressure.

From the angle of natural rights, the current situation can be characterized as one in which the government is gradually returning to defining what is religious truth and what is not rather than leaving this to the citizens themselves. However, the difference with pre-modern times is that the faith in question has taken on an opposite content. As noted earlier, it has become secular or even atheistic, emphasizing values such as liberty and equality. This, according to Paulsen, completes the circle. Indeed, almost unnoticed, we have thus returned to a situation as it existed before the American Founding.

The disappearance of the idea that religious truth exists indicates the disconnection of the right to religious freedom from its natural law context. As argued, it was natural to the Founders that the right should be interpreted and applied against that backdrop. The same can still be argued, at least in part, for the drafters of the *Universal Declaration of Human Rights* and the subsequent *European Convention on Human Rights.*[33]

What is not helpful from this perspective, however, is that the Strasbourg Court has fundamentally chosen to interpret the *European Convention on Human Rights* as a 'living document'.[34] This method corresponds to the progressive mode of interpreting the constitution that Vermeule describes in *Common Good Constitutionalism.*[35] Even for those who do not adhere to a static conception of natural law, it will be apparent that such an approach does not necessarily assist in preserving the relationship between the natural right to religious freedom and a natural law interpretation framework. The same is true for the EU *Charter of Fundamental Rights*, which has the ambition to want to keep up with the times and, therefore, may even already be constantly changing textually. The recent discussion on the possible addition of a right to abortion is a mere illustration of this.

Some authors have suggested, as a remedy, that when it comes to religious freedom, the Strasbourg Court could draw inspiration from the jurisprudence of, say, the Canadian Supreme Court or the South African Constitutional Court.[36] This partly dovetailed with the resurgence of comparative constitutional law at the beginning of the 21st century, which seemed to hold promises of increased use of 'judicial' and 'constitutional borrowing'. The Canadian

33 See, e.g., Commission on Unalienable Rights (2021), *Report of the Commission on Unalienable Rights*, https://www.state.gov/wp-content/uploads/2020/07/Draft-Report-of-the-Commission-on-Unalienable-Rights.pdf, p. 31.

34 European Court of Human Rights, 'Judicial Seminar 2020 The Convention as a Living Instrument at 70. Background Document', https://www.echr.coe.int/documents/d/echr/seminar_background_paper_2020_eng.

35 Vermeule, *Common Good Constitutionalism*, Chapter 4.

36 F.H.K. Theissen, *Sincerely Believing in Freedom. A Reconstruction and Comparison of the Interpretation of the Freedom of Religion and Belief on the Canadian Supreme Court, the South African Constitutional Court and the European Court of Human Rights,* (Delft: Ipskamp Printing, 2023).

and South African courts would favour religious freedom more generously. However, it is doubtful, especially in the case of the Canadian court, whether that is still true. After all, that has (also) taken a course in recent years, which has led, for example, to a situation where – unlike a decade before – a Christian law school could no longer obtain accreditation because of the sexual morality requirements it placed on its students.[37]

It is no coincidence that this case, which symbolizes the court's shift in thinking, concerns the collective dimension of religious freedom. For most adherents of a religion, it needs little argument that this right is not exclusively individual in nature. To live out one's faith, it is at least equally important to be able to do so in a collective context. Moreover, this involves more than just religious meetings in houses of worship. It also includes, for example, charitable work in an association context, such as the organization that works from its Roman Catholic identity to adopt children in Philadelphia (Catholic Social Services).[38]

Nevertheless, this collective dimension of religious freedom is at odds with the principles of at least contemporary liberalism.[39] According to these principles, the individual is paramount and should primarily relate to the state. The idea that numerous organizations and other connections of citizens – *civil society* – exist between the individual and the state is not only challenging to place theoretically but also poses a potential threat to realizing the ideal of individual autonomy.

As liberalism continues to secularize and radicalize, it is logical that the current phase in which the collective dimension is still mainly under pressure will be followed by one in which individual religious freedom will also gradually come more into question. According to Paulsen's theory, at least in Europe, we are already in that phase.[40]

Various commentators, including US Supreme Court Justice Samuel A. Alito, Jr at a symposium in Rome,[41] have raised the question of whether it will prove possible to continue to guarantee the right to religious freedom at all at a time when most of the population is no longer familiar with the phenomenon of religion or no longer sees its importance. According to projections, this will happen in the United States within a few decades.[42] This has been the case in several European countries for some time.

Which brings me, finally, to the third question.

37 Barry Bussey, *The Legal Revolution Against the Accommodation of Religion: The Secular Age v. The Sexular Age* (Leiden: Ph.D. Dissertation, 2019).

38 *Fulton v. Philadelphia*, 593 U.S. ___ (2021).

39 Jacob T. Levy, *Rationalism, Pluralism, and Freedom* (Oxford: Oxford University Press, 2015).

40 Paulsen, 'The Priority of God', p. 1179.

41 https://www.youtube.com/watch?v=uci4uni6O8E.

42 Pew Research Center, *Modeling the Future of Religion in America. If Recent Trends in Religious Switching Continue, Christians Could Make up Less than Half of the U.S. Population within a Few Decades*, 13 September 2022.

What Potential Contribution Can Common Good Constitutionalism Make to Overcoming the Problems with Constitutionalism in General and Those with Religious Freedom in Particular?

Loughlin advocates a return to classical constitutional democracy. Or, in other words, restoring the fragile balance between constitutionalism and democracy. This is certainly necessary.[43] It can take the wind out of the sails of populism and increase the legitimacy of European government systems. Moreover, advocating this solution is brave. Many of his colleagues will not thank Loughlin. They are overwhelmingly proponents of the ideology of constitutionalism.

It is interesting to wonder for a moment why this is so. In all likelihood, many public lawyers adhere to a set of ideals that can be most easily implemented with the help of undemocratic constitutionalism.[44] This hypothesis relativizes the difference with common good constitutionalism if it is correct. That is often accused of being 'ideological', but constitutionalism in that case is no less so.

However, Loughlin's classical constitutional democracy does not offer a substantive compass for how best to solve the problems concerning religious freedom set out in the previous section. Yet that seems to be the only way forward in the current situation. The interpretation and application of rights must somehow be related again to an objective idea of the common good as a corrective to their overly subjective character.[45]

Surprisingly, at first glance, Vermeule's book does not mention the importance of religious freedom. Neither in the general section on the theory of common good constitutionalism nor in the concrete elaboration of the rights section, entitled 'Rights and the Common Good', does the topic appear explicitly.[46]

On closer inspection, however, this is somewhat different. In the first place, the book is, in its own words, no more than 'an overall sketch of a view and a program, with illustrative applications',[47] which will therefore require further elaboration in many parts in the time to come. How the application section of the book criticizes the current state of rights suggests that religion may play a crucial role in this. More importantly, the importance of faith is woven into the very notion of the common good itself insofar as it involves, as seen, in a

43 Cf., from the point of view of common good constitutionalism, Conor Casey, 'Constitutional Design and the Point of Constitutional Law', *American Journal of Jurisprudence* 67: 2 (2022): 173–197.

44 See, e.g., Kumm, 'Who is Afraid of the Total Constitution?'

45 Hans-Martien ten Napel, 'Natural Law and the Future of Human Rights', in: Salvador Santino F. Regilme Jr. and Irene Hadiprayitno (eds.), *Human Rights at Risk. Global Governance, American Power, and the Future of Dignity* (New Brunswick, Camden, and Newark, New Jersey, and London: Rutgers University Press, 2022), p. 157–172.

46 Vermeule, *Common Good Constitutionalism*, p. 164–178.

47 Ibid., p. 41.

political sense, 'the flourishing of a well-ordered political community'.[48] With this, then, the theme is represented and, if implicitly, even forms a common thread throughout both the theoretical part and the practical elaboration.

It is also precisely with this in mind that concerns arise among some commentators.[49] Specifically, the fear is that the impact of common good constitutionalism on religious freedom will be, above all, a restricting one, at least relative to prevailing doctrine. The importance of religion will be endorsed and even interpreted generously compared to the current situation. Precisely because of this, the very meaning of religious freedom would paradoxically be construed restrictively. The idea behind this reasoning is that if religion is to be able to play (again) a more prominent role in the state, the freedom of choice of citizens in that area may have to be restricted.

This is not a foregone conclusion, and at least one article provides a nuanced view of the role of religious freedom in common good constitutionalism. Thus, according to Ménard and Su,[50] it depends on whether a light or a heavy variant of 'integralism' will be advocated. Only in the heavier variants is it conceivable, though still not sure, that the role of religious freedom will become substantially curtailed. Moreover, as stated above, when discussing Vallier's distinctions, Vermeule does not advocate integralism in *Common Good Constitutionalism* but rather a post-liberal perspective.

Advocating a 'heavy' variant of integralism would also be an extraordinary development because it is precisely within one of the historical pillars of common good constitutionalism – the Roman Catholic Church – that thinking about religious freedom has evolved significantly. Documents relating to the Second Vatican Council frequently reference the common good. At the same time, particularly in the declaration on religious freedom, *Dignitatis Humanae* (1965), this Council embraced religious liberty as a natural right of all people. An example of a passage where the two converge, in *Dignitatis Humanae* itself, is this:

> So the state, whose proper purpose it is to provide for the temporal common good, should certainly recognize and promote the religious life of its citizens. With equal certainty it exceeds the limits of its authority, if it takes upon itself to direct or to prevent religious activity.[51]

Such a conclusion places the discussion of common good constitutionalism in relation to religious freedom in a somewhat different perspective. From the

48 Ibid., p. 7.

49 Picciotti-Bayer, 'How Would Religious Freedom Fare With Common-Good Constitutionalists?'

50 Xavier Foccrouille Ménard and Anna Su, 'Liberalism, Catholic Integralism, and the Question of Religious Freedom, 47 *Brigham Young University Law Review* 4 (2022): 1171–1219.

51 S J Norman Tanner (ed.), *Vatican II. The Essential Texts* (New York: Image, 2012), p. 307–308.

anxious, critical attitude that can now be observed in some commentaries, the focus shifts to whether elements can be derived from common good constitutionalism that can promote the continued guarantee of religious freedom.

The answer to this question is in the affirmative. The main element of common good constitutionalism that can help here is the concept of the common good itself. Both the phenomenon of faith itself and the principle that people will have to come to a particular belief of their own free will are, in the Christian tradition, traditionally counted among the things essential for 'the flourishing of a well-ordered political community'. While this is not yet the same as the modern notion of religious freedom, it can be retroactively traced to it, according to *Dignitatis Humanae*, among other things.[52]

Next, it is a matter of interpreting and applying rights by the requirements of the common good. In doing so, it is difficult to determine which of the two takes precedence. Instead, it comes down to the interrelationship between the two:

> In the final analysis, it is a mistake to think that rights can be fully understood in abstraction from the good and it would be wrong to think that rights take priority over the common good. But it is also a mistake to think that the common good can be fully understood in abstraction from principles of right action, nor the rights that arise when such principles manifest directed duties. It is similarly a mistake to think that the common good takes priority over fundamental rights; as Finnis notes, 'we should not say that human rights, or their exercise, are subject to the common good; for the maintenance of human rights is a fundamental component of the common good'. The common good can only be achieved when rights are respected but, equally, the scope and character of rights themselves are subject to or limited by each other and other aspects of the common good. Once each is properly understood to conceptually imply the other, it becomes clear that the correct interpretation of their scope and interaction depends upon a process akin to reflective equilibrium. The real issue here is that an exclusive focus on only one side of this relationship can lead us to forget that this is a relationship at all, and that its boundary and scope is determined not by one side or the other, but by both.[53]

As stated, the same cannot be said about the new constitutionalism. In contemporary liberal constitutionalism, there is little discernible awareness of the importance of religion and religious freedom at the individual, group,

52 E.g., John Witte, Jr., *The Blessings of Liberty. Human Rights and Religious Freedom in the Western Legal Tradition* (Cambridge: Cambridge University Press, 2021).

53 Michael Foran, 'Rights, Common Good, and The Separation of Powers', *The Modern Law Review* 86: 3 (2023) 599–628, at p. 615–616.

and systemic levels. It will be necessary to fill this void at the heart of the new constitutionalism with the concept of the common good. In doing so, classical constitutional democracy, as Loughlin advocates, can be a source of inspiration.

The question arises as to exactly how this should be done. The answer to that question is more challenging to give. One starting point might be to examine how this happened in the past. For example, in several continental European countries, after World War II, a political movement such as Christian democracy promoted the concept of the common good.[54] In the countries in which this current held a powerful position in the political landscape for several decades, such as Belgium, Germany, Italy, and the Netherlands, liberal constitutionalism thus became filled with the notion of the common good. With Germany as a partial exception for the time being, Christian democracy has lost a great deal of influence in these same countries.

In some cases, it has even imploded (almost entirely). Moreover, the idea has also taken hold internally that a centre or centre-right course is a better binder than traditional thought. Consequently, for example, the European People's Party, while still the largest group in the European Parliament, has lost such a profile that it is difficult to distinguish it from other, more explicitly liberal party federations.[55]

It is difficult to overestimate the importance of these political developments for the viability of common good institutionalism in the European Union as a whole and within most of its member states. Some of the founders of the organizations from which the European Union emerged, such as Robert Schuman, as is well known, belonged to the Christian democrat movement. While this has motivated many a Christian democrat to this day to continue to support the political project of European integration, the ethos of the organization has changed almost beyond recognition.[56] That this is not perceived as such by those involved, or even welcomed, can be explained by the signalled development of the movement in a socially liberal direction.

It cannot be ruled out that the political programmes of classical Christian democracy are now perceived as so radical that critics would classify them under at least a light variant of 'integralism'. As already mentioned, there is also reluctance or even objection within Christian democratic circles to any longer stand up for a natural-law-based view of the human person and the policy choices that flow from it. This is partly different for various right wing populist parties in Europe, such as the German *Alternative für Deutschland*, which sometimes even 'flirt' with such a view of man. The term 'flirting' has

54 E.g., David Hanley (ed.), *Christian Democracy in Europe. A Comparative Perspective* (London & New York: Pinter, 1994).

55 E.g., Michel Gurfinkiel, 'Christian Democracy', *First Things*, August 2020.

56 Todd Huizinga, *The New Totalitarian Temptation: Global Governance and the Crisis of Democracy in Europe* (New York & London: Encounter Books, 2016).

a negative connotation in this context as it suggests that the love for it is not deep. To some extent, this is indeed the case, as positions are sometimes taken in other areas (such as asylum policy) that are inconsistent with Christian-inspired politics. Therefore, these parties constitute a 'mixed bag', which is not entirely unjustifiably warned against from political-theological perspectives.[57]

However, the term 'mixed bag' suggests that there are also positive elements to these parties' efforts in the relevant areas. This is a controversial thesis, just as much as it is *not done* in mainstream comparative constitutional law or mainstream political science in general to downplay criticism of populism. That is why the appearance of Loughlin's book has evoked mixed reactions.

When the question, however, is how the notion of the common good can be brought back into constitutionalism, right-wing populist parties can paradoxically play a role. In the European Union, this issue plays out in relation to Hungary and, until recently, Poland, among others. The standard view is that such countries were, or still are, acting in violation of the 'rule of law'. Their defence, however, is that the notion of the 'rule of law' as espoused and propagated by the European Union has become detached from its original natural law embedding. This notion is then 'loaded' with liberal hobbyhorses, resulting in what has been called 'conceptual overreach'.[58]

These issues will only become more prominent in Europe in the coming years. There seems to be a contrast not only between Central and Eastern Europe on the one hand and Western Europe on the other but within Western Europe between a social liberal current that is still dominant on the one hand and a right-wing populist current on the other.[59]

From the point of view of common good constitutionalism, it is reasonable to keep the necessary distance from both currents since neither (fully) meets the standards of the classical legal tradition, just as these neither match the Democratic nor the Republican programs in the US. However, that differs from excluding one of the two currents in advance with the help of a *cordon sanitaire*, thereby de facto surrendering to the other.

In Conclusion

What, admittedly, preliminary conclusions does this chapter now lead to? Three things leap to mind.

First, it undeniably takes some effort to clarify the precise meaning and implications of Loughlin's and Vermeule's recent books on constitutionalism

57 Ulrich Schmiedel and Joshua Ralston (eds.), *The Spirit of Populism. Political Theologies in Polarized Times* (Leiden: Brill, 2021).

58 John Tasioulas, 'The Inflation of Concepts. Human Rights, Health, the Rule of Law – Why Are These Concepts Inflated to the Status of Totalising, Secular Religions?', *Aeon*, 29 January 2021.

59 The picture is evolving with, e.g., the 2022 election results in Sweden and Italy and the outcomes of the 2023 Finnish and Dutch parliamentary elections.

for religious freedom. It is necessary to try anyway since religion, in general, and religious freedom, in particular, have significance for citizens, their organizations, and the state. Although a few references to the Second Vatican Council have been made above, a natural law defence of religious freedom from a Protestant (Baptist) perspective, for example, has also recently appeared.[60] *Dignitatis Humanae* received further affirmation several years ago in the *Religious Freedom for the Good of All: Theological Approaches and Contemporary Challenges* document.[61] It is, thus, reasonable, when translating the classical legal tradition to the present time, to incorporate not just rights in general,[62] but religious freedom in particular.

This means, secondly, that it is neither necessary nor desirable from the perspective of religious liberty to bring the differences between the two books on constitutionalism to a head. Although Vermeule does not explicitly address it, the importance of religion is implicit in the constitutional definition of the common good presented in *Common Good Constitutionalism*. Like other rights, it will have to serve, in part, the realization of the common good. This is a thesis that Loughlin is unlikely to take for granted. However, his proposal to return to a form of classical constitutional democracy matches ideas about constitutional design that, although not discussed above as Vermeule himself remains 'agnostic' about it,[63] can be found in circles of common good constitutionalists.[64] In attempts to further explore such convergence of ideas, it is important not to conclude too quickly that changed circumstances stand in the way of a renewed promotion of the common good. After all, as seen above, those same circumstances also hinder the adequate realization of religious freedom. This means that, from the point of view of the political legitimacy of Western political orders, doing nothing is not a choice.

Last but not least, as Pope Benedict XVI notes in his introduction to the compilation of several important documents of the Second Vatican Council, the subject under discussion in this chapter is part of the complex adaptation of both political and theological thought to modernity: 'the Council had to determine in a new way the relationship between the Church and the modern era'.[65] This process has been ongoing for 500 years and has not been concluded. Admittedly, the prevailing view is that it would. The new constitution-

60 Andrew T. Walker, *Liberty for All: Defending Everyone's Religious Freedom in a Pluralistic Age* (Grand Rapids, Michigan: Brazos Press, 2021).

61 International Theological Commission, Sub-commission for Religious Freedom, *Religious Freedom for the Good of All. Theological Approaches and Contemporary Challenges* (2019), https://www.vatican.va/roman_curia/congregations/cfaith/cti_documents/rc_cti_20190426_liberta-religiosa_en.html).

62 Foran, 'Rights, Common Good, and The Separation of Powers'.

63 Vermeule, *Common Good Constitutionalism*, p. 10.

64 Casey, 'Constitutional Design and the Point of Constitutional Law'.

65 Pope Benedict XVI, 'What Has Been the Result of the Council?', in Tanner, *Vatican II*, 3–13, at p. 7.

alism would then no longer need to relate to ancient constitutionalism. The Second Vatican Council would have brought the Roman Catholic Church definitively into modernity so that all frictions would have been resolved in that area as well.

Perhaps the most outstanding merit of Vermeule's book is that he punctures this image, particularly around constitutionalism. On reflection, the questions facing contemporary liberal constitutionalism are too fundamental to warrant any presentism in that area. Once one realizes this, all sorts of theological questions almost inevitably arise. Those who care about constitutional democracy would be wise to address, rather than avoid, these constitutional and theological questions. The thrust of this chapter was that *Common Good Constitutionalism* provides an excellent entry point for this, also in a European context, and religious freedom is a suitable case. This process of recovery and translation can and should go back even further than the rise of modernity and the response to it as provided by the Second Vatican Council. After all, to quote Pope Benedict XVI once again:

> The steps the Council took toward the modern era which had rather vaguely been presented as 'openness to the world,' belong in short to the perennial problem of the relationship between faith and reason that is re-emerging in ever new forms. The situation that the Council had to face can certainly be compared to events of previous epochs.[66]

66 Pope Benedict XVI, 'What Has Been the Result of the Council?', p. 12.

3 Law, Reconciliation, and Human Dignity

Religious Diversity and Managing Religious Harmony in Singapore

Li-ann Thio

Introduction: Law, Human Rights, and Right Relationships as Components of Religious Harmony and Social Well-Being

A perennial problem of governance within religiously plural societies, where most of the population profess a religious affiliation, is the need to ensure that individuals and groups enjoy religious liberty of a sufficiently robust nature while maintaining the harmonious co-existence of plural faiths whether theistic or humanistic. This is important given the fissiparous tendencies of inter-group tensions evident in both history and contemporary affairs, which may pose a heightened threat to public order and societal cohesion.[1]

This quest for ordered liberty as a prescription for human flourishing engages questions of peace, dispute resolution methods, as well as questions of justice and the normative basis for ordering state-society relations. 'Human dignity' is frequently appealed to, as an egalitarian justice principle, and has universal appeal even if it is a mercurial concept with indeterminate content. It is framed as a normative ally of human rights in the *Universal Declaration of Human Rights* (UDHR),[2] the cornerstone instrument for human rights standard-setting. The UDHR is the sacred text of what Elie Wiesel called a 'world-wide secular religion'[3] that propounds a value system seeking 'to unify humankind into a single moral community'.[4]

1 As noted by the Singapore High Court in *Vijaya Kumar s/o Rajendran v AG* [2015] SGHC 244 at [47].

2 Preamble, Article 1, A/RES/217(III)[A]. See Christopher McCrudden ed, *Understanding Human Dignity* (Oxford University Press, 2013); Jimmy Hsu ed., *Human Dignity in Asia: Dialogue between Law and Culture* (Cambridge University Press, July 2022).

3 Elie Wiesel, 'A Tribute to Human Rights' in *The Universal Declaration of Human Rights: Fifty Years and Beyond*, Yael Danieli et al. eds., (Baywood Publishing Co, 1999), 3.

4 Henri Feron, 'Human rights and faith: a 'world-wide secular religion' (2014) 7(4) Ethics & Global Politics 181–200 at 183.

DOI: 10.4324/9781003519188-5

Insofar as human dignity posits the inherent worth of each human being 'endowed with reason and conscience'[5] and sets the value of normative individualism against statism,[6] the link between human dignity and rights is easy to apprehend. Article 18 UDHR, for instance, recognises the individual and communal dimensions of religious freedom.[7] While the individual right to have or to change a religious belief is absolute, the expression of religious freedom in the *forum externum*, such as through worship, teachings, dress, diet, and propagation, may be qualified. Predicating religious profession on the principle of free conscience reflects a concern for spiritual autonomy and self-determination as a facet of identity and integrity. This reflects a vision of human dignity that is liberal, individualistic, and egalitarian, grounded in the intrinsic worth of human persons as abstract right-bearers. However, the UDHR does not conceptualise humans as atomistic beings but persons situated in community. Article 29 is dignitarian in recognising that rights are not absolute values but function within a context where 'everyone has duties to the community' and may be qualified by the rights of others and 'the just requirements of morality, public order and the general welfare in a democratic society'. Tensions may arise not only from negotiating the contours between competing rights, duties, and public goods between government and citizen but where conflict takes places between two private actors.

While rights discourse is central to maintaining a just equilibrium between rights and competing interests, it is an incomplete moral language that does not exhaust the scope of the broader question of what justice and human flourishing may entail. The dominant stream of rights discourse, where driven by the 'liberalism of fear',[8] manifested by distrust against political authorities as restrictors of autonomy often generates a rights-oriented, court-centric brand of constitutionalism. This may fuel agonistic social relations in an age of politicised and proliferating rights-claims.[9] Litigation as a method of dispute resolution in bringing about a 'winner takes all' situation may undermine relational solidarity, even exacerbate alienation leading to the end of cordial relationships. The impact of adjudication on an ongoing relation has been likened

5 Article 1, UDHR

6 There are views that human dignity is antithetical rather than foundational to human rights: John Milbank, 'Dignity rather than Rights' in *Understanding Human Dignity*, Christopher McCrudden ed., (OUP, 2013), 189–205 at 189–190; Govert den Hartogh, 'Is human dignity the ground of human rights?' in *Cambridge Handbook of Human Dignity: Interdisciplinary Perspectives* (Cambridge University Press, 2014). Marcus Duwell et al. eds., at 200–207.

7 See Linde Lindkvist, *Religious Freedom and the Universal Declaration of Human Rights* (Cambridge University Press, 2017).

8 Judith Shklar, *Political Thought and Political Thinkers* (Stanley Hoffman ed, University of Chicago Press 1998) 3.

9 See Marta Cartabia, 'The challenges of "new rights" and militant secularism' in *Universal Rights in a World of Diversity – The Case of Religious Freedom: Proceedings of the 17th Plenary Session, Pontifical Academy of Social Sciences, Acta 17*, Mary Ann Glendon and Hans F Zacher eds., (Vatican City: 2012).

to 'what surgery is to a patient' as a 'traumatic intervention' attempting to give life to a right, but that may in the process 'sometimes kill the patient, the relationship in which it arises'.[10]

While the role of law in enforcing social norms embodied in legislation and in vindicating rights in adjudication is well-established, this chapter seeks to interrogate the role of law as a tool of reconciliation and how this may relate to human dignity, which may be personal and inherent, a function of social status, or even the dignity of groups.[11] It focuses on the management of religious harmony and social strife where inter-group tensions arise between religious groups or religious and irreligious groups within the secular democratic city-state of Singapore, the world's most religiously diverse polity.[12]

This interrogation goes beyond legal liberalism's focus on legal sanctions, rights, and courts. It extends to engaging the role of soft constitutional law[13] as non-binding but influential norms that affect behaviour by generating aspirations and expectations through hortatory persuasion, rather than obligatory compulsion, and resort to non-judicial approaches towards resolving disputes pursuant to the shared value of 'consensus instead of contention'.[14] It engages a broader moral vocabulary that considers rights in relation to duties whether converse or correlative,[15] perfect or imperfect, or civic virtues and public goods. This form of discourse is familiar to communitarian constitutional orders like Singapore,[16] where the state does not pretend to be 'neutral'[17] but explicitly

10 Gidon Gottlieb, 'Relationism: legal theory for a relational society' (1983) 50(2) University of Chicago Law Review 567–612 at 602.

11 Thio Li-ann, 'Human dignity and relational constitutionalism in Singapore' in ***Human Dignity in Asia: Dialogue between Law and Culture***, Jimmy Hsu ed., (Cambridge University Press, 2022) 187–219.

12 Pew Research Center report on Global Religious Diversity, 4 April (2014) at Religious-Diversity-full-report.pdf (pewresearch.org). The Inter-Religious Organisation, a non-government organisation of religious leaders founded in 1949 has members from ten faiths (Hindu, Jewish, Zoroastrian, Buddhist, Taoist, Jain, Christian, Muslim, Sikh, and Bahai). According to a 2020 national census, the religious composition of the population is 31.3% Buddhist, 8.8% Taoist and Chinese folk religion; 18.9% Christian, 15.6% Islam, 5% Hindu, and no religion 20%: Singapore Department of Statistics | Census of Population 2020 Statistical Release 1 – Key Findings (singstat.gov.sg).

13 Li-ann Thio, 'Soft constitutional law in non-liberal Asian constitutional democracies', (2010) 8(4) ICON 766–799.

14 Shared Values White Paper (Parliament of Singapore, Cmd 1 of 1991) at [14]. (hereafter, 'SVWP').

15 John H. Knox, 'Horizontal human rights law' (2007) 102(1) AJIL 1–47 at 1–2.

16 See Thio Li-ann, 'Varieties of constitutionalism in Asia' (2021) 16 Asian Journal of Comparative Law 285–310; *PP v Kwong Kok Hing* [2008] 2 SLR 684 at [17] (identifying communitarian values like preservation of morality, public peace, and respect for institutions); Para 30, SVWP, *supra*, note 14.

17 Liberal states, where liberal values constitute a public morality, seek not only to protect but to produce liberal individuals who are individualistic, experimental, and choice-loving in orientation. Stephen Macedo, 'The Constitution of Liberalism' in *Liberal Virtues: Citizenship, Virtue and Community in Liberal Constitutionalism* (Oxford University Press, 1990) 163, 169, 201.

champions a substantive vision of the good and the good citizen, incorporating a robust vision of communal life informed by history, ethnicity, religion, or communal morality, as well as group-based sensitivities.[18]

Singapore, as a multi-religious polity, has had unhappy experiences with ethno-religious riots; such traumatic incidents are regularly reiterated by the courts[19] and political branches in cautionary tones as something to be assiduously avoided. While Articles 15(1) and (3) of the Singapore Constitution affirms the right of every person to profess, practise, and propagate his religious faith, and recognises the right of religious groups to manage their own religious affairs respectively, these liberties are qualified in terms of 'public order, public health or morality'.[20] While the principle of free conscience is the bedrock of religious liberty within the Singapore model of accommodative secularism,[21] the premium of public order qualifies external expressions of religious liberty; rights are not treated as autonomy-maximising vehicles but as operating within a framework designed to secure certain public goods and civic virtues.

'Public order' may be invoked 'vertically' to justify state restrictions of fundamental liberties, but also has a 'horizontal' dimension caused by intergroup tensions. The state does not seek merely to keep the peace, but to manage these tensions, which may detrimentally undermine social harmony and national unity. Thus, 'public order' must be appreciated capaciously to implicate securing the sustainability or durability of social relations, a certain quality of friendly relationships embodied by the quasi-constitutional value of 'racial and religious harmony'.[22] Preserving religious harmony is considered 'sacrosanct'[23] given its core importance to public peace and relational weal. As the law minister has observed, 'We are religiously diverse, yet live in harmony. That is not a natural state of things'.[24] Pursuant to this, the government has adopted an approach of 'active state intervention' to create an environment where people are committed to 'multiculturalism and a multiracial,

18 Graham Walker, 'The mixed constitution after liberalism' (1996) 4 Cardozo J. Int'l & Comp. L 311, 315, 319. As with any theory of the good, liberal or otherwise, this comes with authoritarian proclivities.

19 *Supra,* note 1 at [49]. The courts recognise a social fault-line where 'different communities' hold 'deeply held and sometimes conflicting views on important issues of moral conscience': *Tan Seng Kee v AG* [2022] 1 SLR 1347 at [3].

20 Article 15(4), Republic of Singapore Constitution.

21 *Nappalli Peter Williams v Institute of Technical Education* [1999] 2 SLR 569 at [28].

22 SVWP, *supra,* note 14 at [16], [52]. See Jaclyn Neo, 'Dimensions of religious harmony as constitutional practice: beyond state control (2019) 20 German Law Journal 966–985.

23 *Public Prosecutor v Gosling Andrew* [2022] SGDC 239 at [67].

24 Minister of Home Affairs K. Shanmugam, Second Reading, Maintenance of Religious Harmony Amendment Bill 2019, Wrap up Speech at [179]: https://www.mha.gov.sg/media-room/parliamentary/second-reading-of-the-maintenance-of-religious-harmony-amendment-bill-2019---wrap-up-speech-by-mr-k-shanmugam-minister-for-home-affairs-and-minister-for-law/ (hereafter, Wrap up Speech).

multi-religious society'.[25]The government calls out religiously offensive online communications, such as a Facebook post suggesting that the Bible and Koran could be used for toilet paper during the COVID-19 lockdown era, to signal that a serious view is taken of 'very offensive' statements, and subjects these to police investigation for a possible religious offence.[26] This helps set the boundaries of anti-social conduct, as a deterrent.

Aside from the option of deploying punitive legal sanctions where religious sensitivities are affected,[27] the government has sought to facilitate reconciliation between individuals and a religious groups or between religious groups. Reconciliation has been understood in various ways[28] and applied in transitional settings.[29] In stable societies, a dominant way of understanding reconciliation in the judicial context entails recognising and reconciling new rights with countervailing rights and interests through a balancing process[30] to settle strife and serve the common good. This fits well with liberal conceptions of human dignity that tend towards favouring individualism and diversity over community interests in seeking their reasonable accommodation and egalitarian precepts that may mandate recognising the dignity of difference by recognising special group rights.

Law as a tool of reconciliation is used here in the sense of adjusting and improving the relationship between people in conflict or at odds. This is motivated by a desire to promote durable, friendly relations with the goal of securing communal solidarity, dovetailing with the goals of relational constitutionalism.[31] What might be called 'relational reconciliation', which seeks the outcome of restoring right relationships and explores facilitative processes, depends on reciprocal respect and goodwill. This resolves disputes arising

25 'State intervention keeps extremism at bay, fosters integration: Shanmugam', *Today* (Singapore) online, 5 June 2017.

26 'Progress Singapore Party expels member behind offensive post on NUS Atheist Society Facebook page', ChannelNewsAsia.com, 21 March 2020.

27 E.g., prosecutions under s292 Penal Code (*Public Prosecutor v Amos Yee* [2015] SGDC 215, relating to the offence of deliberate intent to wound the religious feelings of any persons by causing certain matter to be seen and heard) and the now defunct Sedition Act where sedition encompassed promoting feelings of ill-will and hostility between different races or classes of Singaporeans: *Public Prosecutor v Ong Kian Cheong* [2009] SGDC 163.

28 Mark D. Walters distinguishes between three types of reconciliation in relation to relationship, resignation, and as restoring consistency, which may impact interpretive enterprises: 'The jurisprudence of reconciliation: aboriginal rights in Canada' in William Kymlicka and B. Bashir eds., *The Politics of Reconciliation in Multicultural Societies* (Oxford University Press, 2008), 166.

29 E.g., Alex Boraine, 'Truth and reconciliation in South Africa: the third way' in *Out of and into Authoritarian Law*, (Kluwer, 2003), Andras Sajo ed., 31–52.

30 Carole Blackburn, 'Producing legitimacy: reconciliation and the negotiation of aboriginal rights in Canada' [2007] 13(3) Journal of the Royal Anthropological Institute 621–638.

31 Li-ann Thio, 'Relational constitutionalism and the management of inter-religious disputes: the Singapore "secularism with a soul" model', (2012) 2 Oxford Journal of Law and Religion 446–469.

from past incidents and offences and is also future-oriented in envisaging a continuing relationship between individuals and groups. Adversarial legal processes, where respective parties seek to prove their case and rigidly insist on their rights, may be ill-suited to cultivate such virtues and other-centric duties in service of religious harmony. Human dignity here may attach to social achievement in the honour owed to virtuous citizens who respond to conflict in a normatively desirable manner and the dignity owed to groups as valued members of the broader community who have suffered indignity and offence, warranting recognition and remedy.

The second part of this chapter contextualises the discussion by setting out key features of religion-state constitutional arrangements in Singapore and general approaches towards regulating religious liberty and religious harmony by focusing on the Maintenance of Religious Harmony Act (MRHA), which was introduced in 1990 and amended in 2019. The third part of this chapter examines why and how a normally interventionist government takes a backseat role in relation to inter-religious disputes, whether caused by direct interactions between members of different religious groups or precipitated by third-party conflict entrepreneurs. This has given rise to an informal method of dispute resolution, where, in accordance with 'soft' public law norms and duties pertaining to religious harmony, the offended and offending parties embark upon a reconciliatory public ritual of sorts. This arose in practice out of various 'disharmony' incidents dating back to more than a decade, with the government communicating its approval of the resolution to signal the end of tensions and return to a harmonious equilibrium without formal prosecution or rights litigation. This has generated expectations concerning desired patterns of action in resolving religious harmony disputes.

In particular, the MRHA was amended in 2019 to introduce the novel 'Community Remedial Initiative' (CRI) under section 16H, which came into effect on 1 November 2022.[32] This allows someone who commits an MRHA offence to enter an agreement to make amends rather than face legal prosecutions. This innovation appears to borrow from the public ritual of reconciliation that has been in practice for more than a decade,[33] exemplifying the norms and dispute resolution methodology of relational constitutionalism. This section examines the rationale and hopes for how the CRI is envisaged to work in seeking to bring about reconciliation by soothing wounded religious feelings or emotions and restoring broken stressed relationships. Whether the CRI promotes or demotes human dignity is assessed both in relation to personalist

32 'Stronger laws on religious harmony to take effect on Nov 1', *Straits Times* (Singapore) 1 Nov. 2022.

33 The Lighthouse Evangelism incident in 2010, where videos placed on a church website apparently upset Buddhists and other citizens, is the first instance where this public ritual began to be developed: see Thio Li-ann, 'Contentious liberty: regulating religious propagation in a religiously diverse secular democracy' (2010) SJLS 484–515.

conceptions of dignity based on inherent individual worth and social roles where dignity may confer a hierarchical status by dint of an office or earned through virtuous achievement or accrue to groups. While dignity is a universal value imputed to all human beings, this analysis seeks to elucidate how dignity discourse inter-relates with rights and harmony discourses in the context of religious freedom. In so doing, it concretises the nature and content of dignity and what duties and expectations may flow therefrom by considering the 'several dignities of [the] human being' in their various functions and social roles.[34]

While noting that any theory of law that 'by virtue of its emphasis on law courts and on enforceable remedies' focuses mainly on the individual and state regulation is 'woefully incomplete', [35] the fourth part of this chapter offers concluding observations on the function of law as reconciliation and how this accords with a theory of justice as friendship, indicating what vision of society the law seeks to advance.[36] In examining how religious harmony is maintained in the non-judicial arena, it affirms that a constitutional order is not found only in the text or case law, but that the constitution is a 'living institution'.[37] The constitutional order thus develops formally and informally by practices, conventions, and prescriptive soft constitutional law norms and the legitimate expectations arising from the interactions of state and non-state actors following and developing community mores.

Accommodative Secularism and State-Religion Relations in Singapore

Unlike Malaysia, which recognises Islam as the Federation's religion, while providing that other religions 'may be practised in peace and harmony', Singapore does not have a confessional constitution,[38] but practises a form of anti-theocratic secular democracy.[39] The government does not protect religious orthodoxy or punish heresy, and citizens of religious or irreligious convictions are able to participate in political debate.[40] The government seeks

34 John Milbank, 'Dignity rather than rights' in *Understanding Human Dignity*, Christopher McCrudden ed., (OUP, 2013), 189–205 at 202.

35 Gottlieb, *supra*, note 10 at 567.

36 Tan Seow Hon, *Justice as Friendship: A Theory of Law* (Ashgate, 2015).

37 Karl Llewellyn conceptualised the US Constitution as not primarily a document but as an institution, a 'set of ways of living and doing': 'The constitution as institution' (1943) 34 Columbia Law Review 1, 3.

38 Article 3, Federal Constitution of Malaysia (1957).

39 Singapore at inception rejected adopting Malaysia's anti-propagation law prohibiting evangelism of Malays that would limit religious liberty, as giving special treatment to a religion was not suited to a 'democratic secular state': Para. 38, Report of the Constitutional Commission (1966).

40 See Li-ann Thio, 'Control, co-optation and co-operation: managing religious harmony in Singapore's multi-ethnic, quasi-secular state, (2005) 33 (2) and (3) Hastings Constitutional Law Quarterly 197–253.

to be even-handed towards different religious groups to allow their pacific co-existence in practising their faiths freely without colliding, and protects freedom of individual religious conscience. The courts approach Article 15 religious freedom cases relating to religious practices by applying a reasonableness test and requiring that restrictions be justified by demonstrating a real risk of harm to public order.

There is a certain official ambivalence towards religion: given the history of racial and religiously motivated riots and concerns about contemporary disputes involving a religious element, religion may be seen as a public order threat where the exercise of liberties like religious assembly pose 'a higher order of public order concerns'.[41] Religion is also seen as an important identity marker and a constructive social force that contributes to sustaining social mores, social welfare initiatives, and assisting in building a harmonious cohesive society.

In addition, the government owes a constitutional duty of care towards the Malays as the recognised indigenous people, to promote and protect their political, educational, religious, and socio-economic and cultural interests.[42] A limited degree of legal pluralism is provided through the constitutionally mandated Administration of Muslim Law Act, which created the advisory Islamic Religious Council, religious courts, and Shariah law relating to family and personal matters.[43] Some 99% of Malays are Muslim[44] though, unlike the Malaysia Constitution, there is no constitutional conflation of ethnicity with religion.[45]

The centrepiece of the religious harmony architecture is the MRHA, first introduced in 1990 to address perceived threats to religious harmony, which are detailed in the Maintenance of Religious Harmony white paper.[46] These were identified as aggressive proselytism, the mixing of religion and politics, such as where religious organisations get involved in the political process and radical social action and use religion for subversive activities. Tensions could arise between religious groups and between religious groups and the government. Legislation was considered necessary to maintain religious harmony, which is considered a matter of existential survivability in a multi-religious and racial polity. The MRHA was designed to formalise prudential rules relating to

41 *Vijaya Kumar v AG* [2015] SGHC 244 at [44].

42 Article 152, Singapore Constitution.

43 Li-ann Thio, 'Rule of law, religious liberty and harmony: multiculturalism, legal pluralism and the Singapore model of accommodative secularism' (2017) 5(3) Journal of Law, Religion and State 254–291.

44 Singapore Census of Population 2010: Statistical Release 1 at Singapore Department of Statistics | Singapore Census of Population 2010: Statistical Release 1: Demographic Characteristics, Education, Language and Religion: Key Findings (singstat.gov.sg).

45 Article 160(2) of the Federal Malaysian Constitution defines a Malay as someone who speaks the Malay language, adheres to Malay customs, and who is a Muslim.

46 Maintenance of Religious Harmony white paper (Cmd 21 of 1989) ('MRHWP').

tolerance, respect, and sensitivity in the exercise of religious freedoms and rules prohibiting the misuse of religion for political causes or subversive purposes.

The state is committed to ensuring the freedom to choose one's religion and to ensure that the exercise of religious liberty does not infringe upon 'the rights and sensitivities of other citizens' as 'emotions are quickly aroused' when religious sensitivities are offended, which may 'inflame passions, kindle violence'.[47] The courts have spoken of the right to 'freedom from offence'[48] and of a 'general right to be protected from insults, abuse or harassment',[49] which may be public law interests but are not constitutionally recognised rights. The white paper set forth soft constitutional law norms that operate as persuasive guidelines rather than binding obligations, constituting an executive reading of how constitutional liberties may be responsibly exercised and enjoyed. While acknowledging the constitutional right to religious propagation it noted that 'weaker' religious groups may feel threatened by attempts to convert their flock to another religion in drastic numbers; thus, religious propagation must be exercised 'very sensitively', with respect and tolerance for other faiths, which must not be denigrated.[50] Practically, this means that the positive portrayal of your own faith may be sensitive, while criticism of other faiths slide dangerously into the terrain of insensitivity; however, as there is no bright line or objective standard of how dispassionate or sensitive one should be, this could peg the degree of insensitivity at the level of the thin-skinned emotional religious man rather than the reasonable person who may be more tolerant of offensive speech in the greater interest of protecting free speech. Aggressive evangelism, particularly of the Malay Muslim community, could potentially precipitate great offence, particularly when a religionist feels that his faith has been insulted and he has no interest in being converted. The constitution guarantees the right to practise one's faith through religious teachings, which would involve differentiating one's faith from other faiths that are considered mistaken; while this was legitimate, the white paper warned this could 'go too far' if insulting and intemperate speech is used causing 'great umbrage to entire communities', the dissolution of trust, and even violent action.[51] Certainly, inciting members of a religious group to hostility or violence towards other groups, religious or otherwise, was to be avoided.

The key innovation introduced by the MRHA in 1990 was the non-justiciable restraining order that operates as a pre-emptive strike. It may be imposed against a religious leader for up to two years when the minister is satisfied that he has committed or is attempting to commit any acts within the four grounds listed under section 8, MRHA. One ground applies 'horizontally',

47 MRHWP, *supra*, note 46: [5], [11].
48 *Public Prosecutor v Benjamin Koh* [2005] SGDC 272 at [8].
49 *Chee Siok Chin v Ministry of Home Affairs HA* [2006] 1 SLR(R) 582 at [136].
50 MRHWP, *supra*, note 46: [13], [15].
51 MRHWP [16].

involving discord between religious groups where an act causes 'feelings of enmity, hatred, ill-will or hostility between religious groups'. The other three grounds apply to the 'vertical' relation between a religious person or group and the state, where under the guise of religious practices, acts are carried out that promote political causes, effect subversive activities, and excite disaffection against the president and government.[52] Restraining orders could also be made against a person acting as a conflict entrepreneur by inciting a religious leader or group to commit the listed acts.[53]

The effect of these restraining or 'gag' orders was to prohibit its recipient from addressing a religious congregation either orally or in writing and from involvement in printing or editing religious publications without prior ministerial permission. These orders are subject to ministerial appeal but not judicial review as it was feared that a public trial would 'stoke passions' and be occasion for 'political propaganda'.[54] The MRHA also created the advisory Presidential Council for Religious Harmony,[55] composed of religious and community leaders who may recommend cancelling or confirming a restraining order; where this differs from the advice of the cabinet, the president has the discretion to make the final decision.[56] Breach of these orders are an offence subject to a maximum fine of $10,000 and two years imprisonment[57] and courts are not to try any MRHA offence without the public prosecutor's consent.[58]

The restraining orders reflect the *preventative* function of law, allowing the government to act swiftly, effectively, and pre-emptively outside of the criminal law before an offence occurs, subject to weak non-judicial review. It was designed to give the government an extra, more calibrated, lever to use in managing religious harmony in cases involving religious disharmony and wounded religious feelings unsuited to prosecution under existing legislation such as the Sedition Act and Penal Code Offences Relating to Religion, where penal sanctions, which are by their nature *punitive*, would be 'too severe and disproportionate'.[59] The fact that a restraining order has never been issued since 1990 is hailed as a success and proof of its deterrent power and expressive function in shaping community norms.[60] It has also seeped into the public consciousness, where some Buddhists have urged in a teaching pamphlet that the MRHA was a safeguard against the harassment of 'insensitive proselytizing'.[61]

52 Section 8(1), MRHA (1990).
53 Section 9, MRHA (1990).
54 Para. 31, MRHWP.
55 Sections 3–7, MRHA.
56 Article 22I, Republic of Singapore Constitution, section 12, MRHA.
57 Section 16, MRHA.
58 Section 17, MRHA.
59 Para 31, MRHWP, *supra*, note 46.
60 Wrap up speech, *supra*, note 24 at [43].
61 Agree to Disagree: Conversations on Conversion at 18: Agree to Disagree | conversations on conversion (buddhist.sg).

In 2019, the MRHA was amended to port over religious offences from the Penal Code, pursuant to the project of having an omnibus legislation on religious harmony. New or expanded offences were created, updated to encompass communications in the internet age, with a clearly punitive function. Serious offences that may attract a sentence of up to ten years' imprisonment, and/or a fine, are provided for in sections 17E and F. The purpose here is to punish through enforcing strong sanctions as a form of retribution and deterrence, reflecting the person's culpability for the gravity of the offence.

Section 17E involves urging violence or force against a target person or group in Singapore, which is distinguished by dint of characteristics such as religion, ethnicity, language, political opinion, or 'any other characteristic'. Section 17F(1) relates to the offence of conduct that incites feelings of enmity, hatred, ill-will, contempt, and ridicule against a target group distinguished by religious belief or activity while section 17F(2) relates to insulting another's religion or wounding religious feelings. A distinction is drawn between offenders who are and are not religious leaders; for the latter, their conduct must threaten the public peace or public order in Singapore, whereas a higher degree of responsibility is placed on religious leaders. The motive of offenders for engaging in the relevant conduct are irrelevant: section 17(G). Such laws can restrict religious liberties, given the ambiguity in the scope of offences like wounding religious feelings: for example, if an Islamic teacher says during a sermon that Jesus is only a prophet and not the son of God as Christianity teaches, would this be an insult to many Christians, where the intent was to deliver Islamic teaching?[62]

With an expanded menu of what constitutes a religious harmony threat, the grounds for issuing a pre-emptive restraining order were expanded to include situations where, in the interests of protecting religious tolerance and public peace in Singapore, the Minister may issue an order to prevent or reduce foreign influence affecting a religious group. The religious group may be required not to accept and to return a religious donation and to ensure that all members of a governing body are Singapore citizens by a certain date.[63]

Lastly, a pacificatory or peace-making function was introduced under section 16H in relation to the community remedial initiative. This introduced another tool that might be deployed instead of legal prosecution in the menu of options serving the project of religious harmony, where reconciliation and healing of strained relations is the goal, rather than retribution. This is examined in the next section.

62 A question raised by an opposition Parliamentarian, Faisal Manap, in response to which the Home Affairs Minister stated that people were free to express their views but had to do so responsibly without denigrating another religion or degenerating into insults or incitement to violence: Para. 57, Wrap up Speech, *supra*, note 21.

63 Section 8(1A),(2A) MRHA (2020 Ed.).

Relational Constitutionalism, Public Ritual, and Formal Nudging via the CRI

Section 16H of the MRHA introduced the CRI in 2019, as an alternative non-judicial method of resolving religious disharmony situations. It reflects the spirit of relational constitutionalism and appears to draw from the public ritual that has informally developed in the past decade. This section first examines the norms and methods of relational constitutionalism in relation to how religious disharmony incidents are dealt with to promote reconciliation. It then examines the nature of the CRI mechanism as a formal attempt to utilise law as a functional tool to promote reconciliation and sustain religious harmony, and whether this vindicates or degrades human dignity values in the pursuit of ordered liberty.

Relational Constitutionalism and Religious Disharmony Public Ritual

Racial and religious harmony is treated as a peremptory norm in Singapore, underscoring the importance of a reconciliatory approach towards damaged relations, as compared to a rights-based approach that is adversarial and may sustain bitter hostility. This flows naturally with the goal of relational constitutionalism to secure 'the relational well-being of individuals and groups and to preserve sustainable relationships', allowing citizens to 'maintain their distinct identities, while being unified by a national identity and a shared commitment to the common good'.[64]

Harmony should not be conceived as a demand for conformity by an authoritarian ruler or silence in the face of a human rights violation; instead, it should be seen, in a covenantal setting,[65] as mandating resistance towards injustice and social evil that harms the common welfare.[66] As a way of 'optimizing liberty, solidarity, and order', harmony may be a way to 'realise rights without rightism',[67] to handle disharmony through civil dialogue in a conciliatory fashion.

Rights as a language of entitlement may inhibit the development of a responsibilities-oriented culture, mediated through the language of duty, civility, prudence, forbearance, and common sense, which is needed to sustain tolerance and solidarity as public values. Relationism apprehends human relations holistically, and it is unsurprising that the soft constitutional law norms

64 Li-ann Thio, 'Relational constitutionalism and the management of religious disputes: the Singapore "secularism with a soul" model' (2012) 1 Oxford Journal of Law and Religion 446.

65 Government ministers have invoked the term 'covenant' in relation to a commitment to minority protection in the face of majoritarian populism: 'Singapore must safeguard position of minorities amid growing polarization abroad: Shanmugam', *Straits Times*, 1 Feb. 2017.

66 Stephen C. Angle, 'Human rights and harmony' (2008) 30 HRQ 76–94.

67 Li-ann Thio, 'Irreducible plurality, indivisible unity: Singapore relational constitutionalism and cultivating harmony through constructing a constitutional civil religion' [2019] 20 German Law Journal 1007–1034 at 1021.

deliberately articulated in the Maintenance of Religious Harmony white paper, which are not legally binding but are legally influential, focus on duties and goods, which give rise to hortatory expectations on how to exercise rights and how to respond when action causes emotional grievances, in a manner consistent with a shared sense of public values. These norms have been internalised and elicited expressions of commitment to religious harmony as key to social cohesion in the drafting of the *Declaration of Religious Harmony* (2004)[68] and the *Commitment to Safeguard Religious Harmony* (2019),[69] which religious representatives had a hand in drafting. The commitments therein are regularly recited at inter-faith events and include respect for religious freedom, building friendships and trust, interacting in common good projects, seeking solidarity through unity in diversity, and seeking unity in diversity. These stress the importance of religious sensitivities, forswearing denigration, insult, and violence, and a commitment to resolve disputes 'through respectful dialogue' rather than diatribe.

The soft constitutional law norms form the normative framework for assessing whether a 'disharmony' incident erupts and how to manage it. These incidents and the public ritual of reconciliation and associated patterns of conduct have been examined at length elsewhere,[70] but a typical incident would involve an actor by word or deed causing another religious person or group to take offence. This could be through a provocative online video or a statement made at a meeting that is spread abroad. A complaint may be made and the police or government may issue a warning but otherwise stay in the background and allow for a community-based approach towards rapprochement to develop. The perpetrator then voluntarily visits representatives of the offended religion to tender an apology, with the press in attendance, to make public the reconciliatory hug, the fellowship meal, or inter-faith activities like joint concerts to indicate that anger has been pacified and animosities dispelled, that the relationship is restored or on an even keel, ripe for the future deepening of social bonds.

Where religious actors have publicly reached an amicable settlement, other religious leaders, through non-government groups like the Inter-Religious Organisation, express collective statements of support for the outcome, reiterating the importance of soft constitutional law norms such as non-denigration and the shared value of religious harmony. The relevant government minister through the news media, or increasingly, a Facebook post, may then 'approve' this informal process, underscoring the extension of gracious forgiveness as reflecting the 'Singapore way' of upholding 'mutual respect and harmony for

68 Text of Declaration available at https://irir.sg/declaration-on-religious-harmony-lyrics/.

69 Religious & Racial Harmony Circle: https://www.harmonycircle.sg/commitment-to-safeguard-religious-harmony/.

70 *Supra*, note 67 at 028–1033.

our common good'.[71] This signals equilibrium restored and the resolution of the matter. This the government seeks to support and will not allow this settlement to unravel.

So, when third parties, such as a group of netizens, call for the offending party to be legally prosecuted, perhaps motivated by anti-religious sentiments and driven by manufactured indignation,[72] the government rejects such calls. Otherwise, the law could be weaponised to heap abuse upon a disliked religious community for political gain or for venting one's spleen, spawning a culture of being easily offended rather than a tolerant culture. Where this rises to the level of the abusive and persecutory, such vindictiveness, acrimonious insults, and demand for vengeance through legal sanction could spark retaliatory countermeasures from that religious leader's broader religious community, perpetuating social tensions. Instead, the government prefers, where it can, to encourage the route of apology and forgiveness, the soothing rather than the stoking of social tensions.

Forgiveness is relationally oriented, as it seeks to repair and preserve a relationship through reconciliation, rather than to solidify social divides through sustained acrimony or intimidation. This requires the civic virtues of grace and goodwill, which law alone cannot cultivate; the High Court has suggested that within a secular state, a 'common value' could be 'forgiving those who have trespassed against us'.[73] Moral authority and human dignity come not only from having rights, but from how we use them, whether viciously, to exact our pound of flesh, or virtuously, to extend charity, which is a kind of love.

The Community Remedial Initiative as Part of the Peace Architecture

Nature of the CRI Mechanism

When an alleged offender commits serious offences under sections 17E and F of the MRHA relating to conduct causing feelings of enmity, ill-will, and hostility against a religious person or group or that insults a religion or wounds the religious feelings of a person in Singapore, section 16H(1) empowers the minister to steer the matter away from criminal prosecution by offering the alternative route of a CRI, involving the executive in dispute management.[74]

71 'Imam who made offense remarks to be repatriated', *Today* (Singapore), 3 Apr. 2017.

72 Cherian George, *Hate Spin: The Manufacture of Religious Offense and its Threat to Democracy* (MIT Press, 2017).

73 *Kalpanath Singh v Law Society* [2009] 4 S.L.R.(R.) 1018 at para. 23 (H.C.).

74 Whether a CRI agreement is made may interfere with the discretion of the Public Prosecutor who acts independently. Indeed, a refusal to enter into a CRI agreement is a factor that will be considered in deciding whether criminal prosecution is appropriate, as distinct from a conditional warning. The Law Minister during parliamentary debates stated it was inappropriate to leave the power for calling for a CRI in the hands of the AG's Chambers as it was voluntary and meant to be a community-based way of dealing with issues: Paras 85–86, Wrap Up Speech, *supra*, note 24.

This was introduced as a novel 'community-based tool' that focuses 'on restoration and rehabilitation',[75] entailing 'an opportunity to take one or more remedial actions, participate in one or more activities, or do any other thing'[76] to promote religious harmony in Singapore. The CRI mechanism is meant to be voluntary, such that section 16H(3) provides that the relevant person chooses whether to enter a CRI with the minister, provided this cannot be entered into after trial for the alleged offence commences: section 16H(5). Where the CRI regarding an alleged offence is in force, the alleged offender is deemed to have been given a discharge not amounting to an acquittal, and during the duration of the CRI, the alleged offender cannot be prosecuted for any offence under the MRHA or any other law in any criminal proceedings: section 16H(6). If however, the minister believes that the terms of the CRI agreement have not been complied with, he may terminate the CRI and refer the offence to the Public Prosecutor: section 16(7).

The CRI Mechanism and Human Dignity

The CRI operates against a broader legal framework, which includes the prospect of punitive sanctions. Its distinct purpose is not punishment but correction and repair of communal relations. It appears to formalise the extant public ritual of reconciliation, rather than letting it develop or operate organically according to social expectations. Under the CRI regime, it is the government that determines the viability of the CRI as a harmony restoration measure and monitors its performance to ensure that its objectives are attained. The government decides the type of person suited to an offer of a CRI agreement, what process of reconciliation and what rituals of contrition are appropriate, and whether the actions taken are satisfactory, so as to negate the need for legal prosecution and its retributive goals.

Law is involved, but not in substantive terms, as the law does not prescribe what a remedial action might constitute on the facts, but pragmatically leaves this open-ended to preserve flexibility; law takes on a functional form, as an instrument in service of reconciliation.[77] It does this by fading into the background and creating a non-law space where strained relationships and hurt

75 Minister for Law K. Shanmugam, Second Reading, Maintenance of Religious Harmony (Amendment) Bill, 7 Oct 2019 at [71]; text available at https://www.mha.gov.sg/media-room/parliamentary/second-reading-speech-for-the-maintenance-of-religious-harmony-amendment-bill---speech-by-mr-k-shanmugam-minister-for-home-affairs-and-minister-for-law/.

76 Section 16H(1), MRHA.

77 Antonio Buti, 'Reconciliation: its relationship and importance to law', and Lorna McGregor, 'Reconciliation: where is the law?', both in Scott Veitch ed. *Law and the Politics of Reconciliation* (Routledge 2007), 107–117 and 111–218.

feelings can be addressed, where 'apology and forgiveness are possible'.[78] It thus takes emotions seriously in a manner trial proceedings are incapable of doing, in the hope of mitigating vindictive, vengeful responses, which bode ill for community relations. As the success of a CRI will turn on the willingness of the alleged offender to comply with its terms, this legally provided for option is designed to persuade, not to compel, to encourage common commitment to religious harmony as a public good. Section 16H provides an institutional 'nudge'[79] by which the government can intervene through wielding carrots and sticks to guide people towards beneficial and desirable behaviour in a 'non-legal way', as far as possible.[80] Nudges, rather than shoves, enable people to make a choice that they adjudge is in their personal interest.

The government has indicated that in deciding on the appropriate form of remedy, it will consult religious leaders while retaining the final decision-making power to ensure CRI actions are 'appropriate and beneficial'.[81] Action oriented towards mending ties with the aggrieved community 'could include issuing a public or private apology or participating in activities that promote religious harmony'.[82] CRIs are reserved for cases where the alleged offender and offended community are 'willing to meet to mend relations'[83]; it will not be offered in serious cases involving egregious conduct such as where a person incites violence or acts in a way that threatens Singapore public peace and order, where criminal sanctions are appropriate.[84]

Non-Coercive Mechanism, Freedom of Conscience, and Human Dignity

The CRI is designed to be voluntary in nature and the specific remedial action that the government may propose, is subject to the mutual agreement of the relevant parties. This reflects a concern with human dignity in the sense of securing spiritual autonomy, grounded upon the principle of free conscience.

During parliamentary debates, the law minister noted that 'we should not force people to do what their faith militates against them doing',[85] such as requiring them to go to another religion's place of worship or participate

78 Meghan Clarke, 'Polarization: the role of emotions in reconciliation efforts' [Spring 2009] 72(2) Law and Contemporary Problems 27–31 at 31.

79 See generally Richard H. Thaler and Cass R. Sunstein, *Nudge* (Yale University Press, 2008).

80 Wrap up Speech, *supra*, note 24 at [89].

81 Ibid., at [88].

82 Sun Xueling, Snr Parliamentary Secretary Home Affairs Ministry, Second Reading, Maintenance of Religious Harmony (Amendment) Bill, 7 Oct. 2019 at [41], text available at Second Reading Speech for the Maintenance of Religious Harmony (Amendment) Bill – Speech by Sun Xueling, Senior Parliamentary Secretary, Ministry of Home Affairs and Ministry of National Development (mha.gov.sg).

83 Wrap up Speech, *supra*, note 24 at [165].

84 Examples of egregious conduct are the type of actions contained in sections 267C (inciting violence) and sections 295–298A of the Penal Code.

85 Wrap up Speech, *supra*, note 24 at [86].

in inter-religious activities. Appeal is made to the conscience of the alleged offender as an autonomous moral agent, maintaining respect for the person's understanding of whether a proposed remedial act violates the integrity of his faith. Further, improvement in the alleged offender's understanding and conduct should not be by way of 'forcing someone through the law to 'reform'.[86] This reflects a Confucianist understanding that all people are educable and that education opens the door to transformation and the development of character and moral virtues, which a *junzi* (君子), meaning a superior person or honourable gentleman, possesses. This comes from the internalisation of social values.[87] Law can extract external conformity in terms of behaviour and speech but cannot change the heart; law can, through promoting dialogue, interaction, and conciliatory processes to help human relating, facilitate this process of personal transformation.

Hard to Say You're Sorry? Apologies, Rehabilitation, and Human Dignity

Judicially ordered apologies are a recognised feature of civil suits, such as contempt of court proceedings.[88] Apologies are also a mitigating factor in assessing the quantum of damages in defamation suits. The Singapore Court of Appeal has recognised that apology orders may serve various purposes, such as retribution, deterrence, rehabilitation and an educative, signalling, and corrective objective.[89]

Notably, as far as community-based reconciliation processes are concerned, delivering apologies plays a key role through a recognitive and reparative act of acknowledging wrong-doing that caused suffering, which can soothe anger,[90] combined with allowing the offended community to speak with the offender and accept his apology. An apology as an expression of respect and regret may provide solace for emotional harm, redress indignity, and restore a sense of esteem, indicating that the offended person is wronged and worthy of respect as a fellow human being of equal moral standing. It provides the reassurance and moral satisfaction that the wrongful conduct is recognised as being

86 Ibid., at [87].

87 Rita Ng, 'College and character: what did Confucius teach us about the importance of integrating ethics, character, learning, and education?' (2009) 10(4) Journal of College and Character 1–6.

88 Robyn Carroll, 'Apologies as a legal remedy' [2013] 35 Sydney Law Review 317–347.

89 *Wham Kwok Han Jolovan v AG* [2020] 1 SLR 804 at [74], citing Gijs van Dijck, 'The ordered apology' (2014) 37 Oxford Journal of Legal Studies 562. See further Nick Smith, *I Was Wrong: The Meaning of Apologies* (Cambridge University Press, 2009); Nick Smith, *Justice Through Apologies: Remorse, Reform and Punishment* (Cambridge University Press, 2014); Lee Taft, 'Apology subverted: the commodification of apology', (2000) 109 Yale Law Journal 1135.

90 Jasper Friedrich, 'Anger and apology, recognition, and reconciliation: managing anger in the wake of injustice' (2002) 2(2) Global Studies Quarterly 1–11.

anti-social, affirming social norms and enhancing the prospect that such conduct will not be repeated in future.

Experience indicates that disharmony situations are most effectively resolved 'where the offender displays remorse' for his actions and 'makes amends directly to the offended party as facilitated by their religious groups',[91] as the practice of the public ritual of apology and forgiveness demonstrates.

Nonetheless, the CRI itself does not provide for enforced apologies, which may be inauthentic and deleterious to genuine reconciliation. As a form of compelled speech, it can also be a disproportionate and ineffective response, limiting the freedom to withhold expression; if too humiliating, the dehumanising effect may breed resentment and alienation, disrespecting human dignity and the integrity of each partner in a community. The sincerity of a heartfelt apology and expression of genuine remorse is better fodder for repairing relational well-being than a formulaic scripted apology cynically delivered to avoid criminal prosecution. Good faith and sincerity maximises the power of face-to-face interaction between the victim and delinquent party, as this has an educative effect in nurturing empathy and understanding. This provides a 'teaching moment', an opportunity for personal rehabilitation through a humble acceptance of moral responsibility, stimulating moral reflection and deepening understanding of the sensitivities of the multi-religious context. This may precipitate modified personal behaviour, allowing for moral growth. The introduction of the CRI reflects an appreciation that human nature is imperfect; however, while human beings are not angels, neither are they devils; people can learn through experience and hortatory guidance. While law can only restrain behaviour, the CRI, by facilitating dialogue and interaction, can contribute to healing by soothing 'communal tensions' and repairing 'disrupted ties' between communities.[92]

The dignity of a religious group and its members is also important, insofar as there is a commitment to reconcile with an offending party, rather than demonise another as the enemy who is not worth maintaining or developing relationships with. Treating a religious individual as an enemy or 'other' can escalate tensions as that individual's religious community will feel the injustice of an over-zealous abusive treatment of that individual, particularly where he has made reconciliatory overtures and demonstrated penitence.

Accepting an apology also signals the acceptance and reintegration of the offending party into the community as a valued member of good standing, able to repent and change for the better, which is the basis for restoring and building friendly relations in the future. This is the dignity of friendly relations that we accord each other by committing to salvage strained relations in service of religious harmony as a social good that all benefit from.

91 Sun Xueling, *supra*, note 82 at [36].
92 Ibid., [35].

What Community Initiated Reconciliatory Gestures Can Accomplish: An Instructive Example

During parliamentary debates, a government minister described a situation that captured the 'essence' of the CRI mechanism,[93] which is instructive in how a process of reconciliation can be approached and realised.

This related to an incident in 2019 when Sheena Phua, a social media influencer, posted an Instagram photo of two tall Sikh men wearing white turbans who blocked her view of the concert stage at the Singapore Grand Prix, referring to them as '2 huge obstructions'. Wearing turbans is religiously required in the Sikh religion and Phua received online backlash for being racist and slighting Sikhism. She responded with an online apology to the Sikh community, stating that the post was not intended to be racist or derogatory.[94] The Young Sikh Association (YSA) then took the 'commendable' path in reaching out and inviting Phua to visit their gurdwara so that she could learn about Sikh traditions. This was praised by the minister as 'the better and more sustainable path is not of hate or taking sides, but of friendship, respect and learning about each other'.[95] While the YSA leaders noted that people inside and outside their community demanded an apology, they felt that 'actions speak louder than words' and that an apology per se would not have contributed towards improving awareness and understanding.[96] She willingly accepted the invitation to visit the Central Sikh Temple where she learnt about Sikh culture and religion, Sikh greetings, and participated in an act of service by making chapati in the community kitchen. The YSA president expressed his hope that all involved 'walked away as better people', appreciating the 'humility, kindness, curiosity and sincerity' that Phua showed.[97] A subsequent YSA Facebook post demonstrated moral leadership in expressing the hope that when we make mistakes and unintentionally cause offence, that others would show us empathy, be understanding and forgiving and 'reach out to us in friendship, as opposed to reacting based on emotions and pointing fingers to blame?'[98] Phua, in an Instagram post, declared that after the warm welcome she received from the Sikh community, 'my faith in humanity has been restored' and she

93 Second Reading, Home Affairs and Law Minister K. Shanmugam, Maintenance of Religious Harmony (Amendment) Bill, 7 Oct. 2019 at [72], text available at https://www.mha.gov.sg/mediaroom/parliamentary/second-reading-speech-for-the-maintenance-of-religious-harmony-amendment-bill---speech-by-mr-k-shanmugam-minister-for-home-affairs-and-minister-for-law/.

94 'Blogger Sheen Phua apologises to Sikh community over "misinterpreted" Instagram Post', Yahoo News, 23 Sept. 2019.

95 K. Shanmugam, *supra*, note 75 at [74]

96 'Sikh group invites influencer to gurdwara after viral Instagram post on two men wearing turbans', *Straits Times* (Singapore) 29 Sept. 2019.

97 Ibid.

98 Young Sikh Association, Facebook post 28 September 2019 at https://www.facebook.com/YSA.SGonInstagram/posts/2655918301125859.

had learned about the need for *Charndikala*, the Punjabi term for the Sikh principle of joyful optimism.[99]

This account reflects a successful case of repairing relational rifts and improving the relationship between two sets of people in conflict. This not only restores peace between two communities, but also internal peace within those communities, where there is mutual recognition and respect for the humanity of the other person as a moral interlocutor, worthy of engaging with, rather than demonising.

It sets forth a normative vision of a plural society that is interactive and where harmonious co-existence is an aspirational and realisable norm rather than isolated ghettoes, which all should be committed to securing. It appreciates the dignity of the group and the nature of religion as not only involving belief but religious relationships; as such, other group members may be offended or hurt by words or deeds directed at a member of their community. Religious harmony gives expression to individual rights and to the responsibilities of a socially situated individual balanced with community interests. Collectively, this shapes expectations that while breach of harmony norms may attract opprobrium, the desirable response is that of forgiveness where apologies are tendered and received and efforts to build friendly relations, goodwill, and solidarity are encouraged and supported.

Law, Reconciliation, and Relational Values

Law has functioned as a tool of reconciliation to bring about durable settlements over conflicts in rifted societies undergoing social change, such as transitional post-apartheid South Africa or the relations between indigenous and settler communities in Canada, protecting the interests of marginalised minority groups and according political legitimacy to social movements.

In Singapore, law as reconciliation operates in a stable multi-religious society dealing not primarily with rights but with restoring right relationships in the interests of religious harmony, social cohesion, and ordered liberty. Rights are implicated, of course, such as where the liberty of propagation or religious teachings offends or 'insults' another religious group. The focus is on the responsible exercise of rights as well as the right reaction in the aftermath of a disharmony incident in living a commitment to conciliation and friendly relations. The aspiration is that this commitment be done in a way that vindicates human dignity, both in the sense of being a universal trait of personhood as well as an aspect of social relationship in terms of the respect and honour due to how good citizens behave in service of harmonious co-existence.

99 Sheen Phua, Instagam post of 29 Sept. 2019: https://www.instagram.com/p/B2_BhT9B-kJg/.

While law can influence behaviour, it 'cannot compel emotions and heartfelt speech',[100] mandate genuine moral transformation, nor assure prudent conduct. It can, by promoting social interaction through dialogical and interactive processes, through apology and forgiveness protocols, 'assist in recovery, forgiveness and reconciliation'.[101] This can meet the psychological needs of the parties to a disharmony incident beyond what judicial proceedings and legal remedies can provide; it allows the wrong or misunderstanding to be faced openly and for the therapeutic expression of emotions, providing an opportunity to listen and speak as part of the healing process, which enables perceptions and attitudes towards the other party to shift for the better. Forgiveness is the best way to recover from the wrong and to build relational wellness. Contrariwise, the legal process may aggravate inter-religious relations and deepen fault lines; it may be 'counter-productive' where the offending party is unrepentant – the law may punish him but is unable to deal with communal relations or prevent offending persons from becoming 'martyrs for their communities', further inflaming tensions.[102]

Legal mechanisms like the CRI can provide a personal inflection point for the offending party to realise the importance of making amends to the affected community and to better appreciate the sensitivities of Singapore's multi-religious society. This shores up the vision of the good citizen as one who values racial and religious harmony and will work to preserve it. It provides a form of catharsis for the affected community and an opportunity to be a good citizen with a virtuous disposition that commits to forgiving the repentant, refusing the path of vitriol and vengeance. Thus, both offender and victim are reinforced through the performance of these imperfect obligations owed at large (such as the duty to be patient or charitable) to their sense of belonging to a moral community, making covenantal relationship possible. It may further reinforce expectations that future disagreements will also be settled peacefully, in a generous spirit of solidarity.

In this way, depolarisation occurs, which is a prelude to reconciliation, where negative emotions like resentment, fear, and hate are resolved and positive emotions like mutual respect, empathy, trust, and solidarity may be adopted. This affects not only the immediate parties but third parties and the broader community, affirming social norms and having the potential to secure better future relations. Trust is cultivated when the alleged offender not only expresses contrition but also demonstrates conduct showing both a changed mindset and the promise of changes in future behaviour, as where a pastor berated for insensitive videos on his church website that were publicly

100 Robyn Carroll, 'Apologies as a legal remedy' [2013] 35 Sydney Law Review 317 at 322.
101 Ibid., at 321.
102 Wrap up Speech, *supra*, note 24 at [154].

accessible, not only apologised but took pains to review the entire online catalogue and to excise material that might cause offence and hurt.[103]

There is always the possibility that reconciliation measures like the CRI may be abused and reduced only to the spectacle of apologetic performance; someone may just go through the motions to avoid criminal prosecution, tendering an insincere apology that may sour trust. However, the official position is that 'we should take a chance that the CRI will help some people, and some communities, to mend communal relations', just as YSA members through their outreach had taken in hope, as it is impossible to discern perfectly the heart and mind of a person. Law can nurture not only expectations but aspirations towards desirable conduct that may result in meaningful relational reconciliation.

Law, Religious Harmony, and Reconciliation as *Shalom*

The social fact of religious diversity may give rise to various governance problems, where individuals or religious minorities may assert rights claims to secure autonomy interests against majoritarian interests or where religious disharmony arises out of inter-religious group tensions. The former problem may focus on rights to mitigate the asymmetries of power, while the latter problem may focus on restoring and maintaining right relationships, not through justiciable entitlements but through deploying law as a tool of reconciliation to bring a sense of harmony to situations of discord.[104] Insofar as 'rights talk' conceives of justice exclusively or predominantly in terms of rights, it is not sufficient to settle strife between social actors and may perpetuate personal conflict and inflexibility in relationships. A different theory of justice, to inform the acceptable contours of ordered liberty, is needed as well as a different method of engagement. Indeed, how a society treats transgressors of social norms is revealing of the character of that society, whether depressed by the bleak worldview of perpetual social conflict or buoyed by the hope of positive change and basic human decency.

Reconciliation focuses on what goes wrong with relationships in order to fix them, setting forth expectations or aspirations of right conduct or right response to wrong conduct through hortatory persuasion rather than compulsion; this dovetails with the goals of relational constitutionalism to secure societal cohesion and solidarity after a conflict that disrupts relational equilibrium. This is done by appealing not only to rights but mutual duties and the shared good of community weal to repair relationships. These values must be internalised to build up the notion of what it means to be a responsible, good

103 'Pastor called up by ISD: leader of independent church apologies to Buddhists and Taoists' *Straits Times* (Singapore) 9 June 2010.

104 Daniel Philpot, 'Reconciliation, politics and transitional justice' in *The Oxford Handbook of Religion, Conflict and Peacebuilding*, (OUP 2015) 335–354.

citizen, as such a citizen who appreciates the civic virtue of seeking friendly relations to solidify racial and religious harmony is a person who thinks and acts relationally. This is akin to the core Confucian value of '*ren*' (仁), which literally means two-man mindedness, considering the other, promoting the good that comes when people get along. As such, conflicts should be reduced by people respecting, understanding, loving, and forgiving each other, acting with self-restraint, and in being educated in the *li* (礼) or moral law with its emphasis on good manners and propriety.[105] Indeed, relationships may flourish when one is not simply given his due but more than his due, as an act of generous, unsolicited goodwill.

Thus, these imperfect obligations not to denigrate other faiths, or where offence is given, to take reciprocal reconciliatory steps to apologise and accept an apology, is the attempt of the law to secure a general level of social trust, to fortify behavioural expectations that induce desirable conduct and to reinforce a sense of belonging to a moral community. If this fails, the Law may default to punitive sanctions.

The prioritisation of right relationship bears some resonance to a theory of justice as friendship[106]; the relationship of friendship, which is posited as a universal phenomenon or universal ideal, generates reasonable expectations and obligations for friends by dint of their relationship. If citizens are regarded as a community of friends, even in disputes, justice requires that citizens should inter-relate in a way that recognises the intrinsic worth of all parties, which shows concern for the well-being of others and the holding of reciprocal obligations to seek peace and pursue it. This comports with human dignity values grounded in reciprocal respect for all, a commitment to remedy dignitary harms and to build friendly relations rather than casting the parties as victim and villain to perpetual antagonism. To be willing to reconcile is to accord human dignity to the offending person, to view that person as a friend, a fellow human being who is worth retaining a relationship with rather than as a demonised other. A shared valuation of community weal in the form of religious harmony makes possible stronger social bonds through what might be called a 'covenantal' perspective towards relationship rather than reducing citizenship to transactional relations shaped by a utilitarian calculus. This posits an enduring partnership between citizens from multiple backgrounds united by shared burdens and values. It speaks to a commitment towards a certain 'way of thinking and conduct' enabling persons to 'live free while being bound together in appropriate relationships, to preserve their own integrities while

105 Lihua Yang, 'Chinese schools of wisdom on conflict resolution and their relevance to contemporary public governance: a contingent framework' (2018) 12 International Journal of Conflict and Violence 1–19.

106 Tan Seow Hon, *Justice as Friendship: A Theory of Law* (Ashgate, 2015).

sharing in a common whole' and 'to pursue both the necessities of human existence and the desiderata of moral response in some reasonable balance'.[107]

Law may facilitate reconciliation in the event of social rifts; reconciliation as a concept of justice contemplates a comprehensive set of obligations that define right relations in all spheres of human activity; reconciliation as a legal tool is also a concept of peace, but not merely the thin concept of peace as an absence of agitation or conflict, but a thicker version of peace. This may encompass something akin to the Greek concept of *eiréné* (ειρήνη), which connotes harmony and concord,[108] and the Hebrew concept of *shalom* (שָׁלוֹם) that entails 'completeness, wholeness, health, peace, welfare, safety, soundness, tranquility … fullness, rest, harmony'.[109]

To attain peace in the face of broken human relationships, a holistic vision of the human person is necessary, where individuals are viewed not as atomistic, utility and autonomy maximising agents, but whole and complex persons with feelings, psychological needs, emotions, rationality, and conscience. Reconciliation, which appreciates that human beings are relational creatures, is able to capture understandings of human dignity not only as an inherent property, but in the quality of relationships and how we are treated by others, which can strengthen the foundation for harmonious relations.

Indeed, the meaning of religion, from the Latin root *ligare*,[110] means to 'bind up what is broken', to reconnect and restore relationship, whether with the divine or fellow humans. In the Book of Isaiah in the Hebrew Bible, an unhealthy wound is described as one that is 'not pressed out, nor bandaged nor softened with oil'.[111] Thus, reconciliatory initiatives like the public ritual of apology, forgiveness, and fellowship, which the government through the CRI may now 'nudge' parties towards in the absence of their proactive measures, can address the wound caused by disharmony in three stages. First, by recognition of the offence and ministering to it by removing what is toxic and harmful; second, by bandaging it and forestalling infection by apologies and reassurances of non-repetition, showing an understanding of hurt sensitivities and the need for remedy; and last, soothing the wound by the oil of contrition and the restoration of 'lost' dignity and respect. Internal peace within persons and communities reinforces peace-making and external amity between persons and groups.

Thus, the imperative of maintaining religious harmony, which contours the scope of religious freedom through deploying law as a pacificatory tool of

107 Daniel J. Elazar, Chapter III, The Covenant Tradition in Politics, Volume 1, Introduction, archived by the Jerusalem Center for Public Affairs at https://www.jcpa.org/dje/books/ct-vol1-int.htm.

108 Strong's G1515, at https://www.blueletterbible.org/lexicon/g1515/kjv/tr/0-1/.

109 Strong's Concordance 7965, at https://biblehub.com/hebrew/7965.htm.

110 Sarah F. Hoyt, 'The etymology of religion' (1912) 32(2) Journal of the American Oriental Society 126–169.

111 Isaiah 1:6, English Standard Version.

reconciliation may further facilitate the beneficial efforts of religion as a public good, insofar as it has reconciliatory, restorative, and redemptive force. The ordered liberty struck by keeping the faith and keeping the peace by keeping relational health is a factor key to securing the sustainable development and flourishing of religiously plural, inter-cultural societies, where both human dignity, in its personal and social forms, and human rights, are taken seriously.

4 On the Importance of the Distinction between Human Dignity and Honour in the Inter-Cultural Debate

Lara Scaglia

Premise

The philosophical and legal debate on human dignity saw a point of no return in 1948, when the *Universal Declaration of Human Rights* – defending freedom and equal dignity and rights of all human beings – was adopted by the UN General Assembly in Paris on 10 December 1948 during its 183rd plenary meeting.[1] While in Western countries many documents followed the path opened by the Declaration and aimed at defending human dignity (for instance, the first article of the German Fundamental Law of 1949 and the Preamble of the International Covenant on Civil and Political Rights of 1966), in Islamic countries, there was no general recognition of its value.[2] However, attempts to adapt its content to the local Islamic context have been made.

More specifically, in 1981 the Muslim World League (established and funded by Saudi Arabia) drafted the *Universal Islamic Declaration of Human Rights* but this document was highly criticised because of the conflation of dignity and honour and because in the original version (but not in the English translation) law is intended exclusively as Shari'ah.[3] Later, in 1990, the *Cairo Declaration of Human Rights* aimed to guide the decisions of all member states in matters of human rights; the language of the document was inspired by the *Universal Declaration of Human Rights* and declared that human rights are dependent on the recognition of human dignity. Still, in the Cairo Declaration

1 However, the notion of dignity was already mentioned in the constitution of the Weimar Republic in 1919, followed by the Portuguese constitution in 1933, and the Irish constitution in 1937.

2 Saudi Arabia abstained from voting on the Declaration because of the lack of reference to God as the source of right. Differently, Pakistan welcomed it, seeing no conflict with the content of the Qur'an (see Gurewitsch, A.D. (1973), *Eleanor Roosevelt: Her Day*. New York, Interchange Foundation: 25).

3 See Mayer, A.E. (2013): *Islam and Human Rights, Tradition and Politics*. NY, Routledge.

DOI: 10.4324/9781003519188-6

of 1990, art. 24 declared that "All human beings are Allah's subjects"[4] and that all rights are subject to Islamic Shari'ah thus undermining the universality of those rights. However, in the revised version of the Cairo Declaration (of 2020) the text is more in line with a universal and modern interpretation of dignity: there is no longer a proclamation of the subordination of all rights to the Shari'ah and the first article does not contain anymore the claim that human beings are Allah's subject, but just that "All human beings form one family. They are equal in dignity, rights and obligations, without any discrimination on the grounds of race, colour, language, sex, religion, sect, political opinion, national or social origin, fortune, age, disability or other status".[5] These changes demonstrate at least the willingness of the member states that signed it to recognise human dignity independently of origin, religious beliefs, and merits, thus suggesting that it is distinguished from honour.

Now, the different reactions to the Declaration of 1948 and the different practical values ascribed to the Cairo Declaration of 2020 demonstrates the absence of a common line in Islamic jurisprudence and philosophy of right concerning the status of human dignity and human rights in general. I will now provide an overview of some of the major positions in the Islamic debate on dignity and focus on the possibility of distinguishing it from honour.

Karamah: Universalists versus Communalists

The term "*karam*" has a pre-Qur'anic origin and was used to describe someone who had a high social rank or was – for some reasons – worthy of being esteemed.[6]. This meaning is therefore similar to the Latin *dignitas*, which refers to the social status of a person. Now, in the Qur'an, *karam* usually describes God's generosity and someone who acts in a noble manner so that he deserves to be treated as honourable.[7]. However, in verse 17:70, dignity is attributed to every human being as such, independently of her behaviour and merits: "We have bestowed dignity [*karamah*] on the children of Adam [...] and conferred upon them special favours above the greater part of Our creation".[8] This verse is the one used to ground the main argument of universalistic interpreters, who defend the attribution of dignity to every human being, independently from her religion, conduct, sex, and social status. But given this ambiguity, which might lead to translating *karamah* as honour as well as dignity, it is important to try to understand the distinction between the two meanings.

4 Cairo Declaration 1990 cairo.pdf (fmreview.org).
5 Cairo Declaration 2020: oic_cairo_dec_hr_19_11_2019_ar.pdf (oic-oci.org).
6 See Dehkhoda (2011), *Dictionary*, Vol. 1, 2nd ed, Tehran, The University of Tehran Press.
7 Rahiminia, M. (2007), transl. of *Mufradat* of Raqib, 1st ed. Tehran, Sobhan Publishing House.
8 Qur'an 17:70.

Honour should be regarded as the recognition of a rank or value attributed to someone because of her behaviour (e.g., be brave, honest) or having some specific characteristics (e.g., having a noble origin). This produces a hierarchical social structure in which everyone has her own status and if she fails to maintain it, the consequence is dishonour.[9] In modern times, a new paradigm and self-awareness spread, namely one in which the subject is considered as "naked", freed from stereotypes. According to Taylor, this separation between the world of honour and the world of dignity characterises a modern sphere deprived of hierarchical structure, in which dignity is attributed to an individual because of her unicity and differences from the community. While in pre-modern societies someone has honour insofar as she shares the values and goals of the community, in modern times someone has dignity independent of her alignment to common ideals.[10]

Now, as Andishan[11] correctly points out, the problem is that in the scholarship on dignity and human rights in Islam, sometimes the two terms have not been distinguished. While in many translations[12] ***karamah*** is rendered as honour, scholars such as Abdulaziz Sachedina[13] and Mohammad H. Kamali[14] translate it as dignity for a practical reason, namely, to make it easier to compare the Islamic moral and legal discourse with the Western one. However, to Andishan, it is clear that the most adequate translation is honour given the number of passages of the Qur'an in which the term is related to the status of the believer[15] rather than to something analogous to the modern notion of human dignity. For instance, "And honour belongs to God, to His Messenger and the believers"[16]; "The most honourable among you in the sight of God is the most pious of you".[17]

Now, in the religious-philosophical Islamic scholarship, ***karamah*** is often related to other concepts and it might be helpful to focus on them to

9 Berger, P. (1983): "On the Obsolescence of the Concept of Honour", in: S. Hauerwas and A. MacIntyre (eds.) *Revisions: Changing Perspectives in Moral Philosophy*. University of Notre Dame Press, Notre Dame: 172–181.

10 Taylor, C. (1991): *The Malaise of Modernity*. Toronto, House of Anansi Press.

11 Andishan, H. (2019): "Honour or Dignity? An Oversimplification in Islamic Human Rights" *Human Rights Review*, Vol. 20: 461–475.

12 Arthur John Arberry, Ahmed Ali, Ahmed Reza Khan, Daryabadi, Hilali and Khan, Itani, Maududi, Mubarakpuri, Pickthall, Qarai, Qaribulah and Darwish, Sarvar, Shakir, Wahiduddin Khan.

13 In his *Islam and the Challenge of Human Rights*, published by Oxford University in 2009.

14 Kamali, M.H. (2007): "Human Dignity in Islam", *International Institute of Advanced Islamic Studies* (IAIS).

15 For this, Andishan believes that the discourse on dignity cannot but remain secular because every reference to any kind of religion, or political status, will inevitably create a hierarchical structure.

16 Qur'an 63:8.

17 Qur'an 49:13.

understand the content of such "special favours"[18] attributed to mankind. The Hanafi school,[19] which defends the universalistic position, focuses on *'ismah*, i.e., inviolability, which, according to Imam Abu Hanifah (d.767) is inseparable from ***adamiyyah*** (being a descendent of Adam, independent of being Muslim or not). As Ibn Abidin (d.1834) stated: "a human being is honoured, even if he is a non-Muslim (***al-adami mukarram wa law kefiran***)".[20]

Besides being related to inviolability, ***karamah*** is linked to the exercise of freedom, in particular, in moral and religious matters, even if it is contrary to Islam.[21] The relationship between man and God, namely, must be defended as a free one, as repeatedly written in the Qu'ran: "there shall be no compulsion in religion"[22]; "Let whosoever wills, believe, and whosoever wills, disbelieve".[23] Freedom is what gives meaning to responsibility, morality, and religious belief; there is no sense, then, for this account, to regard religion as the condition to be treated as having dignity.[24] Opposing this universalistic interpretation, the Imam al-Shafi''i (d.820) saw the condition of belonging to Islam as the necessary condition for dignity. His arguments found further support in Ahmad Ibn Hanbal (d.855), Malik (d.795), Daud al-Zahiri (d.885), and the Shiite al-Tusi, whose lines regard ***karamah*** as being acquired and faith as the condition of its acquisition.[25] So, universalistic and communalist interpretations differ insofar as the former regard ***karamah*** as close to the modern conception of dignity, while the latter consider it as a consequence of honourable behaviour, i.e., be a believer.

Modern Islamic Approaches

Modern Islamic authors discussing dignity and human rights follow – implicitly or explicitly – the universalistic notion of ***karamah*** (regarded as dignity, rather than honour) and link this discourse to that concerning the possibility of modernising Islam. I will provide here some examples of this. The Sudanese scholar and reformer Ustadh Mahmoud Mohmed Taha, who was executed for apostasy, developed what he called the "Second Message of Allah". He stated that it is important to distinguish between the verses revealed in Medina, which were appropriate in their time only, from the ones revealed in Mecca, which

18 Qur'an 17:70.

19 However, there are prominent scholars who do not belong to the Hanafi school who defend this position: Abu Hamid al-Ghazali (Shafi'i), Ibn Rushd al-Qurtubi (Maliki), and Ibn Qayyim al-Jawziyyah (Hanbali) support the universalist position on human dignity.

20 ibn Abidin, M.A. (1386/1966) *Hashiyah ibn 'Abidin*. Cairo: Mustafa al-Babi al-Halabi, Vol. V: 58.

21 Al-Sarakhsi (1986) *Usul al-Sarakhsi*, ed. Abu''l-Wafa al-Afghani. Istanbul, Kahraman Yay: 86.

22 Qur'an 2:256.

23 Qur'an 18:29.

24 Al-Marghinani, A. (1989): *The Hedaya or Guide: A Commentary on the Mussulman Laws*. C. Hamilton (transl.), Karachi. Daru''l- Ishaat, II: 221.

25 Yadollahpur, B. (2012) *Human Dignity According to the Qur'an*, 1st ed. Tehran, Adyan Press.

represent the core of the ideal religion. Taha claims that the verses emphasising freedom of choice and individual responsibility for such choice before God should be the bases of modern Islamic law and that the verses encouraging discrimination against non-Muslims should be abrogated.[26] One of his followers, Abdullahi Ahmed An-Na'im proposes to localise the debate, i.e., in case of disagreement – concerning the content of dignity, the application of human rights, etc., – we should go deeper into the local context of each issue threatening dignity to find points that can be shared by the local community:

> It is imperative to engage in an internal discourse within the framework of the religious community in question, in order to overcome objections to human rights norms [...] The way out of the vicious cycle of the "universality-relativity debate" is to go deeper into the local context of each issue in order to find sustainable points of mediation.[27]

A similar approach is shared by the Iranian Shiite scholar Mohsen Kadivar, who wants to adjust the boundaries between religion and jurisprudence to modernise Islam[28] and the neo-'Mu'tazilite Abdolkarim Souroush, who aims at reforming religion in a rational and plural way:

> By lighting the flame of reason, theologians rescue believers from the chilling aridity of mindless dogmas and contribute to the warmth of wisdom. Theological religion is a hundred times better and sweeter than common, emulative religiosity, and it nurtures within it a plurality of which there is neither sight nor sound in the parched desert of common religiosity. This is a plurality that is built on doubt, not certitude, and it is a pluralism that is negative, not positive.[29]

This emphasis on reason and its role in the religious as well as secular discourse on human dignity is stressed in a recent book by Schroeder and Bani-Sadr. They interpret dignity in Islam as having features similar to the Catholic doctrine of dignity as God-given and the Kantian notions of freedom and

26 An-Na'im, A.A. (1986) "Religious Freedom in Egypt: Under the Shadow of the Islamic Dhimma System", in *Religious Liberty and Human Rights in Nations and in Religions*. L. Swidler (ed.), Philadelphia, Ecumenical Press, Temple University: 59.

27 An-Na'im', A. (2000) "Islam and Human Rights: Beyond the Universality Debate", *Proceedings of the Annual Meeting* (American Society of International Law). New York, Cambridge University Press, Vol. 94: 101.

28 He proposed to distinguish the "sacred message" from "sediment" (which derived from historical circumstances) by separating precepts whose harms or benefits are fixed (for example: fairness) and those that regard actions whose value depend on circumstances. See: Matsunaga, Y. (2011): "Human Rights and New Jurisprudence in Mohsen Kadivar's Advocacy of 'New-Thinker' Islam", *Die Welt des Islams*, Vol. 51, Issue 3/4, 358–381.

29 Soroush, A. (2009) *The Expansion of Prophetic Experience: Essays on Historicity, Contingency and Plurality in Religion*. N. Mobasser (transl.), F. Jahanbakhsh (ed.), Leiden, Brill, 150.

dignity.[30] They seem to distinguish between having dignity, i.e., being an end in itself, and being noble or honourable, i.e., not neglectful of God and acting according to virtue, which is realised through the pursuit of justice, knowledge, and care for others.[31] Dignity, therefore, is here considered as an intrinsic property of rational beings that justify rights that cannot be lost by disbelieving in Islam.[32] They explicitly refer to Kant's account on dignity (on which I will focus later) to stress the similarity with the Qur'anic one (in the universalistic view): for the Qur'an one should not follow the law of force that leads to corruption and alienation[33]:

> Violence – including violence in the form of extreme poverty – can destroy life and the environment. When a people submit to force, its members also start to perceive themselves as objects. Again, one can observe a similarity to Kant's formula of humanity, which forbids seeing and treating other people solely as means to one's own ends[34]

Interestingly they stress not only the importance of the recognition of the dignity of the other but also of oneself: one is not possible without the other. I cannot treat others as having dignity if I do not perceive myself as having dignity, too. In their description of dignity, they relate it essentially to reason and freedom:

> With dignity, God has also given human beings freedoms. 1. The freedom to choose one's guiding principles. No one can be forced to accept the guiding principles of power. This freedom can be linked to the Kantian foundation of dignity, namely the human intellect's power to be self-legislative. 2. The freedom to choose goals. 3. The freedom to choose to establish free relations. [...] 4. The freedom to choose information, ideas and discourses (whether of power or freedom). 5. The freedom to attain knowledge. Learning is a human talent, and a human right. [...] 7. The freedom of leadership, which coordinates the activities of all other human talents according to certain guiding principles.[35]

In evaluating the world's progress toward greater realisation of these freedoms, the authors identify fourteen criteria. Among them, there are the prosperity of

30 Schroeder, D. and Bani-Sadr, A. (2017) *Dignity in the 21st Century Middle East and West*, NY, Springer, 69.
31 See Bani-Sadr, A. (1992) *Osoole Raahnemaye Eslam* (The guiding principles of Islam). Enghelab Eslami Publications.
32 Qur'an 2:256.
33 See Qur'an 24:18; 89:12.
34 Schroeder, D. and Bani-Sadr, A. (2017) *Dignity in the 21st Century Middle East and West*. New York, Springer: 70.
35 Ivi: 74–75.

nature, defence and respect of rights in each country, de-violentisation of relationships, right to know and duty to state the truth, respect of cultural identities and at the same time acknowledgement of how every individual belongs to a universal human culture.

Now, as we can see, there are different trends in the Islamic debate on dignity: communalist, universalist, and grounded in religion or/and in reason. This variety of approaches does not affect the Islamic debate solely, but also the Western one, where the debate on human dignity is carried out in several fields,[36] for instance, in ethics, it is usually used to ascribe to human beings their status as autonomous agents and willing subjects[37]; in politics it is as a normative criteria to improve the systems[38] and to preserve freedom; in jurisprudence, it remains undecided if it is foundational to human rights or if it is a sort of restrictive principle, prohibiting, for instance, cruel and unusual punishment, as it is stated in the Eighth Amendment of the US Constitution.

I believe that to open a path of philosophical, political, and legal dialogue on human dignity, it is necessary to split the discourse on honour from the one on dignity. For this, it is helpful to look at some authors from both Eastern and Western philosophical and legal traditions who stressed this distinction. Besides the above-mentioned authors from the Islamic context, I want to focus now on Kant and Hegel because their accounts of dignity might help in distinguishing it from honour.

Human Dignity in Kant

While discussing human dignity in Kant's ethics, scholars refer to the literal occurrences of the term, which first occurs in the *Groundwork to the Metaphysics of Morals*. As *karamah*, dignity carries the ambiguity of signifying both having an innate worth and having a privileged status or rank.[39] Besides, dignity is not a primary concept of Kant's ethical theory, but rather a secondary one, as

36 I agree with Bos and Riley, who propose an interstitial reading of human dignity,

> that links international law, politics and morality in supporting a more individual-focused, less state-focused account of international relations. This, in turn, strengthens a link between human dignity and (moral and institutional) cosmopolitanism given that the value of individuals transcends state boundaries (Bos, G. and Riley, S. (2019) "Human Dignity", *Internet Encyclopedia of Philosophy*: 13).

37 Sensen, O. (2011) "Human Dignity in Historical Perspective: The Contemporary and Traditional Paradigms", *European Journal of Political Theory*, 10 (1): 71–91.

38 See Boylan, M. (2004) *A Just Society*. NY/Oxford, Rowman & Littlefield Publishers.

39 AA VI:57.

In this chapter, I refer to Kant's works by means of the Academy pagination (AA roman numerals and page numbers). I have used the translations of the editions of the Cambridge University Press, namely: Kant, I. (1996) M. Gregor, (ed. transl.), *Practical Philosophy*. New York, Cambridge University Press; and Kant, I. (1996) A. Wood and di Giovanni (ed. transl) *Religion and Rational Theology*. New York, Cambridge University Press.

Sensen puts it, because it has no justificatory role *per se* but is rather justified by autonomy.[40] But what is the content of dignity and how does Kant describe it? Kant relates it to reason as a law giving function and freedom. The core of Kant's ethics, namely, regards freedom as the capacity to set ends according to and because of practical reason[41]:

> Reason accordingly refers to every maxim of the will as giving universal law to every other will and also to every action toward oneself, and does so not for the sake of any other practical motive or any future advantage but from the idea of the dignity of a rational being, who obeys no law other than that which he himself at the same time gives.[42]

Human beings, then, have dignity insofar as they are a moral person:

> As a person (*homo noumenon*) he is not to be valued merely as a means to the ends of others or even to his own ends, but as an end in itself, that is, he possesses a dignity (an absolute inner worth) by which he exacts respect for himself from all other rational beings in the world. He can measure himself with every other being of this kind and value himself on a footing of equality with them.[43]

Dignity, here, is described as an absolute inner worth that depends on (or is the same as) being an end in itself. It is not entirely clear how Kant understood the relationship between dignity, *homo noumenon*, autonomy, and rationality and I will not deal here with this problem but just point out that dignity implies the possibility to recognise oneself and the other as normative equal authorities, i.e., autonomous lawgivers, generating value[44]:

> And now, then, what is it that justifies the morally good disposition or virtue in making such lofty claims? What justifies it is nothing less than the share that the disposition provides to the rational being in universal lawgiving. By providing this share in universal lawgiving, the disposition makes the rational being fit to be a member in a possible empire of ends.

40 AA IV: 435–436.

41 As Varden puts it:

> Kant's moral philosophy is a theory of freedom in that it views the single-most important moral feature of human beings as their capacity to set and pursue ends of their own, subject only to and motivated by their practical reason; having this capacity is what gives human beings dignity (unconditional value) (Varden, H. (2020) *Sex, Love & Gender: A Kantian Theory*. Oxford, Oxford University Press: 79).

42 AA IV: 434.

43 AA VI: 434–435.

44 See Bojanowski, J. (2015) "Kant on Human Dignity", *Kant-Studien*, 106 (1): 78–87.

> The rational being was already destined by its own nature as an end in itself and therefore as a lawgiver in an empire of ends to be fit to be such a member and to be free with regard.[45]

But can one lose dignity? This question is fundamental to draw a distinction between honour and proper dignity. If dignity is related to a type of lawgiving and lawgiving is not always adequate to the categorical imperative, then it seems that there is a chance for it to be lost.

As Horn[46] points out, proper full dignity is not intrinsically given to every human being but must be constituted by the agent. As it is written in *Moral Philosophie: Collins's Lecture Notes*:

> The duties towards oneself are the supreme condition and the *principium* of all morality, for the worth of a person constitutes the moral worth; the worth of the dexterousness is related only to her state. Socrates was in an evil state which had no worth at all, his person, however, was in this state of the biggest worth. Even if all the commodities of life are sacrificed, *the preservation of the dignity of humanity compensates the loss of all of these commodities*, and receives the acclamation; if all gets lost, one still has one's inner worth. *Under this dignity of humanity we only can practise the other duties. Who has no inner worth, has thrown away his person and cannot fulfil any other duty.*[47]

Kant has a position in between an absolute and a contingent reading; dignity, namely, is an inner absolute worth but it is generated by the adequacy of the will of the subject to the categorical imperative. For this, dignity can be lost. Kant himself writes that if someone commits serious crimes[48] or is not committed to truthfulness,[49] then she can lose dignity:

> By a lie a human being throws away and, as it were, annihilates his dignity as a human being. A human being who does not himself believe

45 AA IV: 435–436.

46 Horn, C. (2020): "Absoluteness and Contingency. Kant's Use of the Concept of Dignity", in Kato, Y. and Schönrich, G. (ed.). *Kant's Concept of Dignity*. Berlin/Boston: de Gruyter.

47 AA XXVII: 1.344, 1–14. transl. Horn, C. (2020): "Absoluteness and Contingency. Kant's Use of the Concept of Dignity", in Kato, Y. and Schönrich, G. (ed.). *Kant's Concept of Dignity*. Berlin/Boston, de Gruyter: 21.

48 See AA VI: 329

49 When lying, not only a subject makes it impossible to interact rightfully with others, thus making it impossible to exercise freedom according to a universal law (lying is not universalisable), but she commits a wrongdoing against humanity in general, herself included, which has a moral (and sometimes empirical) cost. For more on the topic of the immorality of lying see: Varden, H. (2010) "Kant and Lying to the Murderer at the Door ... One More Time: Kant's Legal Philosophy and Lies to Murderers and Nazis", *Journal of Social Philosophy*, 41 (4): 403–421.

> what he tells another (even if the other is a merely ideal person) has even less worth than if he were a mere thing; for a thing, because it is something real and given, has the property of being serviceable so that another can put it to some use.[50]

According to this account, it appears that an agent loses dignity while treating others and oneself as deprived of dignity, while the victim (in the case that she is not the agent) does not lose her dignity. Still, it seems that a sort of minimal dignity must be owned even by a criminal, given that Kant states that respect cannot be denied even to a vicious man and that one cannot lose the predisposition towards the good:

> The same thing applies to the censure of vice, which must never break out into complete contempt and denial of any moral worth to a vicious human being; for on this supposition he could never be improved, and this is not consistent with the idea of a human being, who as such (as a moral being) can never lose entirely his predisposition to the good.[51]

By predisposition to good, Kant means three main tendencies that human beings have and cannot not have. As living and reasonable beings, humans aim at preservation (animality), and they can use reason to decide the means for achieving their ends (humanity), and cannot free themselves from the imperative of reason (personality).[52] The fact that Kant distinguishes predisposition to good from the propensity to evil means that in his view, the former is somehow more fundamental than the latter and cannot be lost. A propensity, namely, can be contingent:

> By propensity (*propensio*) I understand the subjective ground of the possibility of an inclination (habitual desire, *concupiscentia*), insofar as this possibility is contingent for humanity in general. It is distinguished from a predisposition in that a propensity can indeed be innate yet may be represented as not being such: it can rather be thought of (if it is good) as acquired, or (if evil) as brought by the human being upon himself.[53]

Unlike propensity, predisposition cannot be contingent and cannot be lost. This means that reason is always self-legislating and it will always command the categorical imperative, no matter if we follow it or not. It "calls us", so to say, and is always a duty for ethical subjects.

50 AA VI: 429.
51 AA VI: 463–464.
52 AA VI: 26.
53 AA VI: 29.

To conclude, I believe that in Kant, dignity should be separated from honour and that we can distinguish between a strong and a weak sense of dignity: dignity in a strong sense, as unalienable, an inner worth that can never be lost and it depends on personality, while dignity (or honour) in a weak sense can be lost and depends on the performance of personality.[54] In this sense, we can relate the weak sense of dignity to the conception of *honeste vive*:

> Be an honorable human being (*honeste vive*). Rightful honour (*honestas iuridica*) consists in asserting one's worth as a human being in relation to others, a duty expressed by the saying, "Do not make yourself a mere means for others but be at the same time an end for them". This duty will be explained later as obligation from the right of humanity in our own person (*lex iusti*).[55]

Honeste vive might be regarded as the counterpart of dignity in the juridical field[56] insofar as it constitutes the duty of right to treat oneself and the other as an end (even if one does not internally want it). The difference, namely, is that while in the realm of ethics freedom is conceived as internal as so when we say that one should be treated as having dignity, we are considering mostly only their maxims or intentions; in the case of *honeste vive* we are concerned with external actions.

On the Possibility of a Hegelian Account of Human Dignity

Writing on the notion of human dignity in Hegel might sound controversial given that many interpretations of his philosophy of right are centred on the supremacy of the whole – the group or the state – thus depriving the individual of value "*per se*" and that some readers have seen in Hegel's doctrine a theoretical root for the development of theories of totalitarianism.[57]

However, Hegel himself uses both the notions of honour and dignity, thus making it reasonable to question if and in which sense it is possible to speak of human dignity in Hegelian terms.

54 Schönrich, G, 2020: "Kant's Theory of Dignity: A Fitting-Attitude Analysis of a Value", in Kato, Y. and Schönrich, G. (ed.). *Kant's Concept of Dignity*. Berlin/Boston, de Gruyter: 71.

55 AA VI: 236–237.

56 See Pinheiro Walla, A. (2021) "Honeste Vive: Dignity in Kant's Rechtslehre", in Adam Cureton and Jan-Willem van der Rijt (eds.). *Human Dignity and the Kingdom of Ends: Kantian Perspectives and Practical Applications*. Milton Park/NY, Routledge.

57 See: Goodfield, E. (2017) "Negating Negation. A Century of Revision in the Reception of Hegel's Political Philosophy", *History of Political Thought*, 38(2), 295–322; Kiesewetter, H. (1974) *Von Hegel zu Hitler. Eine Analyse der Hegelschen Machtstaatsideologie und der politischen Wirkungsgeschichte des Rechtshegelianismus*. Hamburg, Hoffmann und Campe; Hürstel, S. (2010) *Au nom de Hegel. Les juristes néo-hégéliens et la philosophie du droit de la République de Weimar au Troisième Reich*. Rennes, Presses universitaires de Rennes.

The term "honour", used several times in the *Phenomenology of Spirit*,[58] refers, in the *Philosophy of Right*,[59] to *Standesehre* (class-honour), namely as the condition or status in which someone is an active and recognised member of the civil society. Her honour, here, depends on belonging to a group, thus implying that, on the one hand, the subject is somehow limited by the group, but, on the other hand, it is through this limitation that she recognises the others and is recognised as a subject. The use of the notion of honour, here, seems to open a path towards a conception of dignity in a modern sense: it is not just the case that the belongingness to a group provides honour, but that each and every member of the group must be recognised and that their being persons must be defended against any other member of the group. *Standesehre* leads to mutual recognition for and by all members of the group.[60] Now, this conception of the individual person as carrier or subject of a relationship with someone or something else (the social group, the state, the divine), can be easily seen in Hegel's account of the development of religion from more figurative forms to more universal and abstract ones. In the introduction to the *Lectures on the Philosophy of Religion* we explicitly find reference to human dignity:

> All that has worth and dignity for man, all wherein he seeks his happiness, his glory, and his pride, finds its ultimate centre in religion, in the thought, the consciousness, and the feeling of God. Thus, God is the beginning of all things, and the end of all things. As all things proceed from this point, so all return back to it again.[61]

And later on, at the end of the section, "The Objective Characteristics of the Religion of Magic":

> For man does not possess dignity through what he is as immediate will, but only in virtue of having knowledge of something which exists in-and-for-itself, and of something substantial, and only because he subjects his natural will to this, and brings it into accordance with it. Only by the annulling of natural unruliness, and through the knowledge that a

58 For instance, Hegel refers to the honour of the proud vassal in Hegel, G.W.F. (2018) *The Phenomenology of Spirit*, T. Pinkard (ed. tr.), New York: Cambridge University Press: 293; the actions of the noble consciousness (ivi: 294) and the honour of the god (ivi: 413).

59 Hegel, G.W.F. (1896) *Philosophy of Right*, S.W. Dyde (tr.), London, Bell and sons: 203–204.

60 See Seelman, K. (2021) "Menschenwürde bei Hegel Ein Schnittbereich von Religionsphilosophie und Rechtsphilosophie" in M. Kühnlein und H. Ottmann (Hrsg.), *Religionsphilosophie nach Hegel, Neue Horizonte der Religionsphilosophie*. Berlin, Metzler: 205.

61 Hegel, G.W.F. (1895) *Lectures on the Philosophy of Religion*, London, K. Paul, Trench, Trübner, 2.

> Universal that exists in-and-for-itself is the True, does he acquire a dignity, and then only does life itself too become worth something.[62]

In the Christian dogma of incarnation, Hegel sees not only that the divine is human, but also that the human is divine, i.e., has an infinite incommensurable value because of his freedom.[63] In Christianity, the individual subject – insofar as the object and end of the divine love – has an infinite value (*das Individuum als solches einen unendlichen Wert hat*)[64] and supreme freedom.

Freedom has in Hegel's works a variety of meanings; it changes according to the level of development of the self-consciousness. Here, he wants to stress that the subject has not just a power of choice (*arbitrium*, *Willkür*), but rather a capacity to comprehend and determine oneself and the world. The different political and social structures are modalities of self-understanding of the subject. The aim is an organisation that guarantees that everyone's freedom is promoted. The state, therefore, has not to be conceived as a power opposing and alienating the individual but rather as what can mediate between the individual and society. Before the modern times, there was nothing but the community: it was the time of honour and loyalty; while with modernity, the individual is regarded in her autonomy, independently of the role she assumes in society. But for Hegel, this modern, Kantian, conception of autonomy becomes an abstraction, a causal element of separation between individuals and an absolutisation of the particularity that must be sublated. The individual's autonomy, therefore, needs to be recognised within a communitarian sphere, which is not just a mere sum of particularism – as society might be – namely the state where:

> The conjunction of duty and right has the twofold aspect that what the state demands as duty should forthwith be the right of individuality, since the state's demand is nothing other than the organization of the conception of freedom. The prevailing characters of the individual will are by the state brought into objective reality, and in this way first attain to their truth and realization. The state is the sole and essential condition of the attainment of the particular end and good.[65]

In the state, individual freedom finds its realisation and recognition, not as just *arbitrium* but as power for the realisation of the good. Dignity in Hegel's account is therefore strictly related to recognition, i.e., to the practice by

62 Ivi, 316.

63 See Ferreiro, H. (2021) "Valor y dignidad del individuo en el pensamiento político de Hegel", *Resistance Journal of the Philosophy of History*, 2 (4): 1–17.

64 Hegel, G.W.F. (1992) (GW 20). *Enzyklopadie der philosophischen Wissenschaften im Grundrisse* (1830). In W. Bonsiepen y H.-Ch. Lucas (eds.), Hegel: *Gesammelte Werke*, Vol. 20. Hamburg, Meiner: 477.

65 Hegel, G.W.F. (1896): *Philosophy of Right*, S.W. Dyde (tr.), London, Bell and sons: 251–252.

which one gains the self-awareness and appreciation of being a moral and free reasonable subject. In the *Phenomenology of the Spirit* we encounter the famous dialectic "Master and Servitude", in which two consciousnesses fight against each other not just for life, but for recognition:

> The relation of both self-consciousnesses is thus determined in such a way that it is through a life and death struggle that each *proves its worth* to itself, and that both *prove their worth* to each other. – They must engage in this struggle, for each must elevate its self-certainty of *existing for itself* to truth, both in the other and in itself. And it is solely by staking one's life that freedom is proven to be the essence, namely, that as a result the essence for self-consciousness is proven to be not *being*, not the *immediate* way self-consciousness emerges, not its being absorbed within the expanse of life – but rather, it is that there is nothing present in it itself which could not be a vanishing moment for it, that self-consciousness is only pure *being-for-itself*. The individual who has not risked his life may admittedly be recognized as a *person*, but he has not achieved the truth of being recognized as a self-sufficient self-consciousness.[66]

In the fight, if one of the two consciousnesses surrenders to the other, she affirms herself as a mere member of the living nature, which desires to live more than to be and to be recognised as free, as being capable of setting her own aims in a relational context, i.e., having dignity. However, this creates a situation in which none of the two consciousnesses gain actual recognition because the two consciousnesses will not be equal anymore (one has the status of master, the other of slave and actual recognition must be given by an equal being) and the master will depend on the slave for his own survival. For this, according to Hegel, the only situation of mutual adequate recognition is the one in which there is an institutionalised system of rights securing it. To conclude, we could say that it is possible to elaborate an account of Hegel's notion of dignity but that this must be accompanied by an inquiry into the idea of subject: dignity, namely, changes according to the stage of the consciousness. The pre-modern conception of dignity as honour turns into the modern exaltation of autonomy which, however, remains abstract without a mutual full recognition, which is possible only in the state. Then, we could say, the main feature of Hegel's notion of dignity is relationality: without relationships with others, it would be impossible to have a moral sense of oneself.[67]

66 Hegel, G.W.F. (2018): *The Phenomenology of Spirit*, T. Pinkard (ed. tr.), New York, Cambridge University Press: 111.

67 For more on a relational account of dignity, see Miller, S.C. (2017) "Reconsidering Dignity Relationally", in *Ethics and Social Welfare*, 11 (2): 108–121.

Conclusive Note

In this chapter, I wanted to argue that a fundamental condition for the intercultural debate on human dignity is to clarify the difference between the notion of honour and human dignity itself. In Islam, such a distinction has paved the way for universalist interpretations of *karamah*, thus enabling a dialogue with the post-World War II notion of human dignity, which saw one of its most significant theoretical roots in Kant. In the course of this chapter, we have seen that once the notion of honour is separated from that of human dignity, it becomes easier to find common characteristics related to dignity and belonging to different cultural traditions, such as European and Islamic. I believe that, although there is no agreement on the reasons why human beings have dignity (e.g., being a child of God, etc.), in all the theories presented here, there are recurring common features that make it reasonable to consider dignity as something that everyone wants to preserve, regardless of their cultural background. These common traits are those properties that determine the human being as a relational being (in Hegelian terms) and endowed with predispositions, i.e., personality, humanity, and animality (in Kantian terms) or, in other words, being rational, free, deserving of bodily integrity, care, love, and respect. Furthermore, these considerations on the content and universal value of human dignity could lead to reflection on the role of the notion of dignity, which seems to function not as a substantive term *per se* but rather as a Kantian regulative idea[68] that provides unity, limits, and organisations to the multiplicity of substantive moral accounts given in different contexts, offering different reasons and justifications.[69]

68 AA V: 372–383.

69 For Mosayebi, human dignity and human rights are not reducible to one another, although correlated: a violation of human rights is a violation of human dignity but not the other way around. For instance, cheating on someone is a violation of human dignity but not necessarily of human right (Mosayebi, R. (2020) "A Semi-Kantian Account of Dignity. Passing the Buck whilst Regulating Reasons for Human Rights", in Kato, Y. and Schönrich, G. (ed.). *Kant's Concept of Dignity*. Berlin/Boston: de Gruyter. 2020: 93).

5 Is there a Central European Approach to Human Dignity?

Piotr Szymaniec

Introduction

The aim of this paper is to answer the question of whether it is justified to talk about a specific Central European approach to the constitutional concept of dignity. In order to answer this question, I will analyse the constitutional regulations and – as far as possible – the constitutional jurisprudence of the countries of the region, focusing on the four countries of the Visegrád Group, which are the core of the Central European region, i.e., Poland, Czechia, Slovakia, and Hungary. Secondly, I will deal with the issue of how this constitutional concept of dignity is adapted to the differences regarding the dominant worldview existing in these countries, which undoubtedly have historic and religious background.[1]

Briefly characterising the legal framework for regulating relations between the state and institutional religions in all Visegrád Group countries, it can be stated that the legacy of the Austro-Hungarian monarchy has had an impact on these relations to some extent. Therefore, none of these countries has introduced the separation model based on the French one. The Polish constitution of 2 April 1997 introduces a model of relations based on co-operation between the state and churches and other religious associations, as well as on respect for mutual autonomy, i.e., religious associations in relation to the state and the state in relation to religious associations (Article 25).[2] The new

1 With regard to Czechia and Poland, cf. Piotr Szymaniec, "Cultural Heritage and the Regulation of Religious Freedom: The Case of Poland and Czech Republic", *Revista de Direitos Fundamentais & Democracia* 23, no. 3 (2018): 4–41.

2 Cf. Piotr Stanisz, *Religion and Law in Poland*, 2nd ed. (Alphen aan den Rijn: Wolters Kluwer, 2020); Piotr Stanisz, "The Status of Religious Organizations in Poland: Equal Rights and Differentiation", in *Religion, Pluralism, and Reconciling Difference*, ed. W. Cole Durham and Donlu D. Thayer (Abingdon and New York: Routledge, 2019), 147–158; Wojciech Brzozowski, "Autonomia związków wyznaniowych jako zasada ustrojowa i prawo podmiotowe", *Przegląd Prawa Konstytucyjnego*, no. 1 (2023), 27–38. In Poland, the dominant position of the Catholic Church is expressed in the fact that the relations between the state and the Catholic Church were defined in the concordat ratified in 1998 (*Journal of Laws* of 1998, no. 51, item 318). However, the relations between the state and 14 other churches and other religious asso-

DOI: 10.4324/9781003519188-7

legal framework for freedom of religion in Czechoslovakia was defined by Law 308/1991 Sb., adopted at the end of the existence of the federal state. This act provided quite restrictive rules for registering a religious association (*náboženské společenstvo*) and generally required that at least 10,000 inhabitants had to declare membership in a newly registering religious association. This law is still in force in Slovakia, but the required number of people was increased first to 20,000 (2007), then to 50,000 (2017). In Czechia, a more liberal Law 3/2002 Sb. on freedom of religion and the status of churches and religious associations and on amendments to certain acts that replaced the act of 1991 in 2002 requires 300 persons with Czech citizenship or permanent residency to register a religious association.[3] Although over 47% of Czech declare themselves to be non-religious persons (2021), autonomy of religious associations is guaranteed in the Czech legal system and the entire Czech model of relations between the state and churches can be named a "co-operative model of secular state".[4] In Slovakia, the position of the Catholic Church is much stronger than in Czechia. More than half of the population declares membership in it. The model for regulating relations between the state and churches in Slovakia is similar to that in Czechia, but this model is highly petrified, and since 2007, no new religious association has been registered. In Hungary, the model of relations between the state and churches and religious associations based on a friendly separation is still formally valid. Article VII of the Hungarian Basic Law of 25 April 2011 officially guarantees the autonomy of churches.[5] However, in 2011, attempts were made to limit this autonomy and as many as 67 churches were temporarily deprived of their previous legal

ciations were regulated by separate laws. This includes, among others, Jewish religious communities and the Muslim Religious Association in the Republic of Poland. The Act of 17 May 1989 on the Guarantees of Freedom of Conscience and Religion (consolidated text: *Journal of Laws* of 2023, item 265) introduces quite liberal provisions regarding the registration of a religious association and requires the signatures of only 100 Polish citizens for this purpose. Therefore, there are currently 170 registered religious associations in Poland.

3 Cf. Jiří Rajmund Tretera Tretera, Zaboj Horák, *Konfesní právo* (Praha: Leges, 2015), 118–123; Jiří Rajmund Tretera, Zaboj Horák, *Religion and Law in the Czech Republic* (Alphen aan den Rijn: Wolters Kluwer, 2014); Stanislav Přibyl, *Konfesněprávní studie* (Brno: L. Marek, 2007), 86–99; Zaboj Horák, "Religion and the Secular State in the Czech Republic", in *Religion and the Secular State: National Reports*, ed. Javier Martínez-Torrón, W. Cole Durham, and Donlu D. Thayer (Madrid: Universidad Complutense de Madrid, Facultad de Derecho. Servicio de Publicaciones, 2015), 234–247. The Law 308/1991 Sb. recognised as registered 19 churches and other religious associations existing previously in the territory of Czechia and 14 entities in the territory of Slovakia. Under this legal act only two religious associations obtained registration in Czechia, while under Act no. 3/2002 Sb., 22 churches and religious associations have been registered by 2022.

4 Tretera, Horák, *Religion and Law in the Czech Republic*, 37.

5 Before 2011 it was pointed out that separation between state and churches in Hungary was, on the one hand, more acute than in the German model, but on the other hand, the state was more favourable towards churches and religious associations than in the French model. Thus, it was said the Hungarian system was closer to the Spanish-Italian model. Cf. Balázs Schanda, "State

status.[6] Subsequent changes to the regulations made between 2011 and 2018 clarified the legal situation of churches in Hungary, and thus better secured freedom of religion.

The concept of the dignity of a human being undoubtedly has its roots in the concepts of both the Roman Stoics (especially Cicero) and Christian thought. Immanuel Kant's concept and Christian personalism, developed since the 19th century, were important for the development of the discussion on dignity. It can therefore be considered a secularised religious concept.[7] However, the most important concept of dignity for this discussion is the one developed based on the German Basic Law of 1949. This is especially relevant because German constitutionalism had a significant influence on the constitutional frameworks of Central European countries, particularly in the period immediately after the collapse of the Soviet bloc.[8]

The category of dignity plays a fundamental role in the German constitutional order. The Basic Law (*Grundgesetz*) of 1949 declares human dignity inviolable in Article 1 clause 1, and the second sentence of the same article indicates that respecting and protecting dignity is the duty of the state authority.[9] In German constitutional order, dignity is a constitutional value and a constitutional right. However, as it has been pointed out by an eminent Israeli legal scholar and the Supreme Court Justice, Aharon Barak, the right to dignity rarely becomes the sole or main basis for decisions of the Federal Constitutional Court (*Bundesverfassungsgericht*), since it is understood as an absolute and, hence, unrestrictable right.[10] The substantive concept of dignity used by the Federal Constitutional Court is based on the so-called *object formula* (*Objektformel*), which implies that treating an individual solely as an object of state power is contrary to the requirements of a democratic state. This formula was coined by Günter Dürig (1920–1996) who incorporated

and Church in Hungary", in *State and Church in the European Union*, ed. Gerhard Robbers. 2nd ed. (Baden-Baden: Nomos, 2005), 323–345.

6 Cf. Balázs Schanda, *Religion and Law in Hungary*, 2nd ed. (Alphen aan den Rijn: Wolters Kluwer, 2015).

7 Cf. Ginevra Le Moli, *Human Dignity in International Law* (Cambridge: Cambridge University Press, 2021), 50–85.

8 Cf. Christopher McCrudden, "Human Dignity and Judicial Interpretation of Human Rights", *The European Journal of International Law* 19, no. 4 (2008): 673. Allan F. Tatham, *Central European Constitutional Courts in the Face of EU Membership. The Influence of the German Model in Hungary and Poland* (Leiden: Martinus Nijhoff Publishers, 2013), 41–63. The chapter I refer to has a telling title: "The Predominance of the German Model in Central Europe: Migrations of Legal and Constitutional Ideas".

9 Grundgesetz für die Bundesrepublik Deutschland vom 23. Mai 1949 (BGBl. S. 1). [Basic law for the Federal Republic of Germany of 23 May 1949 (Federal Law Gazette p. 1)]. For English translation, cf. Basic Law for the Federal Republic of Germany, https://www.gesetze-im-internet.de/englisch_gg/englisch_gg.html#p0019.

10 Cf. Aharon Barak, *Human Dignity. The Constitutional Value and the Constitutional Right* (Cambridge: Cambridge University Press, 2015), 229–241.

the category of dignity taken from Kant's ethics into the interpretation of Article 1 clause 1 of the German Basic Law of 1949.[11] Barak present the view that perceiving the right to dignity as an absolute right is unique for German constitutional order. It will be shown, however, to what extent this approach to dignity is present in the countries of Central Europe.

Poland

The Polish Constitution of 2 April 1997 points to dignity in Article 30 as the source of all constitutional human and civil rights and freedoms. In this provision, dignity is characterised as inherent and inalienable. The wording used in this provision clearly refers to Article 1 clause 1 of the German Basic Law. Dignity occupies a very important place in the Polish constitution, as it appears at the beginning of Chapter II on the freedoms, rights, and duties of a human being and citizen.[12] The Polish Constitutional Court, which started to perform its function in 1986 (on the basis of an amendment to the constitution of the People's Republic of Poland, enacted in 1982), referred to the concept of human dignity even before its introduction into constitutional provisions. The first important ruling incorporating this notion is the resolution of 17 March 1993[13] when the Court found it unacceptable to conduct biomedical experiments of non-therapeutic nature without the participant's consent, because the possibility of conducting such experiments would mean treating their participants only as objects of specific research. Hence, the Court clearly utilised Dürig's formula here. This formula was also briefly mentioned in the

11 Cf. Günter Dürig, "Der Grundrechtssatz von der Menschenwürde: Entwurf eines praktikablen Wertsystems der Grundrechte aus Art. 1 Abs. I in Verbindung mit Art. 19 Abs. II des Grundgesetzes", *Archiv des öffentlichen Rechts* 81, no. 2 (1956), 117–157; Matthias Mahlmann, "Human Dignity and Autonomy in Constitutional Orders", in *The Oxford Handbook of Comparative Constitutional Law*, ed. Michel Rosenfeld and András Sajó (Oxford: Oxford University Press 2012), 379–380; Horst Dreier, "Art. 1 I", in *Grundgesetz. Kommentar*, ed. Horst Dreier (Tübingen: Mohr Siebeck, 2004), 166–168. Distinction between things that have dignity and things that have a price, as well as the concept of dignity encapsulated in the third formula of the categorical imperative appear on the ground of Kant's ethics, not his philosophy of law. Therefore, as Olga Rosenkranzová emphasises (referring to Dietmar Pfordten), these concepts were intended to be valid in the realm of *homo noumenon* and were not meant to be employed on the ground of law (i.e., in the sphere of *homo phenomenon*). Thus, Dürig's interpretation of Kantian philosophy was in fact a misinterpretation. Olga Rosenkranzová, *Lidská důstojnost: Právně teoretická a filozofická perspektiva. Giovanni Pico della Mirandola & Immanuel Kant* (Praha: Leges, 2019), 86–89, 128–133. Cf. Immanuel Kant, *Groundwork for the Metaphysics of Morals*, trans. Allen W. Wood (New Haven and London: Yale University Press, 2002), 52–54.

12 The Constitution of the Republic of Poland of 2 April 1997 (*Journal of Laws* of 1997, no. 78, item 483), https://www.sejm.gov.pl/prawo/konst/angielski/konse.htm. In my opinion, the translation available on the website of the Polish Parliament is the most adequate.

13 Resolution of the Constitutional Court of 17 March 1993, file no. W 16/92. The Court's decision was published in *Journal of Laws* no. 23 (1993), item 103.

judgement of 15 October 2002 but the Court did not find the violation of dignity in this case.[14] In the ruling of 13 July 1993, the Constitutional Court linked the category of dignity with social and economic rights and stated that "the obligation of the state existing in the sphere of its social activity to provide an unemployed individual with conditions for exercising his right to existence and freedom" results from the inalienable, inherent human dignity.[15]

The most controversial judgement of the Constitutional Court, which was passed before the entry into force of the 1997 constitution, although after its adoption, concerns the admissibility of abortion. In this judgement, delivered on 27 May 1997, the Court found that the 1996 provision giving the possibility of abortion in the event of "difficult living conditions or a difficult personal situation" of a pregnant woman was unconstitutional. The court found that the terms "difficult living conditions" and "difficult personal situation" are imprecise and can be understood subjectively. Therefore, the challenged provision did not guarantee proper protection of the right to life, which should take place in a democratic state. The dignity of the foetus is mentioned in the judgement only once and generally, and the argument of the Court is not based on this concept. According to the Court, human life is such an important value that it must be protected at every stage of development. The notion of dignity was used to the larger extent only in the dissenting opinion of Justice Leszek Garlicki who tried to present the situation discussed by the Court in terms of conflict between the dignity of a foetus and the dignity of a mother.[16] The lack of broader references to dignity in this judgement may be related to the tendency present in the jurisprudence of the Constitutional Court not to refer to the concept of dignity if the judgement may be based on another fundamental right. Furthermore, it can be explained by the fact that before the entry into force of the 1997 constitution, dignity was not yet a value directly mentioned in constitutional provisions. The result of the judgement of 27 May 1997 was that performing an abortion was allowed only in three narrowly defined situation, namely if there was a reasonable suspicion that the pregnancy had been a result of rape, if the pregnancy endangered the

14 The Court stated as follows:

> Against the background of Article 30 of the Constitution, a situation in which a person would become the sole object of actions taken by the authorities … and his role would be reduced to a purely instrumental form … may, in principle, be considered a violation of dignity: Judgement of 15 October 2002, file no. SK 6/02, point 6.1. Cf. Kamil Jesiołowski, "Kantowskie pojęcie godności a współczesne prawodawstwo", *Societas et Ius* no. 6 (2017): 105.

15 Judgement of the Constitutional Court of 13 July 1993, file no. P 7/92, point 3.

16 Judgement of 28 May 1997, file no. K. 26/96.

life or health of the mother, or there was a "high probability of severe and irreversible impairment of the fetus or an incurable life-threatening disease".[17]

The Polish Constitutional Court follows the German Federal Constitutional Court in perceiving dignity both as a constitutional value and as a constitutional right. Therefore, the Court recognises the existence of the right to respect and protect dignity, which is a separate constitutional right different from other constitutional rights of individuals.[18] As to the content of this right, the Court says:

> The subject of the right to dignity is, in the most general terms, to create (guarantee) such a situation for every human being that he or she has the possibility of autonomous realization of his or her personality, but above all that he or she does not become the subject of actions by others (especially public authority) and is not only an instrument during the realization of their goals.[19]

Since the Polish Constitutional Court, like its German equivalent, perceives this right as an absolute right, and thus not subject to balancing in accordance with the principle of proportionality, this right is very rarely the basis for a decision by the Court. It has become a practice that when the Court may base its decision on a different subjective right, it uses the right to dignity only as a subsidiary in its reasoning. Therefore, Justice Ewa Łętowska is right when she claims that the concept of dignity is used primarily in the axiological assessments of the Constitutional Court.[20] The Constitutional Court presented the view that unconstitutionality based solely on the confirmation of a violation of dignity would then be declared if a specific legal regulation caused that a human being would become only an object of certain actions on the part of state bodies and would be treated purely instrumentally. The Polish Constitutional Court clearly uses the approach to dignity based on the "object formula". The legitimacy of such an approach has been confirmed by one of the most well-known Polish constitutional lawyers, Leszek Garlicki,

17 Act of 7 January 1993 on family planning, protection of the human foetus and conditions for permitting termination of pregnancy (*Journal of Laws* of 1993, no. 17, item 78), Article 4a.

18 Cf. Krzysztof Wojtyczek, "Ochrona godności człowieka, wolności i równości przy pomocy skargi konstytucyjnej w polskim systemie prawnym", in *Godność człowieka jako kategoria prawna (opracowania i materiały)*, ed. Krystian Complak (Wrocław: Drukarnia Centrum Handlu i Poligrafii, 2001), 205–206.

19 Judgement of 15 October 2002, file no. SK 6/02, point 6.2; judgement of 9 July 2009, file no. SK 48/05, point 2.2 (48).

20 Ewa Łętowska, "O godności, jej funkcji w obrocie prawnym i promocyjnej roli Rzecznika Praw Obywatelskich", in *Godność człowieka a prawa ekonomiczne i socjalne. Księga jubileuszowa wydana w piętnastą rocznicę ustanowienia Rzecznika Praw Obywatelskich* (Warsaw: Biuro Rzecznika Praw Obywatelskich, 2003), 248. Professor Ewa Łętowska served as the first Polish ombudsman (1988–1992) and then a justice of the Constitutional Court (2002–2011).

who presented the view that the "object formula" is also valid on the ground of Polish constitution.[21]

The concept of human dignity used by the Polish Constitutional Court is not particularly developed. In addition to references to Dürig's formula, the Court uses a distinction developed on the basis of Polish legal theory and philosophy, often adopted by authors associated with Christian personalism (although not only by them). This distinction includes personal dignity (*godność osobowa*) and dignity connected with personality (*godność osobowościowa*).[22] An individual cannot lose or relinquish her personal dignity which, because of its inalienable nature, cannot be violated by the legislator. This type of dignity is labelled the "transcendent dignity" by the Constitutional Court. Dignity connected with personality refers to the values of one's psychic life and values making a person accepted in society. Dignity of this kind can be violated by the legislator. The Court sometimes uses the term "personality right", which is an equivalent for German *Persönlichkeitsrecht*,[23] in reference to this type of dignity.[24]

When analysing the concept of dignity in the jurisprudence of the Polish Constitutional Court, it is impossible to omit the judgement of 30 September 2008.[25] The issue at stake here was the provision allowing for the shooting down of an aircraft used "for illegal activities, in particular as a means of a terrorist attack from the air" if justified by national security considerations.[26] The Court found this provision unconstitutional because it would result in the instrumental treatment of aircraft passengers in which it made extensive use of the "object formula" in its considerations. Moreover, it was noted by the Court that the situation of the passengers should be seen not only as the result of terrorists' actions, but also as the consequence of a state's failure to fulfil its duty to ensure security.[27] On the one hand, it was the judgement in which the Court dealt with the content of the concept of dignity to the greatest extent. On the other hand, the Court's reasoning, using Dürig's formula, relied

21 Leszek Garlicki, "Artykuł 30", in *Konstytucja Rzeczypospolitej Polskiej. Komentarz*, ed. Leszek Garlicki and Marek Zubik (Warszawa: Wydawnictwo Sejmowe, 2016), vol. II, 34. Professor Garlicki served as a justice of the Constitutional Court between 1993 and 2001 and subsequently as the justice of the European Court of Human Rights between 2002 and 2012.

22 Cf. Józef Krukowski, "Godność człowieka podstawą konstytucyjnego katalogu praw i wolności jednostki", in *Podstawowe prawa jednostki i ich sądowa ochrona*, ed. Leszek Wiśniewski (Warszawa: Wydawnictwo Sejmowe, 1997), 39–42; Franciszek J. Mazurek, *Godność osoby ludzkiej podstawą praw człowieka* (Lublin: Katolicki Uniwersytet Lubelski, 2001).

23 On the concept of *Persönlichkeitsrechte*, cf. Stig Stromholm, *Right of Privacy and Rights of the Personality* (Stockholm: P.A. Norstedt & Soners Fürlag, 1967), 25–44.

24 Judgement of 5 March 2003, file no. K 7/01; judgement of 22 February 2005, file no. K 10/04; judgement of 9 July 2009, file no. SK 48/05, point 2.2 (nos. 49–50).

25 Judgement of 30 September 2008, file no. K 44/07.

26 Article 122a of the Act of 3 July 2002, Aviation Law (*Journal of Laws* of 2005, no. 226, item 1944).

27 Judgement of 30 September 2008, file no. K 44/07, point 174.

heavily and largely on the argumentation presented by the German Federal Constitutional Court in the judgement of 15 February 2006 that concerned an almost identical regulation.[28]

The Constitutional Court's judgement of 22 October 2020 caused huge political controversy as well as impetuous demonstrations and sometimes riots in the largest Polish cities despite the prohibition of larger assemblies valid during the COVID-19 pandemic. I will leave the sociologists to answer the question of whether these protests, which were attended mainly by very young people, were primarily due to the fact that the protesters considered the verdict to represent the position of the Catholic Church.[29] Nevertheless, it must be noted that this judgement was decided by judges elected by the parliamentary majority dominated by the "Law and Justice" party. At the same time, the position of the adjudicating judges was not uniform.[30] The Court declared unconstitutional the provision allowing abortion in the case of severe and irreversible impairment of the foetus or its incurable life-threatening disease, which was not analysed in the 1997 judgement. The majority opinion and dissenting opinions were published as late as three months after the judgement was issued. When analysing the Court's reasoning, it should be emphasised that the presented argumentation is entirely secular in nature and, both in majority opinion and in dissenting opinions, there are no references to the position presented by any church or religious association or to any ideological disputes at all. Somewhat surprisingly, the Court relied heavily on the line of reasoning presented already in the judgement of 30 September 2008 concerning the destruction of an aircraft and emphasised the linkage between dignity and protection of human life. The Court stressed the already mentioned difference between personal dignity (*godność osobowa*) and dignity connected with personality (*godność osobowościowa*) and reaffirmed that the former is vested in a human being regardless of the state in which that being is found. It was pointed out in the majority opinion that "The principle of human dignity should be seen through the prism of the requirement to protect human life".[31] The Court's reasoning can be considered to be built mainly from the views on dignity that have already been expressed in other judgements, but they

28 Judgement of the Federal Constitutional Court of 15 February 2006, file no. 1 BvR 357/05 (Urteil des Ersten Senats vom 15 February 2006), https://www.bundesverfassungsgericht.de/SharedDocs/Entscheidungen/DE/2006/02/rs20060215_1bvr035705.html.

29 It is worth noting that sociological research conducted in 2008–2018 shows that in Poland, among people aged 18–24, the percentage of believers fell from 73% to 55%, and the percentage of people declaring themselves non-believers increased from 5% to 17%. The percentage of people who are deeply religious in this age group has not changed much in recent years and amounts to 8%. Cf. Rafał Boguszewski and Marta Bożewicz, "Religijność i moralność polskiej młodzieży – zależność czy autonomia?", *Zeszyty Naukowe KUL* 62, no. 4 (248) (2019): 31–51.

30 Professor Leon Kieres was the only justice in the panel selected before 2015. The judgement was passed by a majority of votes and two dissenting opinions were presented.

31 Judgement of 22 October 2020, file no. K 1/20, point 3.2.

have been placed in a different context. The novelty of the Court's reasoning consists in the emphasis on the dignity of a foetus ("an unborn child", as it is referred to in the judgement). However, also in this matter, a reference to Dürig's formula can be seen, and it is visible, for example, in the following sentence: "Full dependence of the foetus on the mother does not cause it to lose its subjectivity and, consequently, it can be treated as an object".[32] As can already be seen in this judgement, and as we will see in the judgements of the Slovak and Hungarian constitutional courts, the components of the same understanding of dignity, rooted in German constitutionalism, can be used in very different ways and justify positions that are very different in the axiological sense.

Czechia

The Charter of Fundamental Rights and Freedoms (*Listina základních práv a svobod*), which was passed in Czechoslovakia in January 1991,[33] is the main legal act concerning individual rights in the Czech legal system. Just before the collapse of Czechoslovakia, when the foundations for the constitutional system of Czechia were being prepared, on 16 December 1992,[34] the Presidium of the Czech National Council recognised the Charter as one of the elements of the constitutional order of the newly emerging republic. Article 1 of the Charter states that all people are "free and equal in dignity and rights" (first sentence). Article 10 sec. 1, establishes the right of everyone to "respect for human dignity, personal honor, good reputation and protection of the name". This provision lists dignity as a feature of every human being, as well as honour and good reputation, which are components of a different understanding of dignity.

According to Olga Rosenkranzová, between 1993 and 2019, the term "human dignity" appears in 1,179 decisions of the Constitutional Court of the Czech Republik, out of a total of over 70,000 decisions. Out of this number, in 39 judgements, the concept of human dignity was included in the *ratio decidendi*. In 25 judgements, the Constitutional Court ruled in favour of human dignity. In four judgements, the Court based its argumentation on

32 Judgement of 22 October 2020, file no. K 1/20, point 3.5.

33 Ustavní zákon č. 23/1991 Sb., kterým se uvozuje Listina základních práv a svobod jako ústavní zákon Federálního shromáždění České a Slovenské Federativní Republiky (Constitutional Act No. 23/1991 Coll., which introduces the Charter of Fundamental Rights and Freedoms as a constitutional law of the Federal Assembly of the Czech and Slovak Federal Republic).

34 Zvláštní usnesení Předsednictva České národní rady č. 2/1993 Sb. č. 2/1993 Sb., o vyhlášení Listiny základních práv a svobod jako součásti ústavního pořádku České republiky (Special Resolution of the Presidium of the Czech National Council No. 2/1993 Coll. on the promulgation of the Charter of Fundamental Rights and Freedoms as part of the constitutional order of Czechia).

the Dürig formula taken from German constitutional theory.[35] These judgements were about the protection of the personal sphere of an individual. In the judgement of 18 August 2009, the Court explained Dürig's formula in detail and pointed out that on the basis of the notion of dignity contained in Article 1 and Article 10 of the Bill of Rights, an individual cannot be treated only as an object of actions of state authority. Two judgements are especially worth mentioning. The judgement of 26 September 2013 concerned the protection of the autonomy of mentally ill persons against excessively paternalistic interference by the state (according to the Court, such interference must be justified by the protection of the rights of other people or by the public interest). The judgement of 14 June 2016 concerned, in turn, the constitutionality of the provision indicating that being in a civil partnership is an obstacle to the adoption of a child by a given person.[36] The Constitutional Court found this provision incompatible with the right to human dignity, the right to private life, and the prohibition of discrimination enshrined in Article 1, Article 3, paragraph 1, Article 10, paragraphs 1, 2 of the Charter and in Article 8 (1) and Article 14 of the *European Convention of Human Rights*.[37] Therefore, the Constitutional Court linked the notion of human dignity with the legal situation of homosexual persons. It must be acknowledged that, in this case, the understanding of dignity taken from German constitutionalism and rooted in Christian personalism served to extend the rights of sexual minorities.

Slovakia

The Constitution of the Slovak Republic of 1 September 1992[38] defines the rights and freedoms of individuals in the second chapter. Article 12 sec. 1 repeats sentence 1 of Article 1 of the Charter of Rights of 1991, pointing to the equality of people in their dignity. Article 19 sec. 1 has the same wording

35 Judgement of 6 March 2012, file no. I. ÚS 1586/09; judgement of 18 August 2009, file no. I. ÚS 557/09; judgement of 26 September 2013, file no. III. ÚS 3333/11; judgement of 14 June 2016, file no. Pl. ÚS 7/15.

36 Rosenkranzová, *Lidská důstojnost*, 140–146. Cf. Jaroslav Benák, Ladislav Vyhnánek, and David Zahumenský, "Human Dignity in the Czech Republic", in *Handbook of Human Dignity in Europe*, ed. Paolo Becchi and Klaus Mathis (Cham: Springer, 2018), 197–210. (These authors also emphasise the presence of so-called object formula in the Czech constitutional jurisprudence).

37 Judgement of the Czech Constitutional Court of 14 June 2016, file no. Pl.ÚS 7/15, https://nalus.usoud.cz/Search/GetText.aspx?sz=Pl-7-15_1.

38 Ústava Slovenskej republiky z 1. septembra 1992, 460/1992 Zb. (Constitution of the Slovak Republic from 1 September 1992, 460/1992 Coll.). Amendments to the Slovak constitution were introduced by the following laws: 244/1998 Z.z., 9/1999 Z.z., 90/2001 Z.z., 90/2001 Z.z., 140/2004 Z.z., 323/2004 Z.z., 323/2004 Z.z., 463/2005 Z.z., 92/2006 Z.z., 210/2006 Z.z., 100/2010 Z.z., 356/2011 Z.z., 232/2012 Z.z., 161/2014 Z.z., 306/2014 Z.z., 427/2015 Z.z., 44/2017 Z.z., 71/2017 Z.z., 137/2017 Z.z., 40/2019 Z.z.

as Article 10 sec. 1 of the Bill of Rights, likewise listing dignity, personal honour, and good reputation in one line.

Tomáš Ľalík points out that the Constitutional Court of the Slovak Republic raised the issue of human dignity in three contexts: criminal law (human dignity is related to the principle of humanitarianism, which is to be implemented by criminal law), restrictions on social rights, and in the event of a conflict of freedom of expression with the right to privacy.[39] In the judgement of 9 November 2016 (I. ÚS 689/2014), the Constitutional Court fully expressed the absolute concept of human dignity. It stated that a human being cannot be treated only as an object of a questioned legal relationship. Moreover, this ruling recognises dignity as a value in a horizontal perspective incomparable with other constitutional values. The court also came to the conclusion that the violation of dignity cannot be valued in money.[40] Therefore, reminiscence of Kant's thoughts about things that have a price and things that have dignity can be found in the Court's argumentation. Similar statements can also be found in the jurisprudence of the Czech Constitutional Court. The case concerned the disclosure in the media of information on criminal proceedings instituted against a specific person. The court stated that: "Freedom of speech should not lead to anyone being effectively seen as guilty in the eyes of the general public without the ability to effectively defend themselves against accusations against themselves".

The Slovak Constitutional Court expressed its opinion on dignity in a more abstract way in its judgement of 4 December 2007 (PL. ÚS 12/01) on abortion. The court recognised the dual nature of dignity, which, according to it, is an objective value being the basis of the general constitutional principle and at the same time a subjective right. The Constitutional Court linked human dignity with the right to private life, and more broadly – with the autonomy of an individual's self-determination. According to the Constitutional Court, the life of an unborn child has an objective value (it is worth adding that Article 15 clause 1, second sentence, of the Constitution of the Slovak Republic recognises human life as deserving of protection also before birth). However, the Court also stated that it was human dignity that allowed the conclusion that the right to an abortion in the first 12 weeks of pregnancy fell within the scope of a woman's right to privacy. According to the Court, the right to

39 Tomáš Ľalík, "Ľudská dôstojnosť v právnom poriadku SR", *Justičná revue* 69, no. 3 (2017): 335–337; cf. Tomáš Ľalík, "Human dignity in Slovakia", in, *Handbook of Human Dignity in Europe*, ed. Paolo Becchi, Klaus Mathis (Cham: Springer Nature, 2019), 799–815; Helena Barancová, "Ľudská dôstojnosť – základ právneho štátu", in *Hodnotový systém práva a jeho reflexia v právnej teórii a praxi*, ed. Peter Blaho, Adriana Švecová (Trnava: Trnavská univerzita v Trnave, Právnická fakulta, 2013), vol. 1, 48–64.

40 Judgement of the Slovak Constitutional Court of 9 November 2016, file no. I. ÚS 689/2014, https://www.ustavnysud.sk/docDownload/d43caf60-4a14-4ef5-bd1b-080afa38f696/%C4%8D.%2032%20-%20I.%20%C3%9AS%20689_2014.pdf.

self-determination in this case outweighs the value of the unborn life.[41] It can therefore be noticed that the same absolute concept of dignity – if the emphasis is placed differently – may serve as a justification for both maintaining the possibility of performing abortion (as in the case of Slovakia) and limiting this possibility (as in the case of Poland).

According to Tomáš Ľalík, the Slovak common courts deal with the concept of human dignity in an incidental and non-uniform manner. An example of a judgement in which the absolute concept of dignity was referred to may be the decision of the Supreme Court of 22 March 2007 (4 Sž 9/2006), which concerned showing the external sexual organs of a participant of the *Big Brother* reality show with a mocking commentary by the hosts. In its judgement, the Supreme Court recognised human dignity as an absolute right that is not subject to any restrictions, but this position was not justified in detail.[42]

Hungary

The Hungarian Constitution of 20 August 1949, was largely amended on 23 October 1989 and in the 1990s,[43] and in this form was in force until 2011. In sec. 54 para. 1 the constitution stated that: "In the Republic of Hungary, every human being has the inherent right to life and human dignity, a right of which may not be arbitrarily deprived of anyone". This provision was situated at the beginning of Chapter XII of the constitution on the rights of the individual. This very fact shows that the right to dignity achieved a high position among constitutional rights. It is certain that the Hungarian Constitutional Court took much of the approach of the German Constitutional Court towards the category of human dignity. I should refer to the seminal book of Catherine Dupré who analysed in detail the process of "legal importation", as she names it, in this regard.[44] An example of an approach to dignity by the Constitutional Court in 1990 are two rulings on abortion: No. 64/1991 AB of 17 December 1991 and No. 48/1998 AB of 23 November 1998. In the latter ruling, the Court indicated that because the foetus has no legal personality, "[i]ts life and dignity are therefore not entitled to the absolute protection to which a person who has already been born is entitled under Article 54 (1) of the Constitution".

41 Ľalík, "Ľudská dôstojnosť v právnom poriadku SR", 335–337. Cf. Ingrid Lanczová and Miriam Laclavíková, "Abortion as the Partial Issue of the Right to Life and the Development of the Related Slovak Legal Regulation", *Teka Komisji Prawniczej PAN Oddział w Lublinie* 11, no. 2 (2018): 223–224.

42 Ľalík, "Ľudská dôstojnosť v právnom poriadku SR", 338–340.

43 Act XX of 1949. The Constitution of the Republic of Hungary, https://www2.ohchr.org/english/bodies/cescr/docs/E.C.12.HUN.3-Annex2.pdf.

44 Cf. Catherine Dupré, *Importing the Law in Post-Communist Transitions: The Hungarian Constitutional Court and the Right to Human Dignity* (Oxford and Portland, Oregon: Hart Publishing, 2003), 65–155. Dupré does not like to use Alan Watson's notion of "legal transplatation".

Moreover, according to the Court, "among the rights to be weighed against the State's duty to give increased protection to foetal life, the mother's right of self-determination, as part of the right to human dignity, is the most significant one".[45] Therefore, the Constitutional Court recognised the possibility of abortion in the first three months of pregnancy. In the view of the Court, an absolute ban on abortion would be unconstitutional. However, it also stated that the statutory condition requiring a woman to describe her "severe crisis situation" is consistent with the constitution.

The Fundamental Law of Hungary, currently in force, passed on 18 April 2011,[46] and already in the preamble states that "human dignity is the basis of human existence".[47] Article II expressly refers to the absolute understanding of human dignity: "Human dignity is inviolable. Everyone has the right to life and to respect for human dignity; the life of the human embryo, from conception, is protected". In the Hungarian constitution, dignity appears not only in relation to the human person, but also to the Hungarian nation and communities of various nature. The use of the concept of dignity in various contexts and references provides at least theoretical grounds for constructing the concept of community dignity and contrasting this communitarian notion of dignity with the dignity of an individual. Moreover, the preamble to the constitution also states that "labour is the basis of the strength of the community and the dignity of every person". This formulation suggests that works or deeds of a human being prove his or her dignity. It provides the basis for moving away from the previously accepted concept of dignity in favour of a concept that has a long tradition in history[48] and in which a person's dignity depends on his or her merits. So far, however, the Hungarian Constitutional Court has not followed such an interpretation.

The wording of Article II of the 2011 constitution suggests that dignity is also an attribute of the human foetus. Dignity is used as a concept that delimits the limits of freedom of speech because, according to Article IX paragraph

45 Decision of the Hungarian Constitution Court of 23 November 1998, no. 48/1998, https://hunconcourt.hu/dontes/decision-48-1998-on-abortion.

46 "The Fundamental Law of Hungary (as in force on 1 November 2022)", https://njt.hu/jogszabaly/en/2011-4301-02-00

47 At the same time, in this preamble there is a more collectivist (or communitarian) approach to the rights of the individual, as it was emphasised that "the freedom of the individual can only be realized in cooperation with others". The preamble also uses the understanding of dignity as an honour or social recognition of an individual, as evidenced by the following passage: "the basis of the strength of the community and the dignity of every human being is work, the work of the human spirit". On the notion of dignity under the present Hungarian constitution, cf. Catherine Dupré, "La dignité humaine dans la Loi fondamentale hongroise de 2012", *Revue Est Europa*, special issue no. 1 (2012), 89–110.

48 Such a notion of dignity can be seen in in the thought of the Roman Stoics, and in modern times it was used, e.g., by Francis Hutcheson (1694–1746). Cf. Francis Hutcheson, *An Inquiry into the Original of our Ideas of Beauty and Virtue in Two Treatises* (Indianapolis: Liberty Fund, 2004), 125.

4 and paragraph 5, the use of this freedom in order to violate the dignity of other people, such as the dignity of the nation and "the dignity of any community of a national, ethnic, racial or religious nature", does not enjoy legal protection. It also concerns working conditions that respect the dignity of the employee (Article XVII sec. 3). It is quite obvious, therefore, that the concept of dignity in the Hungarian constitution of 2011 is used in a very awkward way. However, in judgements issued under the 2011 constitution, the Constitutional Court retained much of the approach to dignity it had expressed prior to 2011.[49]

Act C of 2011 on the Right to Freedom of Conscience and Religion, which is no longer in force, tried to define religious activities. According to sec. 6, clause 1 these activities

> Are related to a worldview which is directed towards the transcendental, which has a system of faith-based principles and its teachings are directed toward existence as a whole, and which embraces the entire human personality and has specific codes of conduct that do not offend morality and human dignity.[50]

Therefore, the category of dignity was used here in an unusual way, i.e., as a limitation clause of religious freedom.

Other States of the Region

The constitutions of the Baltic republics contain references to dignity. The constitution of the Republic of Estonia, adopted in the referendum held on 28 June 1992,[51] mentions human dignity only twice. In sec. 10 it is stated that the rights, freedoms, and obligations not explicitly mentioned in the constitution are not excluded, but one of the conditions in this case is that they correspond to human dignity. Paragraph 18 prohibits torture and treatment that is cruel and degrading to human dignity. As Tanel Kerikmäe and Kristi Joamets point out, the Estonian approach to dignity stresses the rights to self-realisation of an individual as the most important components of dignity. In Estonian legal order, the notion of dignity also underpins social rights and the state's duty

49 Cf. Gergely Deli and István Kukorelli, "Human Dignity in Hungary", in *Handbook of Human Dignity in Europe*, ed. Paolo Becchi and Klaus Mathis (Cham: Springer, 2018), 403–411.

50 Cf. Act C of 2011 On the Right to Freedom of Conscience and Religion, and on the Legal Status of Churches, Religious Denominations and Religious Communities https://lapa.princeton.edu/hosteddocs/hungary/Act%20C%20of%202011%20on%20the%20Right%20to%20Freedom%20of%20Conscience%20and%20Religion.pdf; 2011 évi C. törvény a lelkiismereti és vallásszabadság jogáról, valamint az egyházak, vallásfelekezetek és vallási közösségek jogállásáról, https://mkogy.jogtar.hu/jogszabaly?docid=a1100100.TV.

51 The Constitution of the Republic of Estonia, https://www.riigiteataja.ee/en/eli/530102013003/consolide.

to provide individuals with decent living conditions.[52] Dürig's formula is not emphasised in Estonian constitutional law, so the notion of dignity developed in this country is not so much indebted to German constitutional theory. The constitution of the Republic of Latvia[53] goes back to the interwar period; its main framework was adopted on 15 February 1922. Therefore, fundamental rights are specified in its last chapter (Chapter VIII), and its catalogue is not very extensive (Articles 89–116). However, the notion of dignity – understood in many ways – is referred to in Article 95 which states: "The state defends human honor and dignity. Torture, other cruel or degrading dignity treatment of human beings is prohibited. No one may be subjected to cruel or degrading human dignity punishments". As it is stated in the literature, the notion of dignity mentioned in the first sentence of this article is understood mainly as an individual's self-assessment and self-respect. Moreover, the concept of dignity is neither developed nor widely used in the jurisprudence of the Latvian Constitutional Court.[54] The Lithuanian constitution was adopted in a referendum on 25 October 1992.[55] It regulates fundamental rights in Chapter II, entitled in a significant way: "Human being and the state". Article 18 refers to the concept of natural law, emphasising the inherent nature of human rights and freedoms. Article 21 of the Lithuanian constitution indicates in the second sentence that human dignity is to be protected by statute, without, however, indicating any characteristics of dignity. In the constitutional order of Lithuania, the concept of dignity plays a significant role. The Lithuanian Constitutional Court is of the opinion that the right to life and dignity, understood as integrity, belong to natural rights. Dignity is seen as inalienable.[56] Thus, it could be concluded that Lithuanian constitutional jurisprudence recognises the very high place of human dignity among constitutional values and rights, but at the same it time does not interpret dignity in the same way as the German Federal Constitutional Court does.

The constitutions of the countries of the Balkan region contain definitely fewer references to dignity than, for example, in the constitutional orders of the Visegrád Group countries. The Romanian constitution[57] was adopted on 21 November 1991. It indicates that fundamental rights, as regulated in

52 Tanel Kerikmäe and Kristi Joamets, "Human Dignity in Estonia", in *Handbook of Human Dignity in Europe*, ed. Paolo Becchi and Klaus Mathis (Cham: Springer, 2018), 229–244.

53 The Constitution of the Republic of Latvia, https://www.saeima.lv/en/legislative-process/constitution.

54 Dita Plepa and Jānis Pleps, "Human Dignity in Latvia", in *Handbook of Human Dignity in Europe*, ed. Paolo Becchi and Klaus Mathis (Cham: Springer, 2018), 481–502.

55 The Constitution of the Republic of Lithuania, https://e-seimas.lrs.lt/portal/legalAct/lt/TAD/TAIS.21892.

56 Darijus Beinoravičius and Milda Vainiute, "Human Dignity in Lithuania", in *Handbook of Human Dignity in Europe*, ed. Paolo Becchi and Klaus Mathis (Cham: Springer, 2018), 528–531.

57 The Constitution of Romania, https://www.presidency.ro/en/the-constitution-of-romania.

Chapter II thereof, should be understood in accordance with the *Universal Declaration of Human Rights* (Article 20, clause 1). The concept of dignity occurs only in the sense of self-respect, as evidenced by Article 30, clause 6: "The freedom of expression must not violate the dignity, honor, private life of others, or the right to one's own image". In the Romanian constitutional order, dignity is seen both as a value and specific right.[58] The Bulgarian constitution,[59] adopted on 12 July 1991 regulates human rights and freedoms in Chapter II and uses the concept of dignity in a similar sense to the one under the Romanian constitution. Dignity is mentioned in Article 32, clause 1 in the context of the protection of private life. It is about defence against violation of "honor, dignity and good name". The Bulgarian legal order distinguishes individual dignity and collective dignity for the Bulgarian people and the dignity of representatives of specific professional groups.[60] The absolute understanding of dignity is not emphasised in this legal order.

Concluding Remarks

The absolute concept of dignity was transplanted from the German constitutional order to the legal orders and/or constitutional jurisprudence of several Central European states as an expression of the reaction to human rights violations during the communist period. This concept is very flexible and can be combined with Kant's secularised philosophy (as it was done by Günter Dürig), as well as with Christian thought, including Catholic social teaching. Polish constitutional doctrine expresses the view that the constitutional concept of dignity is a specific link between the systems of statutory law and natural law.[61] Such statements, suggesting the connection between dignity and basic Christian values, can be found also in the constitutional doctrine of Lithuania. The jusnaturalist character of dignity has not been highlighted in the other three Visegrád Group countries.

If one can talk about a Central European approach to the legal category of human dignity, it is possible only in relation to the elements of reception of the understanding of dignity expressed on the basis of German constitutionalism and especially the jurisprudence of the German constitution regarding Article 1, clause 1 of the Basic Law of 1949. This reception is present in the jurisprudence of the constitutional courts of Poland, Hungary, Czechia, and Slovakia,

58 Cf. Maria Lia Pop, "Human Dignity in Romania", in *Handbook of Human Dignity in Europe*, ed. Paolo Becchi and Klaus Mathis (Cham: Springer, 2018), 745–769.

59 The Constitution of Bulgaria, https://www.parliament.bg/en/const.

60 Martin Belov, "Human Dignity in Bulgaria", in *Handbook of Human Dignity in Europe*, ed. Paolo Becchi and Klaus Mathis (Cham: Springer, 2018), 129–149.

61 Garlicki, "Artykuł 30", 27–30; Jadwiga Potrzeszcz, "Godność człowieka w orzecznictwie polskiego Trybunału Konstytucyjnego", *Roczniki Nauk Prawnych* 15, no. 1 (2005): 31–33; Judgement of the Constitutional Court of 15 October 2002, file no. SK 6/02.

and concerns in particular the so-called Dürig formula, which indicates that a human person cannot be treated solely as an object of state authority.

The understanding of dignity expressed on the basis of German constitutionalism can be adapted to very different visions of the human being resulting from worldviews or religious views dominant in a given society. All the Visegrád Group countries adopted the so-called co-operative model of the secular state, based on the autonomy of religious associations *vis-à-vis* the state and their co-operation with the state authorities, although the attitudes towards religion vary greatly in them. This diversity partly explains why, as the rulings of the constitutional courts of Poland, Hungary, and Slovakia clearly show, the legal reasoning based on the absolute concept of dignity can go in very different directions and justify very different positions. This very concept was used by constitutional courts in Slovakia and Hungary to justify the right to abortion, while the Polish Constitutional Tribunal, in a controversial 2020 judgement, utilised it to limit this right (in this judgement there were no open references to religion). It is worth noting that the Slovak Constitutional Court used the category of dignity to emphasise the importance of self-determination, in a way that seems surprising when considering the conservative religious structure of this country.

It should be emphasised that in Hungary in 2011 there was an attempt to employ the category of dignity as a general clause limiting freedom of religion, especially its collective dimension. Thus, the legal notion of dignity was used to shake the system of state–churches relationships based on a co-operative model of secular state.

Aharon Barak's view that the absolute understanding of dignity is specific to the German constitutional order can be justified by the fact that if it occurs in other constitutional orders, it is a result of the reception of German concepts. However, the absolute understanding of dignity has undoubtedly been adopted by the constitutional courts of Poland, Hungary, Czechia, and Slovakia. Simultaneously, particular importance was attached to this category in Hungarian and Polish constitutional jurisprudence. Barak plausibly showed, however, that if the right to dignity is seen as absolute and not subject to the proportionality test, it must also be recognised as a right with a narrow scope of application. This is particularly true in the case of the jurisprudence of the Polish Constitutional Court.

Part II

Freedom of Religion or Belief and Other Fundamental Rights

6 Building Bridges between Freedom of Religion and Belief and Other Fundamental Human Rights

Brett G. Scharffs

Introduction

Several people over the last few days, in their remarks from the podium and in private conversations, have referred to this gathering as something like a family reunion. It feels that way to me too. I have been working in this field now for twenty-five years—a relatively short time—but it has been wonderful to see and feel connected to friends and colleagues from around the world, especially after the COVID-19 interlude. I am going to use the metaphor of family to talk about the relationship between religious freedom and other human rights, and in particular, the role of civil society in protecting freedom of thought, conscience, and religion.

Religious Freedom as the Grandparent, Forgotten Stepchild, or Crazy Uncle of Human Rights

Sometimes religious freedom is referred to as the grandparent of human rights.[1] Indeed, it was recognized in early documents such as the *Magna Carta*, which had an early iteration of religious freedom, although of course, focused on

1 E.g., Elder D. Todd Christofferson, "Religious Liberty: The Basis of a Free and Just Society", *Talk About: Law & Religion* (Jan. 8, 2022), https://talkabout.iclrs.org/2022/01/08/religious-liberty-the-basis-of-a-free-and-just-society/ ("Religious liberty is the oldest and most deeply rooted freedom in international human rights law and is essential to the entire structure of human rights. It is widely recognized that religious freedom is the 'grandparent' of all human rights—recognized first in international treaties dating back to the Peace of Augsburg in 1555"); Patrick McKinley Brennan, "The Right of Religious Liberty of the Child: Its Meaning, Measure, and Justification", 20 *Emory Int'l L. Rev.* 129 (2006) ("The right of religious liberty, though 'the oldest of the internationally recognized human rights', has retrogressed into the neglected grandparent of human rights"); W.C. Durham, "Perspectives on Religious Liberty: A Comparative Analysis", in *Religious Human Rights in Global Perspective: Legal Perspectives* 1 (J.D. van der Vyver and J. Witte, Jr. eds., 1996).

DOI: 10.4324/9781003519188-9

institutions and not on individuals.[2] If you think of other important human rights, they also have a deep connection to freedom of religion and belief. Consider freedom of speech. How did this right emerge and warrant protection in Europe? It was in fights over religious dissent, the right to differ with respect to religious orthodoxy.[3]

What about freedom of the press? This emerged from fights over the right to publish the Bible, and in vernaculars that were readable by people.[4] Or consider the right to association, and the related right to assembly. This too was about the right of religious non-conformists to gather and to worship.[5] In the First Amendment of the United States Constitution, all of those rights are gathered under the First Amendment along with religious freedom, suggesting an early understanding of the relationship between these rights.[6] The other

2 E.g., A. Keith Thompson, "The Liberties of the Church and the City of London in Magna Carta", 18 *Ecclesiastical L. J.* 271, 272 (2016) ("the idea of religious freedom addressed in Magna Carta is quite different from the idea of individual religious freedom which is expressed in modern bills and charters of rights. The idea of religious freedom assumed in Magna Carta is more like the idea of religious autonomy said by some contemporary United States (US) commentators to have been confirmed by the establishment clause in the First Amendment to the US Constitution"). See also *Magna Carta, Religion and the Rule of Law* (Robin Griffith-Jones and Mark Hill, QC eds., 2015); Dwight G. Duncan, "Magna Carta's Freedom for the English Church", 6 *Faulkner L. Rev.* 87 (2014).

3 In the 16th century, the Protestant Reformation came about in large part because religious dissenters sought to express their own religious views that diverged from those espoused by the Catholic Church. See, e.g., Joris van Eijnatten, "In Praise of Moderate Enlightenment: A Taxonomy of Early Modern Arguments in Favor of Freedom of Expression", in *Freedom of Speech: The History of an Idea* 35 (Elizabeth Powers ed., 2011) ("During this phase, freedom of expression was treated primarily as an aspect of a wider issue, that of religious toleration"); Jonatas E.M. Machado, "Freedom of Religion: A View from Europe", 10 *Roger Williams U.L. Rev.* 451, 456 (2005) ("The modern defense of religious freedom is inseparable from the rise of ... freedom of speech").

4 See, e.g., David Bogen, "The Origins of Freedom of Speech and Press", 42 *Md L. Rev.* 429, 442 (1983) (noting that prior to the Reformation, those engaged in the printing business were largely left alone by the government in England; however, after the Reformation, subsequent control began to be exercised in order to prevent the spread of various religious texts); Alex Barber, "'Why Don't Those Lazy Priests Answer the Book?' Matthew Tindal, Censorship, Freedom of the Press and Religious Debate in Early Eighteenth-Century England", 98 *History*, 680 (2013).

5 It is interesting to note that prior to the ratification of the Bill of Rights, South Carolina protected only the right to religious assembly in its State Constitution ("No person shall disturb or molest any religious assembly," S.C. Const. of 1778, art. XXXVIII).

6 United States Const. amend. 1 ("Congress shall make no law respecting an establishment of religion, or prohibiting the free exercise thereof; or abridging the freedom of speech, or of the press; or the right of the people peaceably to assemble, and to petition the Government for a redress of grievances".) Several scholars have analyzed the structure and composition of the First Amendment, making the argument that the rights are interconnected. See e.g., Anshuman A. Mondal, "Articles of Faith: Freedom of Expression and Religious Freedom in Contemporary Multiculture", *Islam and Christian-Muslim Relations* 3, 4 (2016) (argues that the various rights of the First Amendment were put together both because of their "conceptual and historical intimacy"); Akhil Reed Amar, "The First Amendment's Firstness", 47 *U.C. Davis L. Rev.*

right enumerated in the First Amendment is the right to petition the government for grievances. And what do you imagine many of those earlier petitions were about? They were about people whose religious freedom and religious identities were being insulted by the state.[7]

In a very similar way, prohibitions on unlawful discrimination, such as Title VII of the Civil Rights Act of 1964 in the United States, include a prohibition not just on discrimination on the basis of race and sex, but also on the basis of religion.[8] The right to be protected from unlawful discrimination includes the right not to be discriminated against on the basis of religion.

As Judge Ann Power and others articulated so clearly at the Sixth International Consortium for Law and Religious Studies (ICLARS) Conference in Cordoba, Spain,[9] we often think of religious freedom as being in a contest or conflict with non-discrimination norms. But the prohibition on discrimination, the early prohibitions especially, always included a prohibition on discrimination on the basis of religion.[10] And if you think about where discrimination takes place in the world today, much of that discrimination is still discrimination on

---

1015, 1027–28 (2014) (argues that the First Amendment rights are gathered together because they are all conceptually, chronologically, doctrinally, and culturally first).

7 One scholar notes that "while religious doctrine itself appears not to have been directly the subject of petitions, virtually every other facet of the organization of religious affairs was", Gregory A. Mark, "The Vestigal Constitution: The History and Significance of the Right to Petition", 66 *Fordham L. Rev.* 2153, 2189 (1998). One of the more well-known petitions, dubbed the "Ten Thousand Petition", addressed church establishment in Virginia and was signed by nearly 10,000 people in 1776, *Petition of the 10,000 for Religious Freedom, 1776*, Document Bank of Virginia (accessed Feb. 27, 2023), https://edu.lva.virginia.gov/dbva/items/show/283. See also Raymond C. Bailey, *Popular Influence Upon Public Policy: Petitioning in Eighteenth-Century Virginia*, 137–58 (1979) (discussing early religious petitions in Virginia).

8 42 U.S.C. § 2000e-2(a) ("It shall be an unlawful employment practice for an employer – (1) to fail or refuse to hire or to discharge any individual, or otherwise to discriminate against any individual with respect to his compensation, terms, conditions, or privileges of employment, because of such individual's race, color, religion, sex, or national origin; or (2) to limit, segregate, or classify his employees or applicants for employment in any way which would deprive or tend to deprive any individual of employment opportunities or otherwise adversely affect his status as an employee, because of such individual's race, color, religion, sex, or national origin".)

9 The Sixth Conference of ICLARS (International Consortium for Law and Religion Studies), was held in Cordoba, Spain, on 19–21 September 2022. I refer here to the oral presentations of Judge Ann Power—former judge of the European Court of Human Rights—and other speakers in that conference.

10 See, e.g., the Fair Housing Act of 1968, which makes it unlawful to discriminate on the basis of race, color, religion, sex, familial status, national origin, or disability, 42 U.S.C. § 3601 et seq.; Title II of the Civil Rights Act of 1964, which prohibits discrimination or segregation at places of public accommodation on the ground of race, color, religion, or national origin, 42 U.S.C. § 2000a et seq.; Title III of the Civil Rights Act of 1964, which prohibits discrimination based on race, color, religion, or national origin in public facilities owned or operated by the state, 42 U.S.C. § 2000b et seq.; Title IV of the Civil Rights Act of 1964, which prohibits discrimination based on race, color, religion, sex, or national origin in public education, including schools and colleges, 42 U.S.C. § 2000c et seq.

the basis of religion.[11] Whether one is a believer or an atheist, discrimination on the basis of thought, conscience, and religion, and limitations of rights on these bases, are commonplace.[12] And so, in a very real sense, religion, the right to exercise one's religion, and religious freedom, is the grandparent of human rights.

A second metaphor that we sometimes hear today is that religious freedom more often feels like the *forgotten stepchild* of human rights.[13] Freedom of religion or belief is sometimes viewed as being redundant, unnecessary, unimportant, or even unrelated to other human rights.[14] Secular human rights discourse almost always completely ignores religious freedom. And indeed, sometimes debates are characterized as a contest between religious freedom and human rights, as if religious freedom isn't even on the list.[15] Moreover,

11 A 2018 Pew Research study reported that harassment against religious groups occurs in more than 90% of countries around the world. This harassment encompasses a wide range of actions, including social and legal discrimination as well as verbal abuse and physical violence. It also is perpetuated by a variety of actors, including both governments and individuals or social groups., Samirah Majumdar and Virginia Villa, "In 2018, Government Restrictions on Religion Reach Highest Level Globally in More Than a Decade", *Pew Research Center* (2020), https://www.pewresearch.org/religion/2020/11/10/harassment-of-religious-groups-continues-to-be-reported-in-more-than-90-of-countries/.

12 Another Pew Research study notes that the total number of countries with "high" or "very high" levels of government restrictions on religion has risen in recent years. In 2019 a total of 57 countries (or 29% of all countries in the study) fell into those categories. The study notes that government restrictions on religion include the official laws, policies, and actions that impinge on religious beliefs and practice, which includes discrimination. Samirah Majumdar and Virginia Villa, "Globally, Social Hostilities Related to Religion Decline in 2019, While Government Restrictions Remain at Highest Levels", *Pew Research Center* (2021), https://www.pewresearch.org/religion/2021/09/30/globally-social-hostilities-related-to-religion-decline-in-2019-while-government-restrictions-remain-at-highest-levels/. For another study focusing on how the COVID-19 pandemic led to an increase in legal restrictions on religious groups, *see* Samirah Majumdar, "How COVID-19 Restrictions Affected Religious Groups Around the World in 2020", *Pew Research Center* (2022), https://www.pewresearch.org/religion/2022/11/29/how-covid-19-restrictions-affected-religious-groups-around-the-world-in-2020/.

13 See, e.g., Judith A. Berling, "Is Conversation About Religion Possible? (And What Can Religionists Do To Promote It?)", 61 *J. Am. Acad. Religion* 1, 2 (1993) ("Religious Studies, the stepchild of a Supreme Court decision in the 1960s, is a newcomer to the university, whose presence is still questioned or threatened in a number of institutions"); Eugene Volokh, "Equal Treatment is Not Establishment", 13 *Notre Dame J.L. Ethics & Pub. Pol'y* 341, 366 (1999) ("Religious speech is not some stepchild of constitutional law: It is fully protected by the Free Speech Clause").

14 See, e.g., Brian Leiter, *Why Tolerate Religion?* (2012); Micah Schwartzman, "What If Religion Is Not Special?", 79 *U. Chi. L. Rev.* 1351 (2012); Anthony Ellis, "What Is Special About Religion?", 25 *L. & Phil.* 219, 220 (2006); Frederick Gedicks, "An Unfirm Foundation: The Regrettable Indefensibility of Religious Exemptions", 20 *U. Ark. Little Rock L. Rev.* 555, 556–57 (1998); James W. Nickel, "Who Needs Freedom of Religion?", 76 *U. Colo. L. Rev.* 941, 943 (2005).

15 E.g., Bekithemba Dube et al., "The Ambivalence of Freedom of Religion, and Unearthing the Unlearnt Lessons of Religious Freedom from the Jonestown Incident: A Decoloniality

religious freedom is somehow viewed as being in opposition to human rights. I was so concerned about this, that I joined the Human Rights section of the American Association of Law Schools. Eventually, I became the Chair of that section and organized a program around the topic of building bridges between religious freedom as a human right and other human rights.[16] There are respectable voices that claim that religious freedom really should not be a human right.[17] So, the challenges of including freedom of thought, conscience, and religion in the human rights discourse is something that we need to be mindful of. For those of us who are specialists in the field of law and religion, I think we need to be especially mindful of building bridges and insisting on being part of conversations with the broader, mostly secular, human rights community.[18]

A third way of thinking about religious freedom is as the *crazy uncle* of human rights. You know this character. He is the one who shows up in mismatched socks and says embarrassing things at Thanksgiving dinner. He has views that are out of fashion on social morality, gender, marriage, family, abortion, and perhaps even issues that seem distantly related to freedom of religion, such as climate change, health care, politics, or the real showstopper in the United States in 2020, Donald Trump. Now, believe it or not, there is literature that appears about a week before Thanksgiving in any given year, mostly in the popular press, about how to cope with your crazy uncle at Thanksgiving.[19] (We never talk about the crazy aunt, by the way; it is only the crazy uncle that gets singled out for analysis at Thanksgiving time.) I studied

---

Approach", 30 *J. Stud. Religion* 330 (2017) (analysis of how freedom of religion in South Africa has led to countless human rights abuses).

16 "International Human Rights, Co-Sponsored by Comparative Law and Law and Religion", *Association of American Law Schools*, (accessed Feb. 27, 2023), https://memberaccess.aals.org/eweb/DynamicPage.aspx?webcode=SesDetails&ses_key=0aa90a30-1698-45f9-9d41-0e134347cd7f.

17 See, e.g., Mark Tushnet, "The Redundant Free Exercise Clause?", 33 *Loy. U. Chi. L.J.* 71 (2001); Gila Stopler, "How Could Religious Liberty Be a Human Right: A Reply to Andrew Koppelman", 16 *Int'l J. Const. L.* (forthcoming 2018), https://ssrn.com/abstract=3245772; Amos Guiora, *Freedom From Religion* (2nd ed. 2012).

18 See generally Jack Donnelly, *Universal Human Rights in Theory and Practice* (3rd ed. 2013); David Weissbrodt et al., *International Human Rights: Law, Policy, and Process* (5th ed. 2021); *Labour Law, Human Rights, and Social Justice: Liber Amicorum in Honour of Ruth Ben-Israel* (Roger Blanpaint, ed. 2001); Michael J. Perry, *The Idea of Human Rights: Four Inquiries* (1998); Dohrman W. Byers, "The Morality of Human Rights: A Secular Ground", 26 *J. L. & Religion* 1 (2010).

19 See, e.g., Kathryn Watson, "How to Survive Thanksgiving With Your Unwoke Relatives", *Brit.co* (Nov. 18, 2020), https://www.brit.co/how-to-survive-awkward-family-thanksgiving-dinner-conversations/; A. Pawlowski, "How to Survive Thanksgiving When Politics Loom Large", *NBC News* (Nov. 19, 2017), https://www.nbcnews.com/better/health/how-survive-thanksgiving-when-politics-loom-large-ncna821206; Ellen Hendriksen, "6 Tips for Thanksgiving with a Difficult Family", *Psychology Today* (Nov. 19, 2019), https://www.psychologytoday.com/us/blog/how-be-yourself/201911/6-tips-thanksgiving-difficult-family.

that literature to see if there were some ideas and suggestions that could help us cope with religious difference, even religious differences of family members, uncles, and aunts.

I have distilled four principles from these "how-to-survive the holidays" articles. The first is empathy.[20] One writer suggests that perhaps the life experiences of your uncle might be quite different than your own.[21] One thing you might want to do is really try to understand where he is coming from. Perhaps this should not be a novel idea—after all empathy is something that hopefully we began to learn in kindergarten—but it is a skill or disposition that is, alas, easily forgotten.

The second principle is familiarity.[22] The point here is that if you only encounter your crazy uncle once a year at Thanksgiving, you are not likely to have a sufficiently deep relationship, notwithstanding kinship, that allows you to really understand him. And so one thing we may need to do with our crazy uncle is spend some time with him, get to know him outside the rituals of Thanksgiving dinner. Again, this seems like a fairly basic concept, but one that is also easily violated. I, perhaps like you, had a crazy uncle whom I only saw once a year, so the lack of real familiarity may be a reality.

The third suggestion is to bond over similarities.[23] Maybe it is Real Madrid or the Dallas Cowboys, but there may be areas of common ground that we can start with to help ease our interactions. It is important not to ignore the differences, but we don't have to start with them, and we don't have to insist that they become the centerpiece of our time together. Perhaps we can talk about things that we share in common, even something as simple as family progenitors or family memories—although it is remarkable the extent to which even the memory of our ancestors, or even childhood events, can vary between different family members.

The fourth suggestion is to focus on something they care about.[24] The idea here is that rather than wanting to showcase and talk about your political perspective or hobby horse, seek to learn something from them. I guess this goes back to Will Rogers' observation that he'd never met a man he didn't like.[25]

20 Mike Pesca, "Taming the Intolerant Uncle: An Enlightened Approach to Dealing with Difficult Family This Holidy Season", *Slate* (Dec. 14, 2015), https://slate.com/human-interest/2015/12/intolerant-uncles-how-to-deal-with-un-pc-family-over-the-holidays.html.

21 Tracy Ross and Melanie Davis-McAfee, "Navigating Thanksgiving with Gratitude, Empathy, and an Open Mind", WKMS (Nov. 20, 2018), https://www.wkms.org/society/2018-11-20/navigating-thanksgiving-with-gratitude-empathy-and-an-open-mind.

22 Pesca, *supra* note 20.

23 Karin Tamerius, "How to Have a Conversation with Your Angry Uncle Over the Holidays", *NY Times*, (accessed Feb. 22, 2023), https://www.nytimes.com/interactive/2018/11/18/opinion/thanksgiving-family-argue-chat-bot.html.

24 Pesca, *supra* note 20.

25 See Joseph H. Carter, *Never Met a Man I Didn't Like: The Life and Writings of Will Rogers*,William Morrow Paperbacks (1991).

Those are some ideas for how we might live with, embrace, and cope with our differences, including different views about religion, social issues that relate to religion, and how religious freedom fits with other human rights.

Tolerance, Respect, and Love

As we strive to live with our deep differences, I want to say a word in defense of a much-maligned value, something that was once celebrated as a virtue: tolerance. We often hear that tolerance is not enough; we must have respect.[26] And then someone will up the ante by insisting that respect is not enough; we must have love.[27] And that is all well and good. But as a legal principle, I think tolerance has a lot to commend itself. Tolerance is something that we can expect and enforce one against each other via law.[28] Respect, on the other hand, is something that is mostly earned or bestowed, and a legal regime that tries to mandate respect would become quite coercive, much less one that mandates love. Can you imagine statutes demanding that we love each other? If you've seen the musical *Hamilton*, as they lampoon King George III in a rather unkind way, King George is portrayed as a callow pop singer, singing a ditty about how he is motivated only by love. He declares:

> Remember, despite our estrangement, I'm your man
> You'll be back, soon you'll see
> You'll remember you belong to me
> You'll be back, time will tell
> You'll remember that I served you well
> Oceans rise, empires fall
> We have seen each other through it all
> And when push comes to shove
> I will send a fully armed battalion to remind you of my love.[29]

A couple of verses later, King George sings, "'Cause when push comes to shove / I will kill your friends and family to remind you of my love".

The truth is, there can be something very coercive about love. I believe tolerance is a very powerful, valid, and valuable legal norm. Respect is a very

26 See, e.g., Monique Deveaux, "Toleration and Respect", 12 *Pub. Affs. Q.* 407, 421–24 (1998); Asher Maoz, "Inter-Religious Relations—Tolerance or Respect?", IF20 *Viewpoints* (May 28, 2021), https://blog.g20interfaith.org/2021/05/28/inter-religious-relations-tolerance-or-respect/.

27 See, e.g., Alex Deagon, "Creating Peaceful Coexistance Through Virtue: A Theological Approach to Institutional Religious Freedom, Equality, and the First Amendment", *Liberty & Law Center* 2 (2022).

28 For a defense of tolerance as a viable legal standard, *see* Catriona McKinnon, *Toleration: A Critical Introduction* (2006); John Stuart Mill, *On Liberty* (1859).

29 Jonathan Groff, "You'll Be Back", (*Hamilton* 2015).

powerful, valid, and valuable political and social norm. And love is a very powerful, valid, and valuable moral and religious norm. But let us not forget that tolerance can do real work as well. We actually need different governing principles in different social realms—the realm of law, the realm of politics, and the realm of morality.

Cut-Flower Culture

If the reality is that religious freedom is the grandparent of human rights, then we should be mindful of what others have described as the cut-flower culture of human rights.[30] If we take religion and clip it, and then take speech, association, the press, non-discrimination, and due process of law and put them in a vase, it is going to be a beautiful bouquet, but it will wither and die. I believe that because there is this deep-rooted wellspring of health and nourishment of human rights that comes from the protection of religious freedom, then if we fail to protect freedom of religion and belief, we are soon going to find ourselves living in a cut-flower human rights culture. For example, if we refuse to protect religious conscience, will we protect conscience for long? If we refuse to protect religious speech, will we protect other forms of speech for long? If we do not prohibit discrimination on the basis of religion, can we expect the norms of non-discrimination to last more than a generation or two? I believe not.

The Generative Power of Human Dignity

My final suggestion is to focus on the generative power of human dignity. For the last four or five years, our Center has been really turning a lion's share of our attention to the generative capacity of human dignity, to help build cultures of respect for human rights.[31] There are several important points I want to share.

First, human dignity as the foundational principle of human rights. When the Human Rights Committee was trying to draft what became the *Universal Declaration of Human Rights* (UDHR), they hit a logjam. That logjam was broken when the Chinese delegate P.C. Chang recalled that human dignity appeared in the preamble to the United Nations Charter, and he said, "Let's

30 Simon McCrosson, "Address at the Twenty-Third International Law and Religion Symposium: Religion & Culture: Personal Observations from the United Kingdom/Europe" (Oct. 2, 2016), https://www.iclrs.org/event.php/2016+Annual+Symposium/Media/English/3667.

31 See, *Punta del Este Declaration on Human Dignity for Everyone Everywhere: Seventy Years After the Universal Declaration of Human Rights*, Dec. 2018; Brett Scharffs et al., *Points of Light: The Punta del Este Declaration on Human Dignity for Everyone Everywhere* (2021); Brett Scharffs and Ewelina Ochab, *Dignity and International Human Rights Law: An Introduction to the Punta del Este Declaration on Human Dignity for Everyone Everywhere* (2021).

start there". That somehow enabled the conversation to be focused and productive in a way that resulted in what must be considered the miraculous achievement of the UDHR.[32]

Second, human dignity builds bridges, as Jan Figel taught us. In our early conversations, he was the EU Special Envoy for Freedom of Religion and Belief, trying to deal with religious freedom in difficult places, like Pakistan. What he found is that if he began the conversation with human dignity, it helped build a bridge that made it possible to begin discussing more controversial issues.[33] Ultimately, his intervention was very important in freeing Azia Bibi, the Christian woman who was convicted of blasphemy and given a very long prison sentence for drinking out of a vessel that was shared with Muslim women.[34]

Human dignity also elevates rather than degrades our human rights discourse.[35] It is very difficult to have a conversation about human dignity and to end it in the ditch. Although it is easy to have human rights conversations that end up stuck in the mud. Human dignity is also a powerful exit ramp from toxic identity politics. Identity politics almost always descend into a zero-sum game, or a contest of oppressors and victims, winners and losers.[36] Human dignity really forces us to think about each other, because it makes no sense to think of my human dignity without thinking of yours as well. As I have mentioned, it is generative. We can all learn something from each other when we ask: what does human dignity mean to you? We have seen this time and again.[37]

32 See Mary Ann Glendon, *A World Made New: Eleanor Roosevelt and the Universal Declaration of Human Rights* (2001); Hans Ingvar Roth, *P.C. Chang and the Universal Declaration of Human Rights,* 153 (2016).

33 Scharffs and Ochab, *supra* note 31 at 1–2.

34 Andrea Gagliarducci, "EU Official: Release of Asia Bibi Shows Promise for Religious Freedom", *Catholic News Agency* (2019), https://www.catholicnewsagency.com/news/42238/eu-official-release-of-asia-bibi-shows-promise-for-religious-freedom.

35 Scharffs and Ochab, *supra* note 31 at 233–34.

36 Many scholars have addressed the criticisms of identity politics. See, e.g., Rajen Harshe and Sujata Patel, "Identity Politics and Crisis of Social Sciences", 38 *Econ. & Pol. Wkly.* 525 (2003); Ananta Kumar Giri, "Civil Society and the Limits of Identity Politics", 50 *Soc. Bulletin* 266 (2001); Martha E. Gimenez, "With a Little Class: A Critique of Identity Politics", 6 *Ethnicities* 423 (2006).

37 Often various cultural, ethnic, or religious perspectives can shed valuable insight into the concept of human dignity. See, e.g., Man Yee Karen Lee, "Universal Human Dignity: Some Reflections in the Asian Context", 3 *Asian J. Comp. L.* 1 (2008) (drawing on principles from Confucianism and Islam to explain how human dignity is understood in many Asian countries); Miklós Maróth, "Human Dignity in the Islamic World", in *The Cambridge Handbook of Human Dignity: Interdisciplinary Perspectives* 155–162 (Marcus Düwell et al. eds., 2014) (discussing Islamic views on human dignity). Declaration from the Seventh Annual Law and Religion in Africa Conference, African Consortium for Law and Religion Studies [ACLARS Declaration], African Perspectives on Human Dignity for Everyone Everywhere: An Endorsement and Elaboration of the Punta del Este Declaration on Dignity for Everyone Everywhere

Our Center recently participated in a project on African perspectives of human dignity.[38] One of the scholars from Zimbabwe said, "In my culture, for a man to have dignity means for him to be able to earn a living sufficient that he can get married and take care of a child". And I thought, that is really important. That is beautiful and lovely. I had never thought about human dignity in that light. Well, not a month later, I was back in the United States reading an article about the crisis of marriage in the United States. Many people are not getting married and not even entering into long-term stable relationships before having children.[39] A large percentage of babies in the United States are born to single mothers.[40] The sociologists who are studying this phenomenon found out that the number one reason women are not marrying is because men are not viewed as good economic partners.[41] They are viewed as people who are going to sit at home playing video games and not make a full contribution to the family financially.[42] Suddenly, I saw that what I had thought of as an interesting and perhaps idiosyncratic view from Africa was much more important to my thinking about what needs to happen in the United States to vindicate the dignity of American men than I had imagined.

Human dignity can also lower the temperature and the volume of human rights discourse. Human rights conversations often descend into finger pointing and assertion of one person's or one group's rights as being more important than others'. Human dignity, in contrast, less easily degenerates into mutual recrimination and defensiveness.

(May 21, 2019), https://www.dignityforeveryone.org/wp-content/uploads/sites/5/2019/10/African-Perspectives-on-Human-Dignity-for-Everyone-Everywhere-2019.pdf (sharing various African perspectives on human dignity).

38 See ACLARS Declaration, *supra* note 37.

39 Gaby Galvin, "U.S. Marriage Rate Hits Historic Low", *US News* (Apr. 29, 2020), https://www.usnews.com/news/healthiest-communities/articles/2020-04-29/us-marriage-rate-drops-to-record-low (In 2018, marriage rates in the United States hit an all-time low; additionally, studies show that people are delaying marriage, and many young people do not expect to ever get married); Gretchen Livingston, "The Changing Profile of Unmarried Parents", *Pew Research Center* (Apr. 25, 2018), https://www.pewresearch.org/social-trends/2018/04/25/the-changing-profile-of-unmarried-parents/ (One-in-four parents in the United States are unmarried.) See also, Juliana Menasce Horowitz et al., "Marriage and Cohabitation in the U.S.", *Pew Research Center* (Nov. 6, 2019), https://www.pewresearch.org/social-trends/2019/11/06/marriage-and-cohabitation-in-the-u-s/.

40 In 2020, the national average was 40%, "Percentage of Babies Born to Unmarried Mothers by State", *Centers for Disease Control and Prevention* (2020), https://www.cdc.gov/nchs/pressroom/sosmap/unmarried/unmarried.htm. The average is much higher for African American children (roughly 60%), see Suzanne M. Bianchi, "The Changing Demographic and Socioeconomic Characteristics of Single Parent Families", 20 *Marriage & Family Rev.* 71 (1994).

41 Drake Baer, "Economic Forces Making US Men Less Appealing Partners, Researchers Say", *CNN* (Sept. 28, 2017), https://www.cnn.com/2017/09/28/health/american-men-less-marriageable-partner/index.html.

42 *Id.* ("The lack of good jobs for these men is making them less and less attractive to women in the marriage market, and women, with their greater earnings, can do fine remaining single".)

Robin Fretwell Wilson, a law professor from the University of Illinois, was instrumental in helping negotiate peace between religious freedom advocates and LGBTQ advocates in Utah surrounding perceived conflicts between religious freedom and non-discrimination. She said that it was really when the group gathered around the table, met each other, and started having dinners and visiting each other in their homes, that the possibility of compromise, what I really see as a mutual vindication of the important interests of both, became achievable.[43]

Finally, it helps move us beyond a rights-only mindset. Heiner Bielefeldt has noted that there is some hesitancy in the human rights movement to talk about responsibility.[44] He distinguishes three levels of responsibility to religious freedom: legal responsibility, moral responsibility, and philosophical responsibility.[45] The first two, legal and moral responsibility, require both states and individuals to act as guarantors or duty bearers of religious freedom. However, the third level of responsibility calls attention to the philosophical considerations of human dignity and how it is at the core of religious freedom.

One of the other contributions P.C. Chang made to the UDHR was in Article 1, where it says, "All human beings are endowed with reason". He said, "That isn't enough. They're also endowed with Ren, which is the Chinese concept for two-person mindedness, the capacity we each possess as human beings to care for and acknowledge the other".[46] Unfortunately that got translated in Article I of the UDHR as conscience. So, Article I refers to human beings endowed with "reason and conscience". Please do not get me wrong, I cherish and value conscience. But something important was lost in translation. Conscience, like reason, is an inward capacity. What *ren* reminds us is that to be human is to also have that outward-focused capacity of regard for others.

Conclusion

As we try to build bridges between FORB and other human rights, I hope that these suggestions might help us in our endeavors to create and sustain cultures of dignity and respect, to cultivate what Judge Ann Power described at the Spain ICLARS conference as strategies of mutual vindication, and to accommodate when possible. This accommodation should not be an unfortunate exception to the rule or an adjustment that the religiously observant must make for state interests, but rather like the accommodation that we have

43 *See*, Robin Fretwell Wilson, "Common Ground Lawmaking: Lessons for Peaceful Coexistence from Masterpiece Cakeshop and the Utah Compromise", 51 *Conn. L. Rev.* 419 (2019).

44 Heiner Bielefeldt, Opening Plenary Speech at the 27th Annual International Law and Religion Symposium: Religious Freedom: Rights and Responsibilities (Oct. 4, 2020), https://talkabout.iclrs.org/2020/11/09/responsibility-on-behalf-of-religious-freedom/.

45 *Id.*

46 *Glendon*, *supra* note 32 at page 35.

received here in Cordoba as visitors.[47] We are staying in hotels where we are safe, where we can rest without a loaded gun under our pillows, and feel that we are not at risk. That is the attitude of accommodation—accommodation of an ethic of hospitality rather than an ethic of right—that I think we need to vindicate, as well as place limitations upon our fundamental freedoms when it is necessary to do so.[48]

47 Brett G. Scharffs, "Conceptualising Reasonable Accommodation", in *Freedom of Religion or Belief* 164–83 (Paul T. Babie et al. eds., 2020).
48 *Id.*

7 Hate Speech, Offences to Religion, and Public Morals in Strasbourg Case Law[1]

Javier Martínez-Torrón

A Recurrent Issue

There is no need to insist that freedom of expression, recognized by art. 10 of the *European Convention on Human Rights* (ECHR), is one of the fundamental rights that have more significance for the structure and dynamics of democratic societies. And it is well known that some people, when exercising their right to publicly express their own ideas and opinions, do it—intentionally or not—in a manner that is disrespectful to those who hold different views.

The Strasbourg jurisdiction has dealt with this type of situation for a long time. In particular, since the *Handyside* judgment in 1976, which involved the judicial seizure of a book for teenage scholars (*The Little Red Schoolbook*) that British authorities considered contrary to public morals. The book, written by an author of philo-Maoist orientation, included some obscene passages and some others inciting rebellion against parental authority.[2]

It is relatively frequent that, through a variety of channels of communication, we find a public discourse that is directly provocative against religion or implies an element of anti-religious offense or derision, direct or indirect; it may be against religion in general or a particular religion—its doctrinal, historical, social, or organizational aspects—or against sacred figures or religious

1 This chapter has been written in the context of the Research Project PID2019-106005GB-I00 (HUDISOC), of the Spanish Ministry of Science. It was also presented at the International Conference on Religion and Freedom of Expression, organized by the International Association for the Defense of Religious Liberty, Lisbon 2023, which will be published in the journal, "Conscience and Liberty" in 2024. A Spanish version of this essay has been published in *Libertad de expresión y libertad religiosa: una perspectiva transatlántica* (ed. by J. Martínez-Torrón - S. Cañamares - M. González), Iustel, 2023.

2 *Handyside v. United Kingdom*, 7 December 1976. For an interesting guide to the Strasbourg case law in this matter, see *Freedom of Expression in Europe: Case-Law Concerning Article 10 of the European Convention on Human Rights* (ed. by M. Oetheimer), Council of Europe, 2007.

DOI: 10.4324/9781003519188-10

symbols.[3] The European Court of Human Rights (ECtHR) has adjudicated on these cases on various occasions since *Otto-Preminger-Institut* (1994), concerning the judicial prohibition of a blasphemous film (*Das Liebeskonzil*), which was to be shown in a cinema club in Innsbruck. The film contained a gross mockery of the main characters of Christianity, including God The Father, Jesus Christ, and the Virgin Mary.[4]

These situations are far from being solved. Just the opposite, they seem to be recurrent, as demonstrated by the various judgments of the Strasbourg Court in this matter in the last few years, with very different profiles.[5]

Thus, the *Sekmadienis* case,[6] in 2018, regarded an advertising campaign introducing a new clothing line in Lithuania, which used characters and expressions of religious connotation, not explicit but clearly visible. More precisely, the campaign showed the image of a man of unequivocal resemblance with the way Jesus Christ was traditionally represented in Christian iconography and a woman with a parallel similarity to customary depictions of the Holy Virgin. In both cases, the images were accompanied by captions that read popular expressions of Christian origin in Lithuania: "Jesus, what trousers!", "Dear

3 For an interesting study on the cases in this matter, in particular with regard to the area of cinema, see G. Moreno Botella, *El conflicto libertad de expresión – libertad religiosa a través del cine*, in "Anuario de Derecho Canónico" 6 Supl. (Febr. 2018), pp. 105–134.

4 *Otto-Preminger-Institut v. Austria*, 20 September 1994. Two years later, the doctrine contained in this judgment was reaffirmed in *Wingrove v. United Kingdom*, 25 November 1996, apropos of a video that, in its author's words, constituted a pornographic version of St Theresa's ecstasy with homosexual connotations. For further details and bibliographical references on this case law of the ECtHR, see J. Martínez-Torrón, *Freedom of Expression Versus Freedom of Religion in the European Court of Human Rights*, in A. Sajó (ed.), "Censorial Sensitivities: Free Speech and Religion in a Fundamentalist World", Eleven International, 2007, pp. 233–269. An update of that essay, in Spanish, can be found in J. Martínez-Torrón, *¿Libertad de expresión amordazada? Libertad de expresión y libertad de religión en la jurisprudencia de Estrasburgo*, in J. Martínez-Torrón and S. Cañamares (eds.), "Tensiones entre libertad de expresión y libertad religiosa", Tirant Lo Blanch, 2014, pp. 83–120.

5 Also, although to a lesser extent, there have been decisions that judged the opposite situation: that is, religious speech that could be offensive, discriminatory, or violent. Among those in recent years, we can mention the decision of inadmissibility, *Belkacem v. Belgium* (Dec. Adm. 34367/14), 20 July 2017, in which a chamber of the ECHR rejected the claim that there was a violation of freedom of expression in the conviction of the leader and spokesperson of the association "Sharia4Belgium", who had been convicted for inciting violent action against non-believers (i.e., non-Muslims) in videos posted on YouTube, where he accused them of being "dirtier than animals" among other things. The sentence was one year and six months of imprisonment, with a suspended sentence, and a fine of 550 euros. More recently, in another inadmissibility decision, *Lenis v. Greece* (Dec. Adm. 47833/20, 31 August 2023), the Court upheld the sanctions imposed on a high priest (Metropolitan) of the Greek Orthodox Church for homophobic hate speech using his personal blog, where he used expressions such as "they are the scum of society", "disgraced people, spit on them", and "they are not human, they are perversions of nature". The applicant had been sentenced to seven months in prison, with suspended sentence, and to pay legal costs of 240 euros.

6 *Sekmadienis v. Lihtuania*, 30 January 2018.

Mary, what a dress!", and "Jesus [and] Mary, what are you wearing!" The campaign was prohibited and the textile company was fined on the grounds that the disrespect it showed for symbols of Christianity—the majority religion in Lithuania—was against public morals. The Strasbourg Court, while recognizing that commercial speech allows for a higher degree of limitation compared to others (such as political or ideological language), found a violation of art. 10 ECHR, holding that the Lithuanian jurisdiction had not adequately balanced the various interests at stake and that the freedom of expression of a minority could not be subject to the acceptance of its ideas by the majority.

In July of the same year, the judgment in *Mariya Alekhina*[7] dealt with the situation of three women belonging to a feminist group of punk music, Pussy Riot, who invaded the Christ the Saviour Orthodox Cathedral in Moscow and began to perform a song that was strongly critical of President Putin and the patriarch of the Russian Orthodox Church. The members of the music band certainly looked for celebrity and visibility; they had invited journalists and broadcast their performance—soon interrupted by security personnel—through a video published on YouTube. They were charged with the aggravated offense of hooliganism motivated by religious hatred and received a two-year prison sentence. The ECtHR held that the Russian authorities had committed multiple violations of the European Convention, including subjecting individuals to inhuman and degrading treatment, as well as denying them basic procedural rights. The Court also ruled in favor of an unjustified limitation on freedom of expression, primarily due to the severity of the sanctions imposed, even though there were no indications of the musical group inciting hatred, violence, or discrimination in their performance.

Hardly a month later, and consequence also of an application against Russia, *Ibragim Ibragimov*[8] regarded a very different issue: an action of the public authorities that restricted the freedom of religious speech. The application was caused by the prohibition and seizure of books written by a Muslim theologian, Said Nursi, which were considered—on unclear factual grounds—to be extremist writings that incited violence and hostility between believers and non-believers. Once again, the European Court observed a violation of freedom of expression, considering that the actions of the Russian courts were based on biased reports and that there was no evidence that the prohibited writings had caused inter-religious tensions or any harmful consequences in society.

Still, in 2018, in *E.S. v. Austria*,[9] conflict was caused by a seminar entitled "Basic information on Islam", organized by an institute linked to a right-wing party, which held hard positions with regard to immigration, and aimed at young voters. In that seminar, the speaker—a woman—made some references

7 *Mariya Alekhina and others v. Russia*, 17 July 2018.
8 *Ibragim Ibragimov v. Russia*, 28 August 2018.
9 *E.S. v. Austria*, 25 October 2018.

to the history and life of Prophet Muhammad, in particular to his marriage with young Aisha, the third of his wives, suggesting that the central figure of Islam did not deserve to be looked at as a role model because he had committed actions that, from a contemporary perspective, would be revealing of a tendency towards pedophilia. The Austrian courts, applying the same legislation used in *Otto-Preminger-Institut*, sentenced the applicant to a fine of 480 euros as guilty of an offense of disparaging an object of veneration of a domestic church or religious society in a manner capable of arousing "justified indignation". In this case, the ECtHR found that the sanction imposed by the national authorities—in its view proportionate—was in accordance with the European Convention, since it involved a type of speech that abusively mistreated the most revered figure of Islam and was therefore likely to arouse "justified indignation" among the Muslim population.

In 2019, the *Tagiyev* judgement[10] declared that the freedom of expression of the applicants—a journalist and the editor of a modest magazine—had been violated by sentencing them to several years of imprisonment, as a consequence of publishing an article criticizing Islam and the Prophet Muhammad for their lack of humanist values in the context of an analysis of Azerbaijan's future in relation to Europe. The applicants were eventually pardoned, but only after spending more than one year in prison. It is worth noting that an important Iranian imam issued a fatwa calling for the death of the applicants. One of them, the journalist, was later stabbed to death by an unknown assailant three years after filing the case in Strasbourg (and it would still take another eight years for the judgment to be delivered). The Court pointed out the disproportionate punishment imposed and the lack of legal and factual analysis by the national courts in criminal proceedings.

In 2020, in the *Baldassi* case,[11] the ECHR decided on a peculiar instance of freedom of expression: the criminal conviction, with economic sanctions of several thousand euros, of a group of individuals from a pro-Palestinian organization who had initiated a campaign at a large shopping center in Alsace. Positioned at the entrance, they put up posters calling on shoppers to boycott Israeli products in protest against Israel's policies in Gaza, which they labeled as criminal. There was no violence or statements of an anti-Semitic nature. Acquitted in the first instance, they were later convicted on appeal of "incitement to economic discrimination" against Israeli suppliers. The European Court concluded that there had been a violation of freedom of expression and that the French courts had failed to conduct any assessment of this fundamental right when applying the provisions of the Criminal Code.

More recently, in 2022, the *Rabczewska* case[12] brought before the ECtHR the case of a popular Polish pop singer—known as Doda—who had been fined

10 *Tagiyev y Huseynov c. Azerbaiyán*, 5 December 2019.
11 *Baldassi y otros c. Francia*, 11 June 2020.
12 *Rabczewska c. Polonia*, 15 September 2022.

just over 1,000 euros by the Polish courts for violating the criminal code by making statements that offended the religious feelings of others by publicly insulting an object of religious worship. The statements in question had been made during an interview in which the singer referred to the Bible as a series of "incredible stories" written by "someone wasted from drinking wine and smoking some weed". It was evident that these were not serious or motivated remarks, but rather a frivolous comment made with the intention of attracting public interest. The Polish Constitutional Tribunal deemed this incompatible with the civilized tone and respect for human dignity that should govern public discourse, avoiding the humiliation of individuals—in this case, by insulting the sacred book of Christians and Jews. However, the ECHR, in a non-unanimous decision, found a violation of freedom of expression on the grounds that the Polish courts had imposed a penalty that was too severe and had not sufficiently assessed to which extent the offensive expressions could endanger peace or religious tolerance.[13]

Shortly afterwards, the *Bouton* case[14] addressed the "performance" carried out by an activist from the Femen group inside the well-known Madeleine church in Paris. A few days before Christmas, with her breasts exposed and her body covered in slogans, the activist performed a parodic simulation of a fictional abortion of Jesus Christ using two pieces of cow liver in front of the altar. The performance was part of a Femen campaign to protest against the Catholic Church's position on abortion. Although it took place outside of the church's worship hours, the activist's intention was to gain as much publicity as possible, and in fact, she had invited a large number of journalists. The French courts sentenced her to one month of suspended imprisonment and ordered her to pay 2,000 euros in moral damages to the parish as well as 1,500 euros to cover its legal expenses. Also, in this case, the European Court found a violation of freedom of expression, noting the disproportionality of the penalty and emphasizing the fact that the national courts had not adequately analyzed the conflicting rights at stake, which included the applicant's right to freedom of expression and also her right to bodily autonomy. Furthermore,

13 In addition to two concurring opinions with the result but disagreeing with the Court's reasoning, the Polish judge (Wojtyczek) wrote a dissenting opinion, noting the inconsistency of this decision with other previous judgements of the ECtHR, and insisting that the applicant's expressions should be understood in the context of a growing phenomenon of physical and verbal attacks in particular against Jews and Christians in Poland. He added that not taking gratuitous offenses against religion seriously—which he described as "religiophobic language"—could contribute to creating an atmosphere of impunity for aggressors, potentially paving the way for more serious episodes of violence.

14 *Bouton v. France*, 13 October 2022. For an interesting comment on this judgment, see G. Gonzalez, *Motivation insuffisante pour la condamnation pénale d'une Femen auteur d'une «performance» pro-avortement dans une église en France: la surprotection de la liberté d'expression selon la Cour européenne des droits de l'homme? (CEDH, 13 octobre 2022, Bouton v. France)*, in "Revista General de Derecho Canónico y Derecho Eclesiástico del Estado" 60 (2022), pp. 1–9

the Court noted that the French courts had convicted the applicant for inappropriate public sexual behavior and not for violating religious freedom—inter alia because French criminal law does not regulate any offense related to the desecration of a sacred place.

In December 2022, the *Zemmour* judgment[15] involved the situation of a political journalist and writer who had been prosecuted for some statements he made with the occasion of the promotion of one of his books identifying Islam and violence; he maintained that French and Islamic values were incompatible and urged to fight against what he understood was a Muslim colonization of France. The French courts considered that such expressions amounted to incitement to religious discrimination and hatred and the applicant was sentenced to pay a fine of 3,000 euros. The Strasbourg Court declared the sentence justified and found no violation of art. 10 ECHR, noting that incitement to hatred or violence could take the shape of categorical expressions that attack, denigrate, or stigmatize an entire group of people encouraging their social exclusion.

It is not my intention, and I do not have the possibility, to provide in this paper a detailed analysis of the foregoing decisions and the legal reasoning that the ECtHR followed in them (as well as some interesting remarks we can find in separate opinions), but it is worth making some brief remarks in addition to other aspects that will be mentioned later. On the one hand, among the mentioned judgments, the only two that justify a restriction of freedom of expression are those involving offensive language against Islam. This may be related to the fact that Islam is a minority religion in the relevant countries—Austria (*E.S.*) and France (*Zemmour*)—but this is not explicitly stated in the reasoning provided by the Court. In any event, those two judgments appear as isolated decisions in the context of a tendency of the European Court, since the mid-2000s, to prioritize freedom of expression over the protection of religious feelings when it had to adjudicate on situations of an offensive speech in the public sphere.[16]

On the other hand, some of the arguments used by the ECtHR do not seem to be consistently applied. Among them are those related to the impact of certain expressions on generating an atmosphere of intolerance; for example, in *E.S.* the potential impact of invectives against a revered figure in Islam—Prophet Mohammed—in a seminar with only thirty attendees is maximized, but in *Rabczewska* the same impact is minimized when it comes to ridiculing the Bible, the sacred book of Jews and Christians, during an interview heard by many thousands of people. We can also mention the difference—difficult to understand—in the criteria for assessing the severity of the sanction imposed for offensive language and its potential chilling effect on the exercise of freedom of expression; for instance, in *Zemmour*, the ECtHR considered it

15 *Zemmour v. France*, 20 December 2022.
16 See the works cited supra, in note 3.

reasonable to impose a fine of 3,000 euro on a journalist, but in *Rabczewska*, a fine of 1,160 euro for a millionaire singer was deemed excessive.

It is also surprising that the Court places little importance on the fact that, in two of the mentioned cases, the offensive expression occurred, intentionally and with the aim of seeking publicity, inside a religious temple (*Mariya Alekhina* and *Bouton*). For the ECtHR, the only significant factor appears to be that no worship service was interrupted, there was no violence, and no one was prevented from practicing their religion. However, it overlooks an essential fact: that the desecration of a sacred place is, in itself, a violation of collective religious freedom,[17] regardless of any other circumstances that may exacerbate this violation, and even if the penal legislation of a country—as is the case in France—does not consider such action as a punishable crime.

The purpose of the pages that follow is, first, to remind the key criteria established by the Strasbourg jurisdiction for an appropriate legal approach to conflicts deriving from the use of offensive language, including that of an anti-religious nature. And, second, to emphasize some of the questions that, in such a delicate matter, the case law of the European Court has left without a proper solution; questions that, in my view, would need a more careful elaboration. As I have to be necessarily selective, I will pay special attention to some of the issues raised by the judgments *Sekmadienis* and *E.S.* with regard, respectively, to the notion of public morals and to the competence of State and international courts to enter into historical debates.

The General Principles Established by the European Court

The first of the general principles formulated by the ECtHR in this area, more than forty years ago, is that freedom of expression, albeit not being, of course, absolute or unlimited, includes the right to use offensive or scandalous language. For the Court, this right, which is an essential foundation of a society that deserves to be considered democratic, comprises not only the freedom to disseminate ideas that society perceives as reasonable or innocuous but also those that "shock, offend or disturb".[18] This implies that, although the exercise of freedom of expression can be restricted, the necessity of every

17 The same mistake was made by Court again, in *Asociación de Abogados Cristianos v. Spain*, Dec. Adm. 22604/18, 30 November 2023, a case involving an exhibition, organized and funded by the municipality, in which the artist had used 242 consecrated Hosts taken from Holy Masses he attended for weeks, secretly putting them in his pocket after receiving the Eucharist. The Spanish courts refused to recognize that such acts constituted an infringement of art. 524 of the Criminal Code, which punishes the profanation of a sacred place or religious ceremony.

18 "Freedom of expression constitutes one of the essential foundations of such a society [democratic society]. … it is applicable not only to 'information' or 'ideas' that are favourably received or regarded as inoffensive or as a matter of indifference, but also to those that shock, offend or disturb the State or any sector of the population. Such are the demands of that pluralism, tolerance and broadmindedness without which there is no 'democratic society'". (*Handyside*, § 49).

restriction must be carefully scrutinized. In this regard, the ECtHR has recognized that national authorities have a certain margin of discretionary appreciation. However, it has also insisted that such a margin is not unlimited and that national authorities' decisions are subject to review by the European Court, especially from the perspective of their proportionality, i.e., if they are proportionate to achieve the legitimate aim pursued by the restrictive measure in question[19] (aim that, besides, must be one of those explicitly mentioned by art. 10.2 ECHR[20]).

Over the years, the European Court has provided some criteria designed to facilitate finding an adequate—and difficult—balance between the states' discretionary power and the Court's competence to review the proportionality of restrictions on free speech. Those criteria can be summarized in the need to contextualize the analysis, taking into account not only the content of the expressions but also the circumstances of the society in which the offensive language has been used, as well as those of the offending speaker and the means utilized to disseminate the offensive expressions.[21] In addition, it is important to assess the nature and severity of the sanctions that may have been imposed; thus, the criminal nature of the sanction or its economic amount may tip the scales in order to determine whether freedom of expression has been violated or not in a specific case.[22]

Beside the need for a contextual analysis, the ECtHR has held that, in the area of political debate, the speech to be protected must be construed in an especially broad fashion. And, correspondingly, the legitimate limitations on political speech must be interpreted in a particularly restrictive manner; i.e., the state must provide persuasive and convincing reasons to justify an interference with freedom of expression. A similar doctrine must be applied to opinions dealing with issues of general interest to society,[23] especially if they are communicated in the context of an academic debate.[24] Conversely, the state has a broader margin of appreciation to regulate and impose limitations on speech in commercial matters or advertising on the basis that such speech does

19 See *Handyside*, § 49.

20 That is, national security, territorial integrity, public safety, the prevention of disorder or crime, the protection of health or morals, the protection of the reputation or rights of others, the prevention of the disclosure of information received in confidence, and the maintenance of the authority and impartiality of the judiciary.

21 A summary description of those criteria can be found in the judgment *Seher Karataş v. Turkey*, 9 July 2002, § 37; and more recently in the above-mentioned *Mariya Alekhina*, §§ 217 ff. See also E. Howard, *Freedom of Expression and Religious Hate Speech in Europe*, Routledge, 2018, pp. 99 ff.

22 See *Sürek v. Turkey* (no. 1), 8 July 1999, § 64; *Chauvy and others v. France*, 29 June 2004, § 78; and *Paturel v. France*, 22 December 2005, §§ 47–51; *Bouton*, § 46.

23 See, for instance, *Lingens v. Austria*, 8 July 1986, § 42; *Castells v. Spain*, 23 April 1992, § 46; *Wingrove v. United Kingdom*, 25 November 1996, § 58; *Fressoz and Roire v. France (GC)*, 21 January 1999, § 45; *Seher Karataş v. Turkey*, 9 July 2002, § 37; *Rabczewska*, § 46.

24 Cf. *Lombardi Vallauri v. Italy*, 20 October 2009, § 43; *Ayuso Torres v. Spain*, 8 November 2022, §§ 51–53.

not pursue per se the general interest of society and citizens must be shielded from expressions that are confusing or even deceiving.[25]

The broad protection of freedom of expression covers, of course, the content of the information or opinion in question but also the way chosen to disseminate it. In other words, it guarantees every person's right to choose a particularly offensive or provocative form to transmit a message that could have been expressed in a more respectful manner.[26] Moreover, it protects not only messages that are spread through words but also those conveyed by images, including artistic expressions.[27]

The Court has also stressed the importance of distinguishing between statements of facts and opinions.[28] The former, as they refer to an objective reality, allow a higher control of their truth or falsity, and therefore they leave more space for limitations or sanctions—freedom of expression does not protect a right to lie. Conversely, opinions are subjective and hence, as far as they have some factual support, are less susceptible to being restricted by the state.

A specific and significant case of language is hate speech, which the ECtHR understands in light of the definitions proposed by other Council of Europe bodies. That is, "all forms of expression which spread, incite, promote or justify racial hatred, xenophobia, anti-Semitism or other forms of hatred based on intolerance".[29] The European Court, when it considers that a certain expression qualifies as hate speech, has always stated unambiguously that such expressions are not protected by the ECHR. Often the Court has done it by applying not art. 10.2 (legitimate limitations on freedom of expression) but art. 17, which prohibits the abuse of rights[30]—despite the fact that the Court itself has declared that, in matters concerning freedom of expression, art. 17 can be applied only exceptionally and in extreme cases.[31] With the consequence

25 See *Sekmadienis*, §§ 73 and 76.

26 See *Oberschlick v. Austria*, 23 May 1991, § 57; *Prager and Oberschlick v. Austria*, 26 April 1995, § 38.

27 See *Müller and others v. Switzerland*, 24 May 1988, § 27; *Bouton*, § 30.

28 See *Lingens v. Austria*, 8 July 1986, § 46; *E.S.*, §§ 47–48.

29 Recommendation No. R (97) 20 on "hate speech", of the Committee of Ministers of the Council of Europe, adopted on 30 October 1997. In Spain, the issue has been studied by I. Martín Sánchez, *El discurso del odio en el ámbito del Consejo de Europa*, in "Revista General de Derecho Canónico y Derecho Eclesiástico del Estado", 28 (2012), pp. 1–33. From a broader perspective, which includes the initiative against the "defamation of religions" in the UN, see Z. Combalía, *Libertad de expresión y difamación de las religiones: el debate en Naciones Unidas a propósito del conflicto de las caricaturas de Mahoma*, and F. Pérez-Madrid, *Incitación al odio religioso o "hate speech" y libertad de expresión*, both in "Revista General de Derecho Canónico y Derecho Eclesiástico del Estado" 19 (2009). See also the collected papers in the monographic issue of the review "Derecho y Religión" 12 (2017), coord. by I. Cano

30 "Article 17. *Prohibition of abuse of rights.*— Nothing in this Convention may be interpreted as implying for any State, group or person any right to engage in any activity or perform any act aimed at the destruction of any of the rights and freedoms set forth herein or at their limitation to a greater extent than is provided for in the Convention".

31 Cf. *Zemmour*, § 26.

that, in those cases, the Court's tendency has been to declare the applications inadmissible as incompatible *ratione materiae* with the Convention (sometimes with a rationale that, in reality, contained a true judgment on the merits, "disguised" as an inadmissibility decision[32]). To put it in different words, in such cases, the ECtHR has maintained that hate speech does not constitute a manifestation of freedom of expression that deserves the potential protection of the *European Convention*. Therefore, once a certain expression is deemed hate speech, there is no need to assess if the restrictions imposed on it by the state were legitimate and proportionate.

This doctrine, naturally, is also applicable to anti-religious hate speech, although the Court has been so far reluctant to accept that any of the situations submitted to its jurisdiction can be characterized as such. An exception is the recent *Zemmour* judgment, mentioned above, where the ECtHR, with unclear reasoning, appears to acknowledge the constitutive elements of hate speech; however, the decision was based on the restrictive clauses of art. 10.2 ECHR rather than on the application of art. 17.[33] Usually, in applications that had their origin in offensive language against religion, or against a particular religion, the ECtHR has stated, at the most, that they were "gratuitous offences" against religious feelings. And in this regard, since the judgment of *Otto-Preminger-Institut* in 1994, the Court's position has been that, in the absence of a clear European consensus about the limits of state action in a matter that is so delicate, and so closely linked to national history and culture, the doctrine of the margin or appreciation has to be generously applied.[34] That is, in those cases national authorities have broad discretion to decide when and how they can resort to the legitimate limitations on freedom of expression foreseen by art. 10.2 ECHR.

No doubt, the ECtHR's doctrine on gratuitously offensive expressions against religion leaves a number of important questions in the air and has been often criticized.[35] And nevertheless, the Court has not explicitly modified its

32 The most emblematic case is probably *Roger Garaudy v. France*, Dec. Adm. on Appl. No. 65831/01, 24 June 2003.

33 See *Zemmour*, §§ 59–61. The judgement, with a curious reasoning, states that

> "in light of Article 17, the Court considers that the applicant's statements do not constitute a category of speech that can benefit from the enhanced protection of Article 10 of the Convention, and concludes from this that the French authorities had a wide margin of discretion to impose a restriction" (§ 61).

34 For an extensive analysis of the doctrine of the margin of appreciation, formulated explicitly for the first time in *Handyside*, see Y. Arai-Takahashi, *The Margin of Appreciation Doctrine and the Principle of Proportionality in the Jurisprudence of the ECHR*, Intersentia, 2002. For a brief explanation, with key references to case law, J. Martínez-Torrón, *Limitations on Religious Freedom in the Case Law of the European Court of Human Rights*, in "Emory International Law Review" 19 (2005), pp. 599–602. For an interesting reinterpretation of that doctrine, with suggestions for future development, see M. Iglesias Vila, *Subsidiarity, Margin of Appreciation and International Adjudication Within a Cooperative Conception of Human Rights*, in "International Journal of Constitutional Law" 15 (2017), pp. 393–413.

35 See, for instance, E. Howard, *Freedom of Expression*, cited in note 19, pp. 28–32; I. Leigh, *Damned if They Do, Damned if They Don't: The European Court of Human Rights and the*

general principles,[36] although the practice of the last fifteen years reveals a tendency to prioritize freedom of expression in that type of conflict.

A Case Law in Need of Development

The above-mentioned principles are not, in general, difficult to accept in the abstract but they require important precisions and nuances when applied to solve particular cases. And in this respect, the judgments of the ECtHR could have been clearer. The Court could have devoted less effort to the grandiloquent exposition of general principles and have been more concerned about providing precise criteria that could actually serve as a guide or orientation to national courts to adjudicate on similar situations.[37]

Indeed, freedom of expression is a matter extremely complex and delicate, which needs a careful and balanced approach. And, when we analyze the Strasbourg decisions, we can easily get the impression that the European Court has not put the necessary energy into defining the boundaries that separate the territory of the margin of national appreciation from the common core of legal criteria that must prevail in all the countries of the Council of Europe. Most often, the Court formulates its principles in a very general fashion, repeating them almost like mantras in every decision, as a sort of wild card that makes it possible to decide on a conflict one way or the opposite, sometimes without being patent which is the reason for those different decisions—and the problem is aggravated by the fact that not all the chambers of the Court apply those general criteria in the same manner.

These dynamics are far from the ideal and leave some important questions without being addressed with sufficient depth. For instance, to mention briefly some issues that I cannot examine in detail in the following pages, to what extent the Strasbourg Court should reconsider some aspects of its doctrine on hate speech in the light of the parallel case law of US courts?[38] I am not

Protection of Religion from Attack, in "Res Publica" 17.1 (2011), p. 71; I. Cram, *The Danish Cartoons, Offensive Expression, and Democratic Legitimacy*, in I. Hare and J. Weinstein (eds.), "Extreme Speech and Democracy", Oxford University Press, 2009, pp. 325–327; J. Martínez-Torrón, *Freedom of Expression*, cited in note 3, pp. 267–269.

36 Indeed, it has recently reaffirmed those principles in *E.S.*, §§ 43–45, and *Rabczewska*, §§ 51–53.

37 In this point I refer to my remarks in J. Martínez-Torrón, *Strasbourg's Approach to Religion in the Pluralist Democracies of Europe*, in R. Griffith-Jones and M. Hill (eds.), "Magna Carta, Religion and the Rule of Law", Cambridge University Press, 2015, especially pp. 284–288.

38 Among the immense legal literature in the United States on this issue, see M. Matsuda et al., *Words that Wound*, Westview Press, 1993; R.C. Post, *Cultural Heterogeneity and Law: Pornography, Blasphemy, and the First Amendment*, in "California Law Review" 76 (1988), pp. 297–335; C.E. Baker, *Harm, Liberty, and Free Speech*, in "Southern California Law Review 70 (1997), pp. 979–1020; M. Minow, *Regulating Hatred: Whose Speech, Whose Crimes, Whose Power?—An Essay for Kenneth Karst*, in "UCLA Law Review" 47 (2000), pp. 1253–1277; R.M. O'Neil, *Hate Speech, Fighting Words, and Beyond—Why American Law is Unique*, in

suggesting that the latter is the paradigm to be followed—indeed, it is significant that US legal literature has included such case law within the so-called "American exceptionalism".[39] But we can probably find interesting middle ground between the US and the European conceptions of which should be the appropriate reaction of the state to that type of abusive language, as well as of the circumstances that can legitimize restrictions on the exercise of freedom of expression, which is an indisputable pillar of democratic societies.[40]

Something similar occurs with regard to the dilemma of whether hate speech situations should be adjudicated under art. 17 ECHR (abuse of rights) or rather art. 10.2 (limitations on freedom of expression). Traditionally, the Strasbourg case law has been inclined to take the first option, which I do not think is the most adequate one because, among other reasons, once some language is labeled as hate speech, public authorities are exempted from providing precise justifications for their restriction on freedom of expression. Nevertheless, the European Court has not always followed easily identifiable criteria, as demonstrated by its position in cases of *negationism*. Thus, situations of denial of the Holocaust of the Jewish people under the Nazi regime have been normally addressed with the most severity under art. 17,[41] and the same has been done some other times with expressions considered as anti-Islamic hate speech.[42] In contrast, the negation of the Armenian genocide perpetrated by the Turkish government in the early 20th century has been dealt with in a different fashion; the Court has meticulously examined if the restriction on freedom of expression was justified under the limitation clause of art. 10.2 (and has concluded, by a narrow majority, that is was not).[43]

Another question that the ECtHR has left without clarification is if, for the purposes of the protection offered by the European Convention, opinions

---

"Albany Law Review" 76 (2012–2013), pp. 467–498. For an interesting comparison between the US and Canada, K. Greenawalt, *Fighting Words: Individuals, Communities and Liberties of Speech*, Princeton University Press, 1996; and S. Tomlins, *The Freedom to Offend? How the "Mohammad Cartoon Controversy" Has Influenced Public Debate on Canada's Hate Speech Regulation*, in "Journal of Church and State" 57 (2013), pp. 44–71.

39 For a detailed analysis of American exceptionalism by various authors, see M. Ignatieff (ed.), *American Exceptionalism and Human Rights*, Princeton University Press, 2005. For a firm and reasoned critique to the prevailing attitudes on hate speech in the United States, J. Waldron, *The Harm in Hate Speech*, Harvard University Press, 2012.

40 For an interesting comparison of US and European notions about how hate speech should be dealt with in contemporary societies, see M. Herz and P. Molnar (eds.), *The Content and Context of Hate Speech. Rethinking Regulation and Responses*, Cambridge University Press, 2012; I. Hare and J. Weinstein (eds.), *Extreme Speech and Democracy*, Oxford University Press, 2009.

41 See *Roger Garaudy*, cited in note 30; also *M'Bala B'Bala v. France*, Dec. Adm. Appl. No. 25239/13, 20 October 2015.

42 See *Norwood v. United Kingdom*, Dec. Adm. Appl. No. 23131/03, 16 November 2004. However, different criteria were used in *Zemmour*, as I pointed out above (see notes 14 and 31, and corresponding text).

43 *Perinçek v. Switzerland* (GC), 15 October 2015. See infra, section 6 of this paper.

conveyed through private channels should be distinguished from those expressed in public spaces.[44] It is possible that these two types of public language do not deserve the same legal treatment by the courts. Probably, it would be appropriate to make further distinctions within the notions of public and private spaces; the public square is not the same as a parliament or a publicly owned radio or TV channel; and private publications or personal Internet blogs are not the same as private TV channels, which are subject to a strict system of public concessions and controls in many European countries. Again, in this area, a comparison with the US judicial doctrine that distinguishes between diverse categories of fora could be useful;[45] not because I think that the Strasbourg case law must be "Americanized", but because the US Supreme Court, irrespective of the opinions we may have of each of its judgments, has put more effort into the elaboration of relatively clear criteria aimed at orientating the future decision of cases by the rest of the US courts (as well as, of course, the Supreme Court itself). Conversely, the Strasbourg Court sometimes seems more concerned about justifying a particular decision in an unassailable fashion instead of tracing an intelligible itinerary of future adjudication for national courts (as well as, of course, for the European Court itself).

Also with regard to the analysis of the legitimacy of limitations on freedom of expression depending on the location, the ECtHR, in my opinion, has not given sufficient significance to the fact that the offensive expressions occur in a place of worship. This was the situation in the cases of *Mariya Alekhina* and *Bouton*.[46] It is true that, in the former, the Court mentions that freedom of expression does not guarantee the right to enter a privately or publicly owned property, nor does it exempt individuals from respecting certain codes of conduct, such as those applicable in a religious temple.[47] But at the same time, the Court emphasizes that the punishment imposed on the applicants was excessive, considering that they had not disrupted any ceremony or caused harm to individuals or property;[48] the Court appears to assume that the gravity of invading a place of worship depends on the extent to which some people find it offensive.[49] The same approach inspires the *Bouton* judgment; the implicit message is that invading a church merely constitutes a breach of "acceptable

44 The Court missed a good opportunity to address such question in the case *Asociación de Abogados Cristianos v. Spain*, which was declared inadmissible as manifestly ill-founded in a disappointing decision published shortly before this text had to be sent to print (Dec. Adm, 22604/18, 30 November 2023).

45 For a critical explanation of the US judicial doctrine that distinguishes between different fora and its consequences, with abundant bibliographical and case law references, see L. Lidsky, *Public Forum 2.0*, in "Boston University Law Review" 91 (2011), pp. 1975–2028.

46 See supra, section 1 of this essay.

47 Cf. *Mariya Alekhina*, §§ 213–214.

48 Cf. ibid., § 215.

49 Cf. ibid., § 225.

codes of behaviour in a place of worship", which is not too serious if it is not accompanied by incitement to hatred or violence or if it does not interrupt a religious ceremony.[50] Furthermore, the Court allows itself to state—for the purpose of maximizing the applicant's freedom of expression—that a church is a "public place",[51] when, in fact, it is a private place that is normally open to the public as long as people respect its sacred character and behave accordingly.[52] Irrespective of our opinion on the proportionality of the penalties imposed on the applicants in these cases—which were particularly severe in the case of *Mariya Alekhina* but less so in *Bouton*[53]—I regret the lack of a clear pronouncement of the ECtHR stating that the invasion of a place of worship constitutes in itself a violation of religious freedom (art. 9 ECHR) and can never be a legitimate exercise of freedom of expression (art. 10 ECHR), one of whose limits is the protection of the rights of others.

I will turn now, in more detail, to other questions that, in my view, require special attention from the ECtHR.

Religious Freedom and Protection of Religious Feelings

A first and crucial question is if the protection of the religious feelings of the majority or a minority of the population constitutes an integral part of the freedom of religion or belief guaranteed by art. 9 ECHR. In my judgment, it is problematic to maintain that one of the functions of a legal system is the protection of feelings, be they religious or of any other kind. The reason is that it would put legal guarantees, which should desirably be objective, in an environment of subjectivity, instability, and unpredictability, for these characteristics are usually intrinsic to the sphere of sentiments.

In any event, the Strasbourg Court has kept an ambiguous and hesitant position in this regard.[54] On the one hand, on the basis that art. 10 ECHR also protects those opinions that "shock, offend or disturb",[55] the Court has held that religions cannot reasonably expect to be free from criticism.[56] Indeed, as mentioned above, according to the ECtHR, art. 10 protects not

50 Cf. *Bouton*, §§ 30, 49, 51, 61 and 62.

51 Cf. ibid., §§ 45 and 53.

52 Indeed, that distinction is present in the judgment of *The Church of Jesus Christ of Latter-Day Saints v. The United Kingdom*, 4 March 2014, in which the ECtHR denied that there was discriminatory treatment concerning certain tax benefits not being applied to a Mormon temple, since it was not open to the public but accessible only to members of that church who fulfilled their religious obligations.

53 This is even clearer if we take into account that the fines would probably have been paid by Femen—on whose behalf the applicant acted—and not by herself.

54 For further details, I refer to J. Martínez-Torrón, *¿Libertad de expresión amordazada?*, cited in note 3, and the references there included.

55 *Handyside v. United Kingdom*, 7 December 1976, § 49.

56 Cf. *Otto-Preminger-Institut*, § 47. This doctrine has been often reiterated by the Court; see, recently, *Rabczewska*, § 51.

only the deliberate choice of offensive content but also a particularly offensive way to convey that content, as well as the resort to some exaggeration and even provocation.[57] But on the other hand, in *Otto-Preminger-Institut*, the Court seemed to declare that religious feelings are included in the scope of protection of religious freedom:

> The respect for the religious feelings of believers as guaranteed in Article 9 (art. 9) can legitimately be thought to have been violated by provocative portrayals of objects of religious veneration; and such portrayals can be regarded as malicious violation of the spirit of tolerance, which must also be a feature of democratic society.[58]

Although the ECtHR has not made clear under which circumstances the protection of religious feelings can prevail over the right to freedom of expression, its tendency has been to interpret that only in extreme cases is it possible to justify limitations or sanctions imposed on anti-religious language that has been intentionally offensive or provocative.[59] At the same time, the Court has emphasized that the doctrine of the margin of appreciation is of importance in this matter; as the European Convention does not impose a uniform criterion about these situations, and in the absence of a European consensus on the issue, national legal systems and authorities have certain discretion to punish those expressions that are deemed "gratuitously offensive" against a religion or its sacred symbols.[60]

The Strasbourg approach is apparently dominated by the notion that the exercise of freedom of religion or belief—by religious or non-religious people—requires an atmosphere of tolerance and respect, free from attacks that may actually inhibit citizens from manifesting their beliefs without intimidation. This is suggested by another of the passages of *Otto-Preminger-Institut*:

> [T]he manner in which religious beliefs and doctrines are opposed or denied is a matter which may engage the responsibility of the State, notably its responsibility to ensure the peaceful enjoyment of the right guaranteed under Article 9 (art. 9) to the holders of those beliefs and doctrines. Indeed, in extreme cases the effect of particular methods of

57 See supra, note 24 and accompanying text.

58 *Otto-Preminger-Institut*, § 47.

59 In Spain there is a specific legal provision to that purpose. Article 525 of the Penal Code criminalizes public derision—orally or in writing—of "tenets, beliefs, rites or ceremonies" of a religious community with the intention to offend the feelings of its members, and it imposes the same penalty to similar conducts with regard to people who profess no religion. This legal provision is almost never applied in practice. On this theme, from a comparative law perspective, see the essays included in the collective book J. Martínez-Torrón and S. Cañamares Arribas (coords.), *Tensiones entre libertad de expresión y libertad religiosa*, cited in note 3.

60 See *Otto-Preminger-Institut*, §§ 49–50.

> opposing or denying religious beliefs can be such as to inhibit those who hold such beliefs from exercising their freedom to hold and express them.[61]

This, for the rest, is a common feature of all fundamental freedoms. A social environment of free discussion and expression, including the free manifestation of beliefs, is essential to democracy. And vice versa, an ambiance of verbal aggression or violence is not the most adequate habitat for the exercise of freedoms. From this perspective, attacks on the grounds of religion are not intrinsically different from attacks on the grounds of sex, race, or national origin; and all those factors are mentioned by art. 14 ECHR, which prohibits discrimination.[62]

Nevertheless, we should not lose sight of the fact that, according to art. 10 ECHR, every restriction on freedom of expression, in addition to pursuing a legitimate aim, has to be justified as "necessary in a democratic society", which means that, in the words of the European Court, it must respond to a "pressing social need".[63]

In my view, the analysis of situations that involve offenses to religious feelings must depart from a basic principle: the protection of religious feelings, per se, is not an integral part of the guarantee offered by freedom of thought, conscience, and religion. Art. 9 ECHR preserves an ambit of freedom but not a space of sentiments or emotions.

The foregoing does not mean that it is not possible to impose legitimate restrictions or sanctions on expressions that are gratuitously offensive in particularly grave cases. More specifically, such possibility exists when abusive language is clearly calumnious; freedom of expression does not protect an alleged right to lie—and therefore to calumny (although this raises interesting questions about historical truth, which I will mention in subsequent sections of this chapter). The same applies to language that, even not strictly qualifying as hate speech, can actually lead, because of the circumstances and the context, to a limitation on the freedom of religion of some people. For instance, when the offense in question not only hurts the feelings of some persons but also seriously damages the reputation of a religious group or its members, with the actual possibility of causing situations of discrimination or making it difficult for some citizens to freely practice their religion.

61 *Otto-Preminger-Institut*, § 47.

62 In fact, the possibility to consider that religion constitutes a legitimate ground to restrict freedom of expression was recognized by the three judges who, *Otto-Preminger-Institut*, wrote a joint dissenting opinion and refused to accept that the freedom of religion enshrined in art. 9 ECHR imply an alleged right to the protection of religious feelings. In their precise words, "tolerance works both ways and the democratic character of a society will be affected if violent and abusive attacks on the reputation of a religious group are allowed" (*Otto-Preminger-Institut c. Austria*, joint dissenting opinion of Judges Palm, Pekkanen, and Makarczyk, § 6).

63 *Handyside*, § 48.

This is probably the sense of the ECtHR's allusion to the inhibitory effect that some public speech may have on the freedom of certain people to manifest their beliefs. It is likely also the intended meaning of the reference of the three dissenting judges in *Otto-Preminger-Institut* to the abusive attacks on the reputation of religious groups.[64] Such situations would not only involve a mere contempt for feelings but an attack on the freedom of others. This is more likely to occur in the case of attacks on religious minorities, which in general are more vulnerable to the consequences of defamation.

In any event, the latest case law of the European Court raises serious doubts as to its consistency in applying its own general principles. For instance, in the judgment of *E.S. v. Austria*, following the reasoning of the *Otto-Preminger-Institut*, the ECtHR considered that the Austrian authorities did not violate the European Convention when they imposed a fine on a speaker at a seminar organized by a political party with around thirty participants, who made critical comments about Muhammad and insulted the memory of a revered figure among Muslims in a way that could offend religious sentiments and generate "justified indignation" in the population. For the Court, such expressions could undermine the spirit of tolerance that should exist in society for the exercise of freedoms and the national authorities had a broad margin of discretion to impose restrictions on freedom of expression as they deemed necessary. However, in *Rabczewska*, the Court reiterated the same general principles apropos of insulting expressions against the Bible—which on this occasion were heard by many thousands of people—but in practice denied the national authorities such broad margin of discretion by replacing their judgment of proportionality concerning the harm that scornful mockery against the sacred book of Jews and Christians could cause to the climate of tolerance and respect in Polish society.

It is possible to conjecture that the different decisions of the Court in these two cases might be associated with the fact that the Catholic religion is the majority religion in Poland, while Muslims are a minority in Austria, and that the political party organizing the seminar in question was particularly harsh on immigration from Islamic countries. Such an interpretation might have been understandable, as the position of minorities is more vulnerable to verbal attacks that can harm their reputation, which in turn may result in greater practical difficulties, or even intimidation, when exercising their religious freedom. However, surprisingly, this point is not explicitly addressed in the reasoning used by the ECtHR in these two judgments. Instead, everything remains in a nebulous application of general criteria to the case in question.

Even more disconcerting, in my opinion, is the emphasis the European Court places on the idea that the state is authorized to limit freedom of expression when some people use words that are likely to cause "justified indignation"

64 See supra, notes 59 and 60 and accompanying text.

among part of the population. This idea originated from Austrian law[65] and could perhaps have some basis—in the light of the doctrine of the margin of appreciation—in the *Otto-Preminger-Institut* and *E.S.* judgments, as this was the applicable national law. However, the Court employs the same argument in *Rabczewska*, even though Polish law does not contain any similar provision.[66] This means that the Court opens the possibility for this argument to be used in the future to support limitations on freedom of expression within the European context and not just in Austria. I find this problematic, especially considering the vagueness of the term "justified indignation", which the ECtHR also links to the maintenance of "religious peace".[67] In practice, such reasoning could lead to establishing a dangerous connection between an offensive expression and the "indignant" reaction of believers of a particular religion, in the sense that the greater predictability of a reaction that would put "religious peace" at risk would lead to easier legitimization of restrictions on those expressions that might hurt certain sensitivities. In other words, if it can be reasonably foreseen that certain sectors of the population will have a strong or even violent reaction to certain types of speech, the state would be more legitimized to limit or sanction such speech.

As acceptable as the argument based on religious or social peace may appear at first glance, I believe that without proper nuances—which the European Court does not provide—it could lead to the opposite effect: generating intolerance instead of tolerance. Let us consider the hypothesis that the authorities of a state would more easily justify offenses against revered objects or persons in Islam because they anticipate a violent response from some Muslims—be they ordinary believers or imams—while, conversely, the same authorities would be more permissive in the case of verbal attacks on Christian symbols or figures because they presume that social peace will not be disturbed. Such unequal legal treatment would not only be discriminatory but it would also follow a highly misguided criterion in view of its potential future effects. Even if unintentional, it could entail an implicit invitation to react disproportionately to anti-religious offenses; in other words, some might think that if the state only shows concern for religious insults that provoke violent reactions, it would be necessary to react violently to make the state take insults to other religions seriously.

Statements of Fact and Subjective Opinions

It has been already mentioned that, for the ECtHR, it is crucial to distinguish between those expressions that consist of statements of fact and those others

65 See *E.S.*, § 24

66 The Polish Penal Code only refers to offenses to religious sentiments through public insults to objects of veneration or worship. See *Rabczewska*, § 21.

67 *E.S.*, §§ 41, 50, 52, and 57; *Rabczewska*, §§ 52, 60, 62, and 64.

that contain an opinion, because the veracity or falsity of facts is more susceptible to control. While opinions are subjective and belong to the legitimate diversity of interpretations of reality, the objectivity of facts is verifiable and sometimes measurable. As a consequence, according to the European Court, a subjective opinion is in principle protected by art. 10 ECHR as far as it is supported by objective and true facts.

The immediate question that comes to mind is how much factual—true—support is needed for a subjective opinion to benefit from the guarantee of art. 10. The question is especially relevant when an opinion interprets real facts in a far-fetched or disproportionate fashion. Naturally, every person looks at reality from a particular perspective, which includes a certain degree of selection, slant, bias, or distortion, even to the extent of manipulation. The important issue is to determine when such views cease to be a mere *interpretation* of facts, no matter how exaggerated or partial, and become a *falsification*, i.e., a lie—to present a mutilated truth is often the subtlest and most efficient way of lying. Certainly, it is not an easy question to answer and even less in the abstract.

Aware that in case of doubt it is preferable to opt for freedom (*in dubio pro libertate*), the Strasbourg case law, as in general the judicature of Western democracies, has tended to a maximalist conception of the freedom to express subjective opinions; these are protected as far as there is a minimum of factual truth, irrespective of how "creative" the speaker's imagination and irrespective of how ostensibly such interpretation of reality leaves aside a part of the facts (even a large part). It is, in my view, a sensible tendency, which is based on the conviction that the hypothetical benefits of correcting the opinions that deform objective facts in an interested way are exceeded by the risks of giving public authorities the power to intervene in the free exchange of ideas to define which is the "orthodox version" of reality—and to illegalize or proscribe all other "heterodox" versions.[68]

If we apply the foregoing to the specific area of offensive expressions against religion, or against a particular religion, which has been the position of the

68 The US Supreme Court expressed this idea vividly long ago, in 1943:

> "If there is any fixed star in our constitutional constellation, it is that no official, high or petty, can prescribe what shall be orthodox in politics, nationalism, religion, or other matters of opinion, or force citizens to confess by word or act their faith therein" (*West Virginia State Board of Education v. Barnette*, 319 U.S. 624, 642). The case involved the conscientious objection of Jehovah's Witnesses to participate in the flag salute ceremony in public schools. For further details, see, in Spanish legal literature, J. Martínez-Torrón, *Las objeciones de conciencia en la jurisprudencia del Tribunal Supremo norteamericano*, in "Anuario de Derecho Eclesiástico del Estadado" 1 (1985), pp. 429–435; J.I. Rubio, *Hacia la primera libertad. Libertad religiosa en los EEUU: de las colonias a la Corte Rehnquist (1600–1986)*, Eunsa, 2011.

Strasbourg Court? The brief answer would be: irregular. Two examples will serve to illustrate it.

One is the *Giniewski* case, in 2006, which originated from a press article against the Catholic Church that the French courts had considered defamatory.[69] The applicant described himself as a journalist, historian, and sociologist who tried, in his work, to encourage an approach between Jews and Christians. In 1994, he published an op-ed piece criticizing the Encyclical *Veritatis Splendor* of Pope John Paul II. In it, he affirmed that the Catholic doctrine of the "fulfillment" (*accomplissement*) of the Old Testament in the New Testament lead to anti-Semitism and contained the theological foundations that made it possible to justify the extermination of Jews in the Nazi concentration camps. The text suggested a parallelism between the "fulfillment" (*accomplissement*) of the Old Testament and the implementation (*accomplissement*) of the Holocaust.[70] A Christian association brought criminal proceedings against the applicant, accusing him of a crime of racial defamation against the Christian community. The applicant was sentenced in the first instance as guilty of publicly defaming a group of persons (Christians) on the grounds of membership in a religion. After a subsequent and complex procedural itinerary, the applicant was absolved from criminal charges but the economic sanctions deriving from the civil action were confirmed.

The European Court, in a unanimous judgment, decided in favor of the applicant, with a brief assessment of the facts, which, unlike the French courts, concluded that there was no serious offense against Christianity. Where the French courts had seen a grave accusation of anti-Semitism directed against Catholics, and a statement that their doctrine was partly responsible for the massacres perpetrated by the Nazis, the ECtHR only saw the exposition of a thesis about the causes of the persecution of Jews in Europe.[71] For the Court, the applicant's press article did not contain any gratuitous attack against religious beliefs as such but rather some thoughts that, even if they could be

69 *Giniewski v. France*, 31 January 2006.

70 These were the passages considered incriminating by the French courts:

> "The Catholic Church sets itself up as the sole keeper of divine truth and assumes the 'duty' of disseminating its doctrine as the sole universal teaching. It strongly proclaims the fulfilment of the 'Old' Covenant in the New and the superiority of the latter, a doctrine which propagates 'the teaching of contempt' for the Jews ... Many Christians have recognised that scriptural anti-Judaism and the 'doctrine of fulfilment' [in French, '*l'accomplissement*'] of the Old Covenant by the New lead to anti-Semitism and prepared the ground in which the idea and implementation [in French, '*l'accomplissement*'] of Auschwitz took seed". The complete text of the article, entitled "The Obscurity of Error", is transcribed in *Giniewski*, § 23 (translation from the French original as provided by the Court).

71 Cf. *Giniewski*, § 50.

hurtful for many, focused on a subject of indubitable significance in our recent history.[72]

The Court remarked that the search for historical truth is an integral part of freedom of expression and that it was not the Court's role or competence to take sides in a historical controversial issue.[73] Indeed, the Court's succinct analysis of the contentious text revealed its intention to refrain from making any judgment about the actual foundation of the author's opinion. The European Court also emphasized that when an author communicates his opinions on issues of general interest, limitations on freedom of expression must be construed narrowly; the threat of a legally imposed sanction—even a reduced economic penalty—could have a deterrent effect and could inhibit the press, or the authors, from freely disseminating their ideas and intervening in public debates on important issues.[74] Such restrictions would be justifiable only in the case of opinions that were gratuitously offensive to the religious beliefs of others, incited to hatred or lack of respect, or denied well-established historical facts.[75]

It is worth comparing the ECtHR's position on *Giniewski*[76] with a recent decision: the aforementioned *E.S. v. Austria*[77]. As I explained at the beginning of this chapter, the conflict had its origin in statements that strongly criticized Prophet Muhammad, which had been expressed by a person giving a seminar entitled "Basic Information on Islam". The seminar was organized by an institute run by the Freedom Party of Austria (*Freiheitliche Partei Österreichs*, FPÖ), characterized by a political nationalist orientation, a conservative and liberal approach to economic issues, and a restrictive stance on immigration matters, especially with regard to Muslims, which the party declares to be based on its interest in preserving Austrian cultural identity. The seminar was held in Vienna and was directed not only at party members and their invitees but also at young voters in general; indeed, it had been publicized on the institute's web pages. Among the approximately thirty attendees, there was an undercover journalist who later asked the Vienna Public Prosecutor's Office to bring criminal proceedings against the speaker at the seminar.

72 Cf. ibid., § 51.

73 Cf. ibid., § 51, with explicit reference to *Chauvy and others v. France*, 29 June 2004, § 69.

74 Cf. *Giniewski*, § 51 & 54, with explicit reference to *Jersild v. Denmark*, 23 September 1994, § 35.

75 Cf. *Giniewski*, § 52, with explicit reference to *Roger Garaudy*, cited in note 30, En droit, § 1. The mention of the *Garaudy* decision is particularly significant, for the case involved the delicate issue of anti Semitism in Europe, more precisely its expression through "negationism", i.e., expression of opinions aimed at denying the existence or the dimension of the Holocaust.

76 Shortly before, in *Paturel c. Francia*, 22 December 2005, a different chamber of the Court had adopted an approach similar to that in *Giniewski*, but with an interesting separate opinion adding nuances to the Court's rationale.

77 *E.S. v. Austria*, 25 October 2018.

The applicant was initially accused of incitement to hatred but, because of doubts about the exact expressions she had used, she was finally convicted of disparaging religious doctrines pursuant to art. 188 of the Austrian Criminal Code; she was ordered to pay the cost of the proceedings as well as a fine of 480 euros.[78] The court found her guilty of publicly disparaging an object of veneration of a domestic church or religious society, namely Prophet Muhammad, in a manner "likely to arouse justified indignation".[79] The statements that the court found incriminating affirmed that Muhammad was far from being an ideal man or a role model and that it was incomprehensible that the central prophet of Islam was a warrior who had several wives; especially considering that he married one of them—Aisha—when he was more than fifty years old and she only six and that he had sexual intercourse with her when she had hardly turned nine years old. The last fact, added the speaker, would qualify today as pedophilia.[80] For the Austrian courts, such statements were intentionally provocative, contained an abusive attack and a gratuitous offense to a religious community, and did not contribute at all to a debate of general interest—they were just aimed at defaming Muhammad. Moreover, the courts refused to recognize any relevance to one of the applicant's allegations, namely that all participants in the seminar knew of her critical approach and it was therefore very doubtful that anyone could feel offended; for the Austrian courts, at least one of the participants had felt offended, as her complaints had led to the applicant's prosecution.[81]

The ECtHR, in its judgment, dispatched as irrelevant—without providing any concrete reason—the circumstance that the seminar had been attended only by about thirty people.[82] The Court also completely deferred to the national authorities the assessment of how much the "religious peace" of the country could be endangered. And, most significantly, the Court approached

78 A day fine of four euros for a period of 120 days, which would result in 60 days' imprisonment in the event of default.

79 Article 188 of the Austrian Criminal Code is part of a section that contains, inter alia, offenses against religious peace. This is its text:

> Whoever, in circumstances where his or her behaviour is likely to arouse justified indignation, publicly disparages or insults a person who, or an object which, is an object of veneration of a church or religious community established within the country, or a dogma, a lawful custom or a lawful institution of such a church or religious community, shall be liable to up to six months' imprisonment or a day-fine for a period of up to 360 days". (translation provided by the Court in *E.S. v. Austria*, § 24).

80 Cf. *E.S. v. Austria*, § 13.

81 For a detailed description of the judicial itinerary and rationale used by the Austrian courts, see ibid., §§ 14–22.

82 Cf. ibid., § 51.

the content of the applicant's statements in a totally different way in comparison with *Giniewski*.[83]

On the one hand, the Court emphasized the obvious offensive and provocative nature of the statements, recalling at the same time that, as such, this does not justify limitations on freedom of expression; art. 10 ECHR not only protects the dissemination of ideas "that are favourably received or regarded as inoffensive or as a matter of indifference, but also ... those that offend, shock or disturb".[84] And on the other hand, and above all, the judgment went into a relatively detailed assessment of the historical rigor and accuracy of the applicant's statements, concluding, and underscoring, that they "they had not been made in an objective manner",[85] and that the applicant "failed to neutrally inform her audience of the historical background, which consequently did not allow for a serious debate on that issue".[86] That is, the ECtHR not only centered its judgment on the characterization of the *tone* of the applicant's speech as offensive, provocative, insulting, and hurtful; it also took a position about the *substance* of the debate, thus acting as censor of what is or not intellectually or historically accurate. In addition, the Court declared that the criminal sanction imposed on the applicant (480 euros or 60 days of imprisonment) was moderate and not disproportionate,[87] when in *Giniewski* it had been considered excessive, and with a deterrent effect on freedom of expression, to order the applicant to pay one franc (= 0.15 euro) as civil damages (there was no criminal conviction) and to publish a notice of the ruling in a national newspaper at his own expense.[88]

It is not my intention to analyze here in detail the ECtHR's case law on freedom of expression and offenses against religion,[89] but it is worth noting the contradiction between the approaches of the European Court in *Giniewski* and in *E.S.*, respectively. If we compare the rationale of these two judgments, the result is puzzling. If a Pope, then alive, is accused in a press article published in a national newspaper of endorsing a doctrine that, for the journalist, is in the origins of anti-Semitism and the Nazi extermination camps, the Court holds that it is a contribution about a historical issue of general interest for society. The Court refrains from evaluating how well-grounded the journalist's opinion was—notwithstanding the fact that most likely it would appear

83 Cf. ibid., §§ 50–57

84 Ibid., § 42.

85 Ibid., § 52.

86 Ibid., § 54.

87 Cf. ibid., § 56.

88 Cf. *Giniewski*, § 55. In *Aydin Tatlav v. Turkey*, 2 May 2006, § 30, the Court had considered disproportionate, and inhibiting for the exercise of freedom of expression, a criminal sanction consisting in a fine of ten euros.

89 I have already done it in other writings, previously cited. See also, including some comparative remark regarding the US law, J. Martínez-Torrón, *Hate speech, libertad de expresión y sentimientos religiosos*, in "Estudios Eclesiásticos" 92 (2017), pp. 749–767.

absurd to anyone who knows something about the life of John Paul II and his relationships with the Jewish communities. Conversely, if in the context of a seminar attended by hardly thirty people, the speaker accuses a person who died centuries ago, but is venerated by millions of Muslims, of having sexual relationships that today would be deemed as pedophilia, then the Court makes a pronouncement on a historical question—objectively of much lesser significance even though it is emotionally important for many—in spite of the fact that, in reality, the relationships of Muhammad with Aisha, and her age when she married the Prophet, are the subject of a historical debate.

Why such a different attitude of the ECtHR? It has been suggested that even the Court could wish to modify its doctrine about gratuitous offenses to religious feelings as expressed in *Otto-Preminger-Institut*, the case of *E.S.* was not probably the adequate opportunity to do so; it could lead to the wrong perception that Strasbourg justifies the legal punishment of insults against Christianity but delegitimizes an equivalent punishment of disparagement of Islam.[90] It is an interesting conjecture but I am not entirely persuaded by it. Among other reasons, it does not look like the European Court has the least intention to change its general principles on this matter—which the Court could likely have done in *E.S.* without the need to alter the outcome, especially considering the manifold ways in which it has applied those principles in the past.

Was perhaps this different approach caused by the fact that in *Giniewski* the targeted religion was Catholicism—i.e., the major church in France—while in *E.S.* it was Islam, a more vulnerable minority in a society, as Austria, that is predominantly Catholic? In reality, it is not easy to find a clear reason, and even less so in the light of Strasbourg precedents. It is true that in *I.A. v. Turkey*, which involved an offensive book against Muhammad and Islam, the Court took the same position as in *E.S.*, but it was a controversial judgment adopted by a divided chamber—four votes against three.[91] And a few months later, in *Aydin Tatlav*,[92] the same chamber of the Court, unanimously, affirmed that freedom of expression had to prevail in a case regarding another book containing statements that were openly offensive against Islam—for instance, that Islam is of "barbaric violence" or that Muhammad founded his main policies on violence and promised men a paradise with "the true parasitic life of an aristocrat".[93]

90 See S. Smet, *E.S. v. Austria: Freedom of Expression versus Religious Feelings, the Sequel*, in "Strasbourg Observers", 7 November 2018, available in: https://strasbourgobservers.com/2018/11/07/e-s-v-austria-freedom-of-expression-versus-religious-feelings-the-sequel/#more-4246.

91 *I.A. v. Turkey*, 13 September 2005. The three judges of the minority wrote a joint dissenting opinion with a vigorous reasoning against the judgment's rationale.

92 *Aydin Tatlav v. Turkey*, 2 May 2006. Nevertheless, the composition of the Second Chamber, had changed: only five of the seven judges were the same as in *I.A.*

93 See *Aydin Tatlav v. Turkey*, § 12.

What is striking and raises particular concern in the rationale of the *E.S.* judgment is the fact that the Strasbourg Court decided to assess the "objectivity", "neutrality", and "rigour" of the statements made by the applicant. The Court had not done it before, and even less so in such a detailed way. Not even in *Otto-Preminger-Institut* or in *Wingrove*, whose outcome was also favorable to the protection of religious feelings, the Court made reference to the historical accuracy of a ridiculing depiction of Jesus Christ and the Virgin Mary, or of St. Theresa's ecstasy. Its arguments focused on the fact that the audio-visual expressions in question were unnecessarily offensive and provocative, without judging their truth or their correctness.

Without going into the particulars of the judgment, I do not deny that, in the circumstances of the *E.S.* case, the European Court could have justified the applicant's conviction by the Austrian courts. But, if that was what the Court thought was the fair thing to do, it should have used different arguments. Intervening in a debate—ongoing in the Islamic world—about the precise facts of the relationship between Muhammad and Aisha, and about her actual age when she married, is not the courts' competence, including the ECtHR, as the Court itself has recognized in previous occasions.[94] And, with regard to the argument that the offense was "likely to arouse justified indignation", the only person who appeared to have been "indignant" at the words of the applicant was an undercover journalist who attended the seminar with the presumable purpose of finding grounds to attack the institute of the Freedom Party of Austria. If there were actually any indignation, it would have been triggered not by the applicant's speech but rather by the publicity that the journalist—intentionally—gave to it.

Manipulation of History and Hate Speech

We could conjecture that, in *E.S.*, the ECtHR intended—like the Austrian courts—to prevent a political party from disseminating, under the guise of a purported historical critique, an image of Muslims as an irrational and fanatical people who profess beliefs that are irreconcilable with Western values. If this were the case, in my opinion, resorting to the concepts of disparagement of religion or likely justified indignation was not the right approach. The Court should have rather analyzed the situation in the light of hate speech, i.e., incitation to hatred, violence, or discrimination.[95] Otherwise, there is the risk of opening the door to the possibility that the European Court decides to assume the role of arbiter in intellectual or historical disputations—a role that, so far, it has rejected. One of the consequences of it would be that the Court might justify new patterns of censorship of provocative expressions that question core aspects of some religions. That would be most unfortunate because, leaving

94 See note 71 and accompanying text.
95 That was the approach in the *Zemmour* judgment; see note 14 and corresponding text.

aside the possible inappropriate tone of such critiques, the debate about those issues is of general interest to society.

The foregoing leads us to raise a third important question: when, and under which circumstances, can we say that the manipulation or falsification of historical truth, by disseminating false information or by hiding relevant true data, is actually a subtler form of hate speech? In other words, when can it be concluded that the apparent intellectual or historical debate, in reality, conceals a discourse that is aimed at promoting hostility towards a particular group of persons?

This is precisely the case of the so-called negationism, whose actual purpose is not to determine accurate historical data but rather to use them, manipulated or just fabricated, to spread a subliminal message. The most well-known type of negationism refers to the intended extermination of the Jewish people perpetrated by the Nazi regime, questioning the true intention or the dimension of such crime, and sometimes its very existence. The publications of such orientation are not aimed at revising or refining the knowledge we have of that tragic episode in our recent history. Its aim is, by undermining the credibility of historical testimonies (including those of the survivors), to transmit a message of anti-Semitism, namely that the Jews are a cunning and parasitic people that have no scruples in distorting the reality and presenting themselves as victims as a strategy for their benefit.

The ECtHR's position has been normally very clear when it has adjudicated on cases relating to anti-Semitic negationism. Two decisions are particularly well known. One is *Roger Garaudy*,[96] which involved the criminal conviction of a notorious French public figure for negation of crimes against humanity and incitement to hatred. The European Court, in a long inadmissibility decision,[97] held that the criminal sentence was justified by art. 17 ECHR. In the Court's view, the work of Mr. Garaudy not only contained a critique of Israeli policies but also, above all, a denial of historical facts that were well-established and proven. For the Court, his work was aimed at the rehabilitation of the Nazi regime through a falsification of history and a negation of crimes against humanity, which in turn was an unequivocal form of hate speech.[98] An identical approach permeated another large inadmissibility decision, *M'Bala*,[99]

96 *Roger Garaudy v. France*, 2003, cited in note 30.

97 The official French text has 40 pages. Such a length reveals that the case deserved a judgment on the merits and not an inadmissibility decision as "manifestly ill-founded". The decision states that it was adopted unanimously.

98 See *Roger Garaudy*, En droit, § 1.i.

99 *M'Bala B'Bala v. France*, 2015, cited in note 39. This time, it was a majority decision of 18 pages. Many scholars have criticized the fact that such important issues have been ended with inadmissibility decisions that are actually, by their length and approach, judgments on the merits. This does not help the transparency of the Court; inadmissibility decisions do not enjoy the same publicity as judgments; in addition, in non-unanimous decisions, it is not known how many judges are in the minority side and these cannot write dissenting opinions.

about a popular French comedian (his artistic name is "Dieudonné") who had been sentenced to an economic penalty for using in his shows sarcastic expressions of anti-Semitic, negationist, and offensive nature. After reminding that freedom of expression also applies to satire—with all it involves of caricature and provocative exaggeration—the ECtHR made clear that this freedom does not protect speech against the fundamental values of the ECHR, as is the case of the denial of Shoah.[100]

A similar approach inspired *Norwood*, another—shorter—inadmissibility decision concerning a curious form of anti-Islamic expression which, rather than "negationist", should qualify as "attributionist", i.e., unfounded and indiscriminate attribution of acts of violence to a religious community as a whole.[101] Despite the brevity of its reasoning, *Norwood* has had a remarkable impact on North American legal literature, perhaps because it involved a case that emerged in another common law country (United Kingdom), and because the legal solution given to the case was in overt contrast with the usual criteria followed by the US judicature. The applicant was a regional organizer for an extreme right-wing political party (British National Party) who had been sentenced to pay a fine of 300 pounds for having displayed in the window of his flat, for two months, a large poster with a picture of the Twin Towers in flames, together with the sentence "Islam out of Britain – Protect the British People" and a prohibition sign with the symbol of a crescent inside. With a very laconic reasoning based on art. 17 ECHR, the European Court held that "[s]uch a general, vehement attack against a religious group, linking the group as a whole with a grave act of terrorism, is incompatible with the values proclaimed and guaranteed by the Convention, notably tolerance, social peace and non-discrimination".[102]

Nevertheless, four years later, the ECtHR, in *Soulas*,[103] rendered a new decision—this time a judgment—concerning anti-Islamic speech apropos of a book against immigration, whose publisher and author had been sentenced to the payment of a fine of 7,500 euro each. The French courts held that some passages of the book contained incitation to hatred and violence against Muslim communities of African origin. The European Court's judgment is confusing and far from the approach taken in *Norwood*. The Court stated the importance of fighting against racial discrimination and agreed that part of the text transmits a negative stereotype of those communities, but it did not describe it as hate speech. For the ECtHR, the circumstances were not sufficiently grave as to justify the application of art. 17 ECHR but they were serious enough to conclude that the restriction of freedom of expression by French authorities was

100 See *M'Bala B'Bala*, §§ 31–33.
101 *Norwood v. United Kingdom*, 2004, cited in note 40.
102 *Norwood*, § The law.
103 *Soulas and others v. France*, 10 July 2008.

well founded and the sanctions imposed were proportionate.[104] This leads me to wonder to what extent the European Court's position on this issue is erratic; a poster in a window is deemed grave enough to invoke art. 17 but the publication of a book is not, even though that work, under the guise of a socio-political analysis, is aimed at stigmatizing a part of the population. The recent judgment in *Zemmour* seems to confirm a tendency of the European Court to avoid the application of art. 17 in this type of case and decide them under art. 10, considering that the sanctions imposed, as far as they are of economic nature, are proportioned and within the national authorities' margin of appreciation.[105]

The clarity of the criteria followed in cases of anti-Semitic speech is in overt contrast with the more tepid posture of the ECtHR in another case concerning negationism, *Perinçek*,[106] with regard to the Armenian genocide at the hands of the Ottoman Empire. The applicant was the leader of a Turkish political party (the Workers' Party[107]) who, in several public events held in Switzerland, denied that any genocide of Armenians by the Turks ever existed and described it as "an international lie". The Swiss courts sentenced the applicant to pay the costs of the proceedings (10,000 Swiss francs), an additional payment of 1,000 francs as compensation to the Switzerland-Armenia Association, and a fine of 3,000 francs. He was also warned that, if in the future he incurred similar conduct in Swiss territory, he would receive a prison sentence. It is not my intention to discuss here the outcome of the case or to analyze the complex and long judgment of the Grand Chamber (122 pages, plus 12 other pages of separate opinions of the seven dissenting judges), but it is worth noting three aspects of it.

First, unlike the aforementioned cases of anti-Semitic negationism, the application in *Perinçek* ended with a judgment on the merits and not with a mere decision of inadmissibility as ill-founded (in reality there were two judgments, one by a chamber and the other by the Grand Chamber). Second, also unlike those other decisions, the case was judged in the light of art. 10.2 ECHR (limitations on freedom of expression) instead of art. 17 (abuse of rights), which the Court affirmed must be applied only "on an exceptional basis and in extreme cases".[108] This difference is significant, for an approach based on art. 10.2 requires determining if the penalties imposed on the applicant can be deemed "necessary in a democratic society" to achieve some of the legitimate purposes enumerated in that article of the Convention. Third, precisely because of it, the Court examined carefully and in detail the factual circumstances and the context of the applicant's statements on the Armenian

104 Cf. *Soulas*, §§ 41–48.

105 Cf. *Zemmour*, cited in note 14.

106 *Perinçek v. Switzerland* (GC), 15 October 2015.

107 This party dissolved in 2015 and was succeeded by the Patriotic Party, also led by Perinçek. Its ideology is a curious mix of socialism, left-wing populism, and nationalism.

108 *Perinçek*, § 114.

genocide (including the international notion of genocide and the actual impact of the public events in which the applicant spoke) in order to ascertain whether the interference with the applicant's freedom of expression was justifiable and proportionate. The Court concluded, by ten votes against seven, that it was not, and therefore there had been a violation of art. 10 ECHR.

I am not in principle against any of those three aspects: deciding the application by a judgment, examining it under art. 10.2 ECHR, and performing a detailed analysis of the factual circumstances. Just the opposite, I think this is the right way to proceed. What I do not understand is the reason why the ECtHR applied in *Perinçek* criteria that were different from those inspiring the aforementioned cases of anti-Semitic and anti-Islamic speech, without any indication at all that it had the wish to change its jurisprudence.[109] To begin with, *Garaudy*, *M'Bala*, and *Norwood* were decided under art. 17, and certainly, it is not easy to accept that they were "extreme cases" that required exceptional action on the part of the European Court. As I said, it is not my intention to discuss here if the Court's decision in these four cases was the right one or not. However, it is difficult not to get the impression that, in comparison with the decisions on conflicts generated by expressions of anti-Semitic negationism, the Court applied different and less strict standards to the speech against the Armenian genocide.[110] And, in such a delicate matter, it is essential to keep homogeneous criteria and justify very persuasively any inequality in the treatment of apparently comparable situations. In any event, the subsequent *Baldassi* judgment seems to reveal that the European Court is performing lately a more careful examination of accusations of anti-Semitism. In this case, the Court refused to accept that a call to boycott Israeli products, as a protest against the policies of the State of Israel towards Palestinians, would qualify either as anti-Semitism or hate speech or would justify the application of the limitation clauses on freedom of expression contained in art. 10.2 ECHR.[111]

Public Morals as a Notion That Could Justify Limitations on Freedom of Expression

I would like to refer now to some questions that relate to the protection of public morals, which is mentioned by art. 10.2 ECHR among the aims that

109 It is true that § 114 of *Perinçek* refers to a "recent" position of the Court. However, although *Garaudy* and *Norwood* are of 2003 and 2004, respectively, *M'Bala* was decided five days after *Perinçek*. And those three cases are cited repeatedly in *Perinçek* without any indication that the Court had the intention to introduce a new jurisprudence (indeed, it looks just the opposite).

110 As the German judge Angelica Nussberger noted in her separate opinion, the explanation provided by the ECtHR to distinguish those situations, in *Perinçek*, §§ 209–212 and 242–250, is not very convincing.

111 Cf. *Baldassi v. France*: see note 10 and corresponding text.

may justify restrictions on freedom of expression—and on other rights recognized by the European Convention.[112] In this regard, it should be borne in mind that, to be acceptable, it is not sufficient that limitations or sanctions on the exercise of freedom of expression are based on the concept of public morals in the abstract; they must be measures specifically "prescribed by law" (with the aim of the protection of public morals).[113]

Of the various notions enumerated by the *European Convention* to justify limitations on freedoms, public morals are probably the most ethereal one, the one that is most difficult to apply and to apprehend in its precise details. It is likely also the one that makes jurists feel less at ease and takes them out of their comfort zone. In fact, so far it has been only rarely used by the Strasbourg Court, thus evincing a reluctance that is shared by many European jurisdictions.[114]

It is perhaps revealing that a number of the few judgments that have made reference to public morals involve either the protection of the life of the unborn[115] or limitations on adoption by persons of non-traditional sexual orientation.[116] With regard to freedom of expression, prior to *Sekmadienis*, in 2018, we find three main judgments: *Handyside* (1976),[117] *Müller* (1988),[118] and *Mouvement Raëlien* (2012).[119] As mentioned at the beginning of this

112 In reality, art. 10.2 ECHR mentions just "morals", but the comparison with other articles of the Convention—including art. 9, on religious freedom—leaves no doubt about the fact that it is the protection of public morals, and not private morals, that could justify the application of restrictive measures to the exercise of freedom of expression. Morals are mentioned specifically in art. 6, 8, 9, 10, and 11 of the European Convention.

113 As is well-known, the reference to the "law" must be interpreted as comprising not only legislation but also case law, regulations, and administrative praxis. The requirement of being "prescribed by law" is inspired by legal certainty, so that citizens can reasonably foresee the consequences of their actions. For a more detailed explanation of it, with references, see J. Martínez-Torrón, *Limitations on Religious Freedom…*, cited in note 32, pp. 597–598.

114 One of the most indicative cases in Strasbourg in this regard is *Gough v. United Kingdom*, 28 October 2014, concerning public nudity. The applicant was a British citizen who, convinced of the benefits of public nudity, attempted to promote it by walking totally naked in various places, earning the nickname "the naked rambler", which got him arrested on multiple occasions. Significantly, the cause used by the British authorities for his detention and subsequent trial was "breach of the peace". The issue of public morals was virtually not mentioned by the courts (at least in the version given by the ECtHR). And the references that the European Court itself made to public morals in its judgment were few and formulaic. The Court concluded that neither art. 8 nor art. 10 had been violated.

115 See *A, B and C v. Ireland* (GC), 16 December 2010; *Evans v. United Kingdom* (GC), 10 April 2007; *Vo v. France* (GC), 8 July 2004; *Open Door and Dublin Well Woman v. Ireland* (plenary), 29 October 1992. Indicative of the significance that the Court recognized those cases is the fact that all of them were decided by the Grand Chamber (or by the Court in plenary session, which was the approximate equivalent before the reform of the Court in 1998).

116 *Fretté v. France*, 26 February 2002; *X, Y and Z v. United Kingdom* (GC), 22 April 1997.

117 *Handyside v. United Kingdom*, 7 December 1976.

118 *Müller and others v. Switzerland*, 24 May 1988.

119 *Mouvement Raëlien Suisse v. Switzerland* (GC), 13 July 2012.

chapter, *Handyside* defined some key principles on the guarantee of freedom of expression; the application has its origin in the judicial prohibition and seizure of a book aimed at teenagers, which was deemed to be against public morals because it contained some obscene passages and some others of anarchist orientation, inciting to rebellion against authority within the family. *Müller* concerned the confiscation, ordered by the Swiss courts, of three large paintings that contained gross obscene representations that included scenes of sodomy, fellatio, and bestiality; the paintings were to be displayed in an exhibition, of free access, held as part of of the celebrations of the 500th anniversary of the Canton of Fribourg's entry into the Swiss Confederation. *Mouvement Raëlien* involved the prohibition of a poster campaign programmed by that group, which described itself as religious, aimed at attracting new followers; the campaign was to be developed in the public spaces of the Swiss town of Neuchâtel but the Swiss authorities considered the campaign immoral and against the public order, based on the references of the Raelians' doctrine to "geniocracy", human cloning, eugenics, and "sensual meditation" (the latter, according to the Swiss authorities, could lead to abuse of children, which in some of the group's sources were described as "privileged sexual objects"). In those three judgments, the ECtHR held that there was no violation of freedom of expression and gave priority to the national margin of appreciation to determine the reach and consequences of the protection of public morals. *Handyside* and *Müller* were adopted by a large majority of the judges, and *Mouvement Raëlien* was decided by a divided Grand Chamber: nine votes to eight.

If we turn now to *Sekmadienis*, probably the most interesting aspect of this judgment is the relationship between public morals, freedom of expression, and religious freedom, especially on account of the reason alleged by Lithuanian authorities to justify the limitation on freedom of expression. As mentioned above,[120] and without any intention to go into the details of the judgment more than is strictly necessary, the case involved an advertising campaign to introduce a new clothing line, which displayed three advertisements in twenty hoardings in public areas of Vilnius, using, humorously, some characters and words of implicit, but clear, religious connotation. Following the complaints of a number of citizens, the State bodies for consumer protection and regulation of commercial publicity initiated review proceedings and concluded that, because of its frivolous attitude towards central figures of Christianity, the advertising campaign had gone beyond the limits of decency that public morals imposed. Having been consulted, the Catholic Bishops Conference of Lithuania expressed the same opinion, declaring that the advertisements degraded sacred persons and offended the feelings of Christians. The removal of the campaign was ordered (it had been active only a few weeks in Vilnius) and a moderate fine (less than 600 euros) was imposed on the company

120 See supra, note 5 and accompanying text.

When we compare the facts in *Sekmadienis* with those in other judgments mentioned above, the most distinctive factor is that the national law considered that respect for the religious beliefs and feelings of others was an integral part of public morals. In *Handyside* and *Müller*, the notion of morals—which was no doubt operative in British and Swiss law—appeared dissociated from religious elements. The same occurred in *Mouvement Raëlien*: the circumstance that the protagonist of the vetoed campaign was a group self-described as religious is accidental. The action of the Swiss authorities would have been the same whatever the nature (real or apparent) of the group involved. In *Otto-Preminger-Institut*, as in other subsequent cases decided in Strasbourg (including *Giniewski* and *E.S.*), the national authorities alleged that certain sanctions on the exercise of freedom of expression were justified as necessary to ensure respect for religious feelings, which they understood was a part of the freedom of religion protected by art. 9 ECHR. Such restrictive measures, therefore, were legitimate as their aim was the protection of the rights of others.

In *Sekmadienis*, the approach of the national authorities was different. They did not affirm that citizens have the right to have their religious feelings protected; what they asserted is that the State must ensure the maintenance of public morals, which included the preservation of an atmosphere of religious tolerance. Lithuanian law envisages the prohibition of advertisements that infringe public morals;[121] and both the courts and administrative practice interpret the law in the sense that public morals demand that every form of expression respects the religious beliefs and feelings of the population. The Supreme Administrative Court was especially clear about this when it declared that religion contributes to the moral development of society and therefore the inappropriate use of religious symbols is contrary to commonly accepted moral norms.[122] The same court also observed that such principle is particularly applicable to expressions that have a purely commercial purpose and are not intended to contribute to any public debate about religion, its symbols, and its proper place in civil society.[123]

If we turn to the judgment of the Court of Strasbourg, probably it is not difficult to agree with its outcome. The Court held that, in the specific circumstances of the case, the restriction on freedom of expression was not sufficiently justified (but this, according to a separate concurring opinion of one of the judges, should not be understood as carte blanche to offend religious symbols in public[124]). However, it is more difficult to share the rationale of the Court, which focussed on a summary and almost formulaic account of general

121 See *Sekmadienis*, § 34–35.
122 Cf. *Sekmadienis*, § 25.
123 Cf. *Sekmadienis*, § 29.
124 Concurring opinion of the Maltese judge Vincent de Gaetano.

principles and passed like on tiptoe through the important issues, beginning with the very notion of public morals.

Indeed, the ECtHR has been reluctant so far to go into the concept of public morals in-depth and has merely referred to it in the minimum possible terms when it was indispensable to justify its decision. It would appear as if the Court felt uncomfortable talking of public morals, perhaps assuming that a secular judge must not speak about morals—this would be a mistake, because public morals, in the sense that it is used by the European Convention as well as by many national laws, are a legal and not a moral notion. As a matter of fact, since *Handyside*—and *Sekmadienis* is no exception—the ECtHR's position on public morals has been characterized by its lack of definition, in spite of how important this concept is, like all concepts that can be used to legitimize limitations on fundamental freedoms. In the few times the Court has referred to public morals, normally it has just reiterated some general statements: that the notion of public morals is unprecise and continuously changing,[125] that it is part of the general interest, and that this is a matter in which, in the absence of a European consensus, a broad margin of appreciation must be granted to national authorities (in the traditional formulation of the margin of appreciation doctrine by the Court, the less consensus there is among European countries on a particular issue, the bigger the national margin of appreciation, and vice versa[126]). Certainly not much.

I am afraid that, in *Sekmadienis*, the ECtHR has lost another opportunity to introduce new nuances in some of its old doctrines. In a number of prior judgments, the Court could have said more about the function of the European consensus vis-à-vis the national margin of appreciation[127]—which would have been very welcome in order to avoid surprisingly odd interpretations of that doctrine, as the ones provided in *Leyla Şahin* or *S.A.S.*[128] In *Mouvement Raëlien*, the Court missed the chance to elaborate on an important aspect of freedom of expression: namely, if the limitations enumerated in art. 10.2 ECHR, including public morals, must be construed differently depending on whether the speech in question goes through private channels or through spaces or media that are controlled and managed by public authorities or institutions.[129] And, also in *Mouvement Raëlien*, it would have been desirable that the Court enunciated clearer criteria to distinguish when a speech can be deemed predominantly commercial despite coming from a religious group (real or alleged); this is a very significant issue characterized by the convergence of proselytism, religious freedom, and freedom of expression.

125 Cf. *Handyside*, § 48.

126 See supra, note 32.

127 In this regard, see the interesting remarks of the ad hoc Irish judge Mary Finlay Geoghegan in her concurring opinion to the judgment *A, B and C. v. Ireland*, cited supra, in note 113.

128 *Leyla Şahin v. Turkey* (GC), 10 November 2005; *S.A.S. v. France* (GC), 1 July 2014.

129 Some judges, in their separate opinions, focused much more on this issue–which in my view is of the utmost importance–than the main judgment did.

In *Sekmadienis*, perhaps the most important issue that the ECtHR left aside was the relationship between public morals and religion, in a double sense. On the one hand, to what extent the notion of public morals used by state law may include elements deriving from secularized religious principles—this issue is only incidentally alluded to by the judgments, in the light of some unclear references to tensions between majority and minority.[130] On the other hand, if a national legal system can adopt the position that public morals involve respect for the religious feelings of people. This was precisely the approach taken by the Lithuanian authorities and it is not per se an unreasonable idea. It needs, however, to be carefully elaborated to avoid the risk that a notion that is valid in itself is transformed in practice into an instrument of moral authoritarianism, thus hindering legitimate expressions of discrepancy with regard to ethical values held by the majority, which would be to the detriment of one of the central freedoms guaranteed by the European Convention. Ultimately, these are questions that connect with the broader theme of the relationships between religion and culture, and which is the role of those relationships in the context of a society that must protect both freedom of expression and freedom of religion—i.e., a society not characterized by the political predominance of a majority religion (even if it is socially predominant).

In my view, *Sekmadienis* was an "easy case" from the perspective of what its fair outcome should be. Nevertheless, because of the importance of the questions it raised, it should have received more attention from the Strasbourg Court. Certainly, we cannot expect from the European Court a treatise on religion and public morals, but some more clear guidance in this area would have been advisable. The Court could—and probably should—have provided criteria that could serve as points of reference for state laws to avoid two mistakes: to eradicate moral dissent from society and to misread the *Sekmadienis* judgment—as one of the judges warned—as a sort of carte blanche to trivialize public offenses against religious symbols in a society that has decided that such offenses run counter the ambiance of tolerance and respect required for the peaceful exercise of freedoms.

Towards an Integrating Conception of Human Rights

One of the main challenges that contemporary democratic societies must face is to mark itineraries that facilitate adequate and reasonable solutions to conflicts between the exercise of fundamental rights by different persons. The proliferation of such situations is a fact that can be read in various ways. Among the reasons that may explain the increase in this type of conflict, there are two which, in my view, are of particular significance.

In the first place, a progressively extensive interpretation of human rights. There is a tendency to enlarge the range of conducts, identities, and life

130 Cf. *Sekmadienis*, §§ 80–82.

attitudes that are included within the protectable content of human rights. And, in parallel, new rights have been added to classic rights, sometimes in a controversial fashion, and not always in binding legal or international documents but often in the political discourse, at least in the West. Such expansion of the legal protection of certain human characteristics and choices naturally multiplies the possibilities of negative interaction between the exercise of fundamental freedoms by different people, especially when there is a remarkable disparity between each other's conception of which is the prevailing or more legitimate claim in case of clash.

In the second place, such negative interaction becomes more frequent as fundamental rights are increasingly exercised from the perspective of a purely individualist position. The beginning of the culture of human rights had its center of gravity in the recognition of the dignity of human beings, which is intrinsically linked to their moral dimension, with all it implies of ethical responsibility—not only individual but also social responsibility. The success of the movement in favor of human rights came in the 20th century, after two devastating world wars that injected into our culture the conviction that reconstructing societies based on peace and justice was only possible if they were founded on human dignity and human rights. A few generations later, however, the same societies, being chronologically and emotionally distanced from those tragedies, have ended up accentuating what human rights have of individual claim in the legislative and judicial realm, and in parallel blurring what human rights have of contribution to social harmony and cohesion. The notion of the essentiality of human rights has been preserved but we have lost sight of *why* they are essential. This paves the way for an implicit social legitimation of any exercise of rights, even though it does not have any other purpose than the instant interest—here and now—of the individual exercising those rights.

If there is a fundamental freedom whose exercise from a strictly individualist perspective is susceptible to causing conflicts, this is freedom of expression and even more in the Internet era. It is a freedom easy to exercise, and its negative effects are not normally either immediate or tangible, and hence there is a tendency to accept them as the "reasonable price" we must pay for freedom in a democracy. No doubt, such a tendency is based on sensible grounds but at the same time we should not underestimate the power—sometimes destructive—of words.

Social conflicts that have freedom of expression as the protagonist require careful legal treatment by legislation and especially by the courts; this applies also to conflicts involving the sensitive realm of religion and beliefs. The purpose of this paper has been to point out some elements that I think should be taken into account in the debate about the criteria that must define such legal treatment. In any event, we should bear in mind that solving this type of conflict is the responsibility of the entire society and not only of the law and state institutions. The pernicious effects of excessive or abusive free speech could often be remedied with a spontaneous and vigorous social response more efficiently than with the use of legal instruments.

Furthermore, if we look beyond conflicts generated by the exercise of freedom of expression, it is urgent that we retrieve the meaning of human dignity as a central notion around which we can build societies based on the respect for the human rights of everyone, and not only the rights of the majority that get hold of political power—or the control of the media. In ideologically and culturally plural societies, it is natural that competing notions of human rights are bound to coexist. The real challenge is to make it possible for those notions to live together, with the maximum degree of mutual respect, instead of having the dominant position trying to banish or conquer the competitor.[131]

131 Some interesting initiatives with this orientation have recently emerged in scholarly circles. For instance, the project "Human Dignity for Everyone Everywhere", which has produced a text already translated into several languages: the "Punta del Este Declaration on Human Dignity for Everyone Everywhere". See https://www.dignityforeveryone.org. For some recent and interesting studies in this matter in the context of religious freedom, see the collective volumes S. Meseguer and M. Domingo (coords.), *Dignidad humana, derecho y libertad religiosa*, and R. Palomino and B. Rodrigo (coords.), *Cultura, identidad, religión y derecho: una perspectiva interdisciplinar*, both published by Editorial del BOE, 2023.

8 State Neutrality, Religion, and Academic Freedom

François Venter

Introduction

Western constitutionalism assumes the neutrality of the state in religious matters. This assumption is however amorphous and open-ended: does 'neutrality' imply disinterestedness, detachment, non-involvement, objectivity, or fair arbitration? If the neutral state is required to arbitrate over religious disagreements, on which epistemic constitutional premises is it to be done, and how does this impact upon the notion of academic freedom?

In this chapter the obstacles that challenge the reconciliation of state neutrality, religion, and academic freedom are canvassed against the background of the difficulties attending the characterisation of each of these notions. Firstly, the notion of academic freedom and limitations thereon are outlined comparatively, followed by a consideration of the nature of neutrality and the achievability of neutrality in science and constitutional governance. In section title 'Religion', the meaning of 'religion' and its relevance for the manner in which states deal with academic freedom is discussed. In the concluding section a remedial approach to resolve the problem of the unattainability of neutrality is suggested.

Academic Freedom

'Academic freedom' concerns the practice of scholarship and teaching. The notion, sometimes constitutionally entrenched as a fundamental right in its own right, or more regularly expressly or by implication subsumed in the right to freedom of expression, implies non-interference by the state in the work of researchers and teachers in higher education. Where science, scholarship, and religion conflate, as they inevitably do, the ability of anyone wishing to maintain neutrality in the matter becomes questionable.

UNESCO defines academic freedom as the 'liberty of educational institutions to decide courses and research, and of teachers to teach subjects,

DOI: 10.4324/9781003519188-11

without outside coercion'.[1] In a General Comment of 2020 the Committee on Economic, Social, and Cultural Rights (CESCR)[2] referred to States parties' tendency not to give much attention to science in their reports to and dialogues with the Committee.[3] After pointing out that Article 15(3) of the Covenant imposes a specific duty on states to 'respect the freedom indispensable for scientific research',[4] the Committee found that –

> States parties should not only abstain from interfering in the freedom of individuals and institutions to develop science and diffuse its results. States must take positive steps for the advancement of science (development) and for the protection and dissemination of scientific knowledge and its applications (conservation and diffusion).[5]

CESCR also emphasised the duty of states to promote the right to participate in and to enjoy the benefits of scientific progress and to take measures to ensure enjoyment of the right without discrimination on various grounds, including religion.[6]

Constitutional protection of academic freedom can be traced back in time to the German Frankfurt Constitution of 1849 (*Verfassung des Deutschen Reiches*), which states in paragraph 152 '*Die Wissenschaft und ihre Lehre ist frei*' (science and teaching science is free).[7] An English translation of Article 5(3) of the current *Grundgesetz* of 1949 reads 'Arts and sciences, research and teaching shall be free. The freedom of teaching shall not release any person from allegiance to the constitution'.[8] Contemporary German constitutional jurisprudence on the subject is quite extensive, beginning with the Federal Constitutional Court's decision of 1972, known as the *Hochschulurteil.* The Court interpreted Article 5(3) to reflect a constitutional value judgement

1 UNESCO, 'Thesaurus' https://vocabularies.unesco.org/browser/thesaurus/en/page/concept1071 accessed 1 August 2022.

2 The CESCR is a body of 18 independent experts that monitors the implementation of the International Covenant on Economic, Social, and Cultural Rights: see United Nations Human Rights Treaty Bodies, 'Committee on Economic, Social, and Cultural Rights' https://www.ohchr.org/en/treaty-bodies/cescr accessed 1 August 2022.

3 Committee on Economic, Social, and Cultural Rights, 'General Comment No. 25 (2020) on Science and Economic, Social and Cultural Rights Article 15 (1) (b), (2), (3) and (4) of the International Covenant on Economic, Social and Cultural Rights' E/C.12/GC/25 30 April 2020 paragraph 2.

4 Para. 13 of the General Comment n 3.

5 Para. 14 of the General Comment n 3.

6 Para. 25 of the General Comment n 3.

7 Article 142 of the 1919 Weimar Constitution expanded this wording to: '*Die Kunst, die Wissenschaft und ihre Lehre sind frei. Der Staat gewährt ihnen Schutz und nimmt an ihrer Pflege teil*' (The arts, science and its teaching are free. The state guarantees their protection and participates in their nurture.)

8 '*Kunst und Wissenschaft, Forschung und Lehre sind frei. Die Freiheit der Lehre entbindet nicht von der Treue zur Verfassung*'.

(*Wertentscheidung*), entailing the core function that free scientific work holds both for the self-realisation of the individual and for the development of society as a whole, and requires the state to protect scientific freedom while also preventing it being hollowed out.[9]

A somewhat unusual south-north, trans-Atlantic conceptual migration occurred in the 1950s when the US Supreme Court adopted the definition of academic freedom reflected in a report of a conference of senior scholars of two South African universities, namely that the 'four essential freedoms of a university is to determine for itself on academic grounds who may teach, what may be taught, how it shall be taught and who may be admitted to study'.[10]

In the United Kingdom the Education Reform Act of 1988 established a body of 'University Commissioners' to oversee academic tenure, having regard to the need –

To ensure that academic staff have freedom within the law to question and test received wisdom, and to put forward new ideas and controversial or unpopular opinions, without placing themselves in jeopardy of losing their jobs or privileges they may have at their institutions.[11]

One notices that some of the characterisations of academic freedom focus on institutional protection against meddling by the state in academic, scholarly, and managerial decisions of universities,[12] and others approach the matter as a liberty claimed primarily by individual scholars. It seems fair to assume that these perspectives are not mutually exclusive, and to employ the concept in a manner that covers both institutional and individual research and teaching. Academic freedom therefore entails both the autonomy of the university against state and other interference, and a fundamental right that may be defended by individual scholars against both the university, the state, and other role-players. These notions of academic freedom are borne by and expressed in terms of *liberal* ideals, and are concerned with the unfettered generation and dissemination of knowledge and the security of scholars and their employment, regardless of the principles they choose to express in their approach to research and teaching.

9 BverfGE 35, 79, 114

10 *Sweezy v New Hampshire* 354 US 234, 263. The approach was also followed in the famous *Regents of the University of California v Bakke* 438 US 265, 312.

11 Section 202(2)(a) of the Education Reform Act 1988.

12 See, e.g., Klaus D. Beiter 'Where have all the scientific and academic freedoms gone?' – four caveats to guide the interpretation of the Right to Enjoy the Benefits of Scientific Progress and Its Applications (REBPSA) in Article 15(1)(b) of the International Covenant of Economic, Social and Cultural Rights (2019) 52,2 *Israel Law Review* 233, who (at 265–269) condemns research management as a flawed concept, and states (at 281) that universities have since the 1980s experienced dwindling independence and that the erosion of individual academic freedom has occurred, 'precipitated by the implementation of neoliberal higher education and science policies'.

The bundle of fundamental rights collectively expressed as 'academic freedom' can naturally, like all legal rights, not be deemed to be absolute. Examples of the limitability of the rights are the second sentence of Article 5(3) German *Grundgesetz*, which makes it clear that allegiance to the constitution precedes the freedom, and the UK's Education Reform Act, which grants the freedom 'subject to the law'. In any disputation of the boundaries of the right, the question of the justification of limiting the rights of universities or scholars, will therefore arise. It is exactly at this juncture where considerations of fundamental premises and religion unavoidably come into play.

A relatively obvious instance of religious limitations on academic freedom may be found in Islamic states. Thus, for instance, in Saudi Arabia Islamic doctrine is entrenched as a prime constitutional purpose leading to the proscription, without qualification, of the expression of views that violate Islamic laws. Stating ideas that may collapse the Islamic social order (*al-fitnah*) are forbidden in the Quran as conduct considered worse than murder.[13] Interestingly, such limitations on academic freedom should not usually be much of a burden on those who approach the natural (or 'hard') sciences as the domain of value-free empirical factuality – much as it is seen by agnostic and atheistic scientists working in liberal constitutional orders. Where more than the laws of nature come into play, as is the case in the social sciences, it is however quite different.

The apparent protection of academic freedom in constitutional orders not founded upon the Western liberal tradition, such as those found in Islamic, socialist, and other autocratic states, can readily be recognised as being subject to a religion or ideology that compels strict limitations upon all freedoms, including academic freedom. However, where limitations are imposed in a liberal democracy, the ideological substrate for such limitation is more difficult to identify because it is usually couched in terms such as 'secularism' and 'neutrality', and as Andrew Koppelman correctly points out, 'The secularist commitment to human rights is curiously ungrounded'.[14]

Neutrality

At the end of the introductory chapter of a book on neutrality in science, culture, and politics in Europe, the editors concluded: 'Neutrality may not be a "negative word"; but it is not neutral either'.[15]

13 Ashwaq Mohammed Aldossari, 'Academic freedom in Saudi Arabia: a comparative analysis' (Doctoral Thesis, University of Lincoln 2021) 63. See also Sari Hanafi, 'The pen and the sword: the narrow margin of academic freedom in the Arab world' https://trafo.hypotheses.org/28464 accessed 19 July 2022.

14 Andrew Koppelman, *Defending American Religious Neutrality* (Harvard University Press 2013) 170.

15 Rebecka Lettevall, Geert Somsen, and Sven Widmalm (eds), *Neutrality in Twentieth-Century Europe* (Routledge 2012) 13.

Since the end of the 18th century, liberal democracy, also identified as 'liberal constitutionalism', has been publicised as the ideal form of state and government, not only in and for the Western world, but around the globe, and continues to be a prominent standard against which the quality of statehood is measured.[16] State neutrality, especially in matters of religion, may be described as a cornerstone of liberal democracy because of its foundational precepts of the equality of all and individual liberty to pursue personal belief. Much has been written on neutrality by especially North American liberal legal theorists such as John Rawls, Jeremy Waldron, William Kymlicka, Charles Larmore, and William Galston.[17]

What exactly neutrality should be understood to entail is however all but clear. In a recent dissection of the notion of neutrality, Matt Watson found that –

> Many theorists writing about neutrality as a political ideal are operating without the benefit of a coherent and plausible conception of what it is to act neutrally, and that in the interests of conceptual clarity it would be preferable if they spoke not of 'neutrality', but rather of 'public justifiability', or 'equal accommodation', or 'equal impact' (depending on the particular emphasis of particular scholars).[18]

A key question is what it is that moves proponents of state neutrality to extol its merits. A fair answer might be that non-neutrality implies explicit preference for one approach above others. In reality, all but a very few contemporary states harbour pluralistic citizenries insofar as cultural, ethnic, religious, social, and economic views and statuses are concerned, which complicates the making of basic choices. A government or judiciary seen to be preferential in especially the cultural, ethnic, and religious contexts is exposed to readily justifiable charges of prejudice. Enter 'neutrality' as the solution.

Despite neutrality being the rote liberal response, the polysemic nature of the concept challenges its value as a solution to the pluralistic demands of the inhabitants of a country. Being presented as the way out is in itself, for better or for worse, ideologically coloured and is by no means represented uniformly by its proponents.[19] The depth of the fault lines in the thinking of various leading liberal scholars is well described by Denise Meyerson, who concluded –

16 See, e.g., François Venter, *Constitutionalism and Religion* (Edward Elgar 2022) 50–51.

17 See, e.g., Leni Franken, *Liberal Neutrality and State Support for Religion* (Springer 2016) 3–10.

18 Matt Watson, 'Rethinking neutrality: a conceptual analysis' (2021) 46,1 *Journal of Legal Philosophy* 1, 27.

19 Watson (n 18) 2, e.g., proposes 'volitional neutrality' (refraining from differentially helping or hindering one party over others) as the correct approach, distinct from notions of neutrality of effects, neutrality of intentions, neutrality of justification, and neutrality of treatment.

> That a neutral state–one that refrains from restricting people's liberties or discriminating against them on the ground that their way of life is intrinsically inferior–is the only respectful response to the fact that disagreements on matters of the good life come down to a bare clash of personal convictions. This is not a morally neutral justification for liberal tolerance. On the contrary, it relies on the power of the moral idea that we are all equal in moral status. It is, however, methodologically neutral because, unlike Dworkin's approach, it is neutral about the nature of the good life. Dworkin's approach does not give people who reject the value of autonomy a reason to accept state neutrality and it gives rise to the apprehension of unfairness.[20]

Dissention over the nature and effect of state neutrality was highlighted in the 2002 *Zelman* judgement of the US Supreme Court concerning the constitutionality of a programme of vouchers issued by the State of Ohio to allow the children of low-income families to attend schools of their choice, regardless of their choice being for a religious school or not. The Court was split five to four, especially due to differences in opinion on the kind of neutrality required by the Establishment Clause. Justice O'Connor encapsulated the difference in the approaches in a judgement concurring with the majority:

> There is little question in my mind that the Cleveland voucher program is neutral as between religious schools and nonreligious schools. … JUSTICE SOUTER rejects the Court's notion of neutrality, proposing that the neutrality of a program should be gauged not by the opportunities it presents but rather by its effects. In particular, a 'neutrality test … [should] focus on a category of aid that may be directed to religious as well as secular schools, and ask whether the scheme favors a religious direction.' [Justice Souter] … surmises that the cap on tuition that voucher schools may charge low-income students encourages these students to attend religious rather than nonreligious private voucher schools. … But JUSTICE SOUTER's notion of neutrality is inconsistent with that in our case law. As we put it in *Agostini*, government aid must be 'made available to both religious and secular beneficiaries on a nondiscriminatory basis'.[21]

In June 2022 the *Zelman* judgement figured prominently in a case from Maine dealing with similar considerations. This time the split was six to three, and Justice Sotomayor delivered a particularly sharp dissenting judgement, holding that the Supreme Court 'continues to dismantle the wall of separation

20 Denise Meyerson, 'Three versions of liberal tolerance: Dworkin, Rawls, Raz' (2012) 3 *Jurisprudence* 37, 69.

21 *Zelman v Simmon-Harris* 536 U.S. 639 (2002) 670.

between church and state that the Framers fought to build', and stating that the decision –

> Is especially perverse because the benefit at issue is the public education to which all of Maine's children are entitled under the State Constitution. As this Court has long recognised, the Establishment Clause requires that public education be secular and neutral as to religion.[22]

Edward Eberle describes the majority's approach to neutrality in *Zelman* as having only 'a formal, facial meaning', whereas the minority supported a 'substantive' approach, holding that supporting religious schools by allowing state support to be channeled to them should not be seen as neutral because it implied coercion of conscience. He concluded that 'The Court's fight over neutrality illustrates our fight over religious freedom and why this may, indeed, be a mission impossible'.[23]

This is true not only for the US. The German state Saxony-Anhalt provides an annual grant to the Jewish religious community by means of a lump sum paid to a regional association of Jewish congregations, which then distributes the funds proportionally to congregations according to the size of their membership. A congregation of liberal Jews contested the administratively determined statistics of their membership before the administrative courts, which ordered the regional association to revise the numbers. After further unsuccessful litigation up to the Federal Administrative Court, the regional association submitted a constitutional complaint (*Verfassungsbeschwerde*) to the *Bundesverfassungsgericht*, which was rejected in January 2022 in a reasoned decision by a panel of three judges.[24]

The reasoning involved the understanding of the judges of the nature of the religious neutrality of the state. The point of departure was the foundational principle of religious and ideological neutrality of the state (*Grundsatz der religiösen und weltanschaulichen Neutralität des Staates*) required by a reading of various provisions of the *Grundgesetz*.[25] The panel stated that this meant that the state is, in accordance with the principles of *Rechtsstaatlichkeit*, required to orient its approach to the various religious and ideological communities according to the principle of equality. This should be understood to

22 *Carson v Makin* 596 U.S. _ (2022) at 1 and 4 of Sotomayor J's opinion.

23 Edward J. Eberle, 'A comment on Mark Weiner's "Neutrality between church and state: mission impossible"' in Winfried Brugger and Michael Karayanni (eds), *Religion in the Public Sphere: A Comparative Analysis of German, Israeli, American and International Law* (Springer 2007) 453, 459–460.

24 BVerfG, Beschluss der 3. Kammer des Zweiten Senats vom 20. January 2022 – 2 BvR 2467/17 – Rn. 1–36 http://www.bverfg.de/e/rk20220120_2bvr246717.html accessed 5 August 2022.

25 Articles 4 Abs. 1, 3 Abs. 3, 33 Abs. 3, 140 GG read with Article 136 Abs. 1, Abs. 4 and Article 137 Abs. 1 of the Weimar Constitution 1919.

mean that where the state cooperates with or supports religious communities, such collaboration may not amount to the state's identification with specific religious communities or to the privileging of specific confessions, thus avoiding the danger of arbitrary state conduct (*Staatswillkür*).

The panel of constitutional justices found that the payment of the grant may not put one religious community in a stronger competitive position than another that has an equal claim to rely on a constitutional right. In the circumstances of the case that would have been the case if the regional association were to be allowed to determine the size of the proportional claim to the grant of a congregation that is not one of its members. The manner in which the various administrative courts dealt with the matter amounted to the making of judicial decisions regarding membership of various religious communities, not in the sense of replacing the determination of membership made by the regional association, but by finding its determination of the statistics to unconstitutionally reduce the benefits of state subvention due to a non-member. Stated more concretely, the courts sought to resolve an intra-religious dispute by invoking the neutrality of the state.

The approach of European Union law to neutrality exhibits similar tensions. Various EU directives provide for a qualification of neutrality through 'indirect discrimination', which is generally deemed 'to occur where an apparently neutral provision, criterion or practice would put persons … at a particular disadvantage compared to other persons'.[26] Several EU directives qualify this general rule with the proviso 'unless that provision, criterion or practice is objectively justified by a legitimate aim, and the means of achieving that aim are appropriate and necessary'.[27] One might well ask how the notion of an 'objective' test should be understood to be different from neutrality: what distinguishes objectivity from neutrality? To this question we will return.

Under certain circumstances, however, EU law allows for differential or discriminatory treatment, among others, where religious institutions 'require individuals working for them to act in good faith and with loyalty to the organisation's ethos'.[28] This is demonstrated in various European 'headscarf' cases in which the wearing of that religious symbol in public institutions, such as a hospital, was found to be justifiable in order to *maintain* the institution's neutrality.[29] It may therefore be said that, on the basis of liberal premises, EU law allows for a certain degree of subjective preference in the name of neutrality.

These examples from leading liberal democracies confirm the truth of the statement by Lettevall, Somsen, and Widmalm that 'neutrality' is not a neutral

26 See, e.g., European Union Agency for Fundamental Rights and Council of Europe, *Handbook on European Non-Discrimination Law* (Publications Office of the European Union Luxembourg 2018) chapter 2.2.

27 *Handbook on European Non-Discrimination Law* (n 26) chapter 3.2.

28 *Handbook on European Non-Discrimination Law* (n 26) chapter 3.3.2.

29 See, e.g., the decision of the European Court of Human Rights in *Ebrahimian v. France*, No. 64846/11, 26 November 2015. Also the *Handbook on European Non-Discrimination Law* (n 26) chapter 5.8.

word.[30] Having sifted through various liberal approaches to neutrality, Leni Franken also concluded that '*external neutrality* (a neutral legitimation for a neutral policy) is impossible, and every liberal theory ... is based on a particular comprehensive doctrine or a conception of the good'.[31]

For present purposes the conclusion must therefore be that one's understanding of the nature and content of neutrality is based on a *subjective* choice, thereby in effect defeating the purpose of avoiding ontological (state) preference: in short, as is the case with all worldviews, the liberal *Weltanschauung* upon which liberal democracy is founded, is based on foundational premises that cannot claim to be neutral.

When it comes to scholarship, neutrality is unattainable because the history, terminology, and methodology of empirical, deductive, and comparative research cannot be filtered out of the work of a scientist, regardless of the field or discipline.[32] This truism is more easily accepted in the social and human sciences than in the scientific study of phenomena governed by the laws of nature. However, 'hard' or 'physical' sciences such as physics, chemistry, and mathematics cannot avoid foundational questions about the origins of the laws of nature, the reasons for their immutability and the inexplicability of the existence of essential notions such as time, gravity, and molecular polarity – without compromising profundity. Attempting to ignore or gloss over the cosmological, ontological, and epistemic premises of scholarship is to reduce its depth, thereby rendering its results or products unconvincing to those who maintain different points of departure. And yet, neutrality in science is often hailed to be a *sine qua non* for validity.

This form of neutrality seems to imply detachment, disinterest, non-engagement, uncaring blandness, and disregard for one's personal convictions – an attitude incompatible with honest scientific investigation. Watson seems to propose a remedy by requiring volition as a means of active engagement.[33] I would in fact argue that acknowledgement of involuntary prejudice speaks for sound scholarship in all fields of scientific endeavour, but that labelling acceptance that one's worldview affects one's work as a version of 'neutrality' conceptually disregards the customary understanding of the essence of neutral detachment.

Questioning the viability of scientific neutrality should not be understood to be a negation of the existence of objective truth: thus, for instance, neither the injustice of premeditated murder, nor the mathematical reality of the number

30 See text at n 15.

31 Franken (n 17) 43. At 8 Franken explains the difference between external neutrality (neutrality as a principle) and internal neutrality (neutrality of principle) as the difference between the legitimation of neutral rules being external and the rules or policy being internal.

32 Cf. Venter (n 16) 225–226.

33 In his dissection of the notion of neutrality, Watson (n 18) 27 proposed the notion of 'volitional neutrality', 'according to which acting neutrally requires that an actor refrains from conduct engaged in for the purpose of helping or hindering a particular party in a given contest, as well as conduct that the actor believes is likely to cause such an effect'.

of pi (π) being a mathematical constant can be contested credibly. However, answering the questions *why* murder is wrong and how it came about that the ratio of a circle's circumference to its diameter is always π, require deeper, more often than not inconclusive, thought. Such further thinking inevitably produces different results depending on diverse worldviews. Put differently, what may on the surface appear to be a neutral given, will frequently be explained dissimilarly, depending on the explainer's ontological and epistemic stance. In the next section it is argued that such a stance is essentially religious.

Religion

'Religion' is instinctively, and often exclusively, understood to mean faith in and worship of deity usually associated with liturgical ritual.[34] Such a narrow understanding of the word suggests that persons or institutions that do not profess an instituted religion (e.g., agnostics and atheists) do not hold any religious belief. However, although one's beliefs may not be related to deity or ritual, no conscious person can exist in an emptiness where profound belief is absent. Belief (whatever form it might take) is a foundational attribute of the human condition that determines opinion, attitude, understanding, and responses to the impulses of one's experiences. It is therefore not far-fetched to employ 'religion' in an expanded sense to include all beliefs.[35] Consider for instance Koppelman's atheist confession:

> What contemporary atheists are committed to might be called Naked Strong Evaluation: the idea, unsupported by any particular metaphysical claims, that the commitment to decent treatment for all human beings is a nonoptional criterion for judging our own desires and actions. It is difficult for many theists to imagine how such an atheist humanism can be coherent. Yet the nakedness of this commitment does not necessarily weaken it, as a basis for either morality or social solidarity. [36]

34 Under 'religion' the *Oxford English Dictionary*, e.g., provides the following entries:

1. A state of life bound by religious vows; the condition of belonging to a religious order.

3. a. Action or conduct indicating belief in, obedience to, and reverence for a god, gods, or similar superhuman power; the performance of religious rites or observances.

5. a. Belief in or acknowledgement of some superhuman power or powers (esp. a god or gods) which is typically manifested in obedience, reverence, and worship; such a belief as part of a system defining a code of living, esp. as a means of achieving spiritual or material improvement.

35 It is also not unusual to do so. See, e.g., Franken (n 17) 75, citing Ninian Smart, *Secular Education and the Logic of Religion* (Faber 1968) 104, who describes religion 'as a coherent system of beliefs and practices which relates man to a supernatural or transcendent realm, without necessarily believing in a transcendent entity'.

36 Koppelman (n 14) 169. See also note 41.

In order to avoid repeated explanation, 'religion' is assumed, at least for the present analysis, to convey more than institutional and ritual confession of deity. The reason for such an extended use of the notion is that *Weltanschauung* – signifying every form of ontological predilection, including attitudes dismissive of institutional structures or rites, acknowledgement of any form of deity, and adherence to scriptural authority – determines one's approach to life. This means that the individual's understanding of the world and all that may be encountered and investigated therein scientifically or inductively, determines one's attitude to fundamental moral and ethical matters. Thus one's understanding of the nature and viability of freedom (academic or otherwise) and state neutrality essentially depends on one's religion (in both its conventional and extended senses).

An influential case in point is to be found in German constitutional law. In protecting the fundamental right to freedom of religion and of conscience, the German *Grundgesetz* simultaneously provides in Article 4(1) for the protection by the state of religion and *Weltanschauung*: 'Freedom of creed, of conscience, and freedom to profess a religious or non-religious faith are inviolable'. The original of the expression translated in this version as 'non-religious faith' is *weltanschauliches Bekenntnis*,[37] which is better translated as 'belief/creed based on worldview'. The following key *dictum* of the *Bundesverfassungsgericht* concerning the state-religion relationship captures the German approach well, warranting full quotation:[38]

> The Basic Law lays down for the state as the home of all citizens the duty of religious and ideological neutrality. It bars the introduction of legal structures in the nature of a state church and forbids giving privileged treatment to particular faiths and excluding those of a different belief. The state must be careful to treat the various religious and ideological communities with regard to the principle of equality and may not identify with a particular religious community. The free state of the Basic Law is characterised by openness towards the variety of ideological and religious convictions and bases this on an image of humanity that is marked by the dignity of humans and the free development of personality in self-determination and personal responsibility.
>
> However, the religious and ideological neutrality required of the state is not to be understood as a distancing attitude in the sense of a strict separation of state and church, but as an open and comprehensive one,

37 'Die Freiheit des Glaubens, des Gewissens und die Freiheit des religiösen und weltanschaulichen Bekenntnisses sind unverletzlich'.

38 The English version provided on the court's website https://www.bundesverfassungsgericht.de/SharedDocs/Entscheidungen/EN/2003/09/rs20030924_2bvr143602en.html accessed 8 June 2022. The translation of *weltanschaulich* in this version is also not satisfactory, 'ideological' representing an over-reduction of an iconic notion for which a direct equivalent is not available in English.

> encouraging freedom of faith equally for all beliefs. Article 4.1 and 4.2 of the Basic Law also contain a positive requirement to safeguard the space for active exercise of religious conviction and the realisation of autonomous personality in the area of ideology and religion. The state is prohibited only from exercising deliberate influence in the service of a particular political or ideological tendency or expressly or impliedly identifying itself by way of measures originated by it or attributable to it with a particular belief or a particular ideology and in this way itself endangering religious peace in a society. The principle of religious and ideological neutrality also bars the state from evaluating the faith and doctrine of a religious group as such.[39]

The last sentence of the first paragraph quoted significantly explains neutrality as being based on a particular 'image of humanity' (*ein Menschenbild*). At the potential cost of reluctance to accept the notion, this might be described as anthropological philosophy, or perhaps more safely, as an ontological perspective on the place of humans in reality.

The German approach differs from the American, in that the 'wall of separation between church and state' is usually deemed to be higher (or thicker) in the US. Nevertheless, consider for instance the following statement by Koppelman in the American constitutional context:

> Contrary to the radical secularists, First Amendment doctrine treats religion as a good thing. It insists, however—and here it parts company with the religious traditionalists—that religion's goodness be understood at a high enough level of abstraction that the state takes no position on any live religious dispute. It holds that religion's value is best honored by prohibiting the state from trying to answer religious questions.[40]

Here we find an acknowledgement by clear implication that the choice to be made regarding the nature and role of religion in law is founded upon a worldview – in this case an undefined stance somewhere between radical secularism and religious traditionalism. Such a choice can obviously not be made in a vacuum of ontological neutrality,[41] nor does a prohibition on the state to

39 BverfG 2 BVR 1436/02 delivered on 24 September 2003, margin numbers 42 and 43 (references omitted).

40 Koppelman (n 14) 2.

41 Koppelman (n 14) 169–170 seems to subscribe to this view in the following nonchalant statement:

> I'm not prepared to claim … that there is no transcendent basis for my commitment, that it is a purely contingent historical formation … I just don't know. So there's what appears to be a permanent gap in my belief system. If I were a religious person, I guess I'd be entitled to call it a Mystery. It doesn't trouble me, because every belief system has Mysteries of its own. My agnosticism is the

attempt answering religious questions isolate the state or its organs from the bonds of worldview. In short, secularism cannot claim to be neutral.

The question therefore arises inevitably whether the (any) state can in its constitutional, legislative, executive, administrative, or judicial functions completely avoid taking a position on religious questions. The answer is 'no', because the state's stance on religion is (or should be) rooted in the *Weltanschauung* upon which its constitution and law are founded, and as it has been argued, ontological neutrality is impossible. Law as such cannot be deemed to be a mere collection of abstract rules or norms that are to be applied mechanically – a constitution even less so. Making and applying law are actions that are rooted in worldview.

The inability of the state to avoid religion should not be understood to mean that the state, composed as it routinely is of an ontologically pluralistic citizenry, would be justified to conduct its business and exercise its authority in a manner that discriminates against some religions and worldviews in favour of others. A core function of the state should be to establish and maintain a just social order, and discrimination does not provide the means to preserve social justice. And yet, religion, especially in its extended sense, is demonstrably the foundation upon which contemporary states deal with religious diversity.

States whose constitutions are explicitly founded upon some doctrine other than liberal democracy provide obvious examples. Among them are one-party states, especially Communist states such as China. Article 36 of the *Constitution of the People's Republic of China* 1982 purports to guarantee 'freedom of religious belief' for Chinese citizens. However, the preamble to this constitution ideologically commits the state to Marxist–Leninist atheism. Furthermore, in China religious freedom may be restricted by ordinary legislation and citizens are obliged to comply with the law regardless of their beliefs. Religious practices 'disrupting the public order' or that 'interfere' with official state education are proscribed and 'foreign domination' of religious bodies and religious affairs is not allowed.[42] Article 47 grants citizens 'the freedom to engage in scientific research', but reserves control over 'creative endeavours conducive to the interests of the people'.[43]

Another clearly recognisable category of forms of state are those that explicitly profess their statehood as a manifestation of a religion, such as the Islamic

functional equivalent of atheism in many ways; I don't rely at all on a belief in God as the basis for any of my commitments. I don't think I have to.

42 Cf., e.g., Sonfeng Li, 'Freedom in handcuffs: religious freedom in the constitution of China' (2020) 35,1 *Journal of Law and Religion* 113.

43 See also Articles 89 (7) listing among the State Council's functions and powers the direction and administration of 'the affairs of science', Article 14, which makes it the task of the state to disseminate advanced science and technology, and Article 19, providing under the heading of 'Education' in the last paragraph: 'The state promotes the development of natural and social sciences, disseminates knowledge of science and technology, and commends and rewards achievements in scientific research as well as technological innovations and inventions'.

kingdoms and republics. Among these are Saudi Arabia. Article 1 of Saudi Arabia's Basic Law of 1992 provides that 'The Kingdom of Saudi Arabia is a sovereign Arab Islamic State. Its religion is Islam. Its constitution is Almighty God's Book, The Holy Quran, and the Sunna (Tradition) of the Prophet' and Article 29 proclaims that 'The State shall patronize sciences, letters and culture. It shall encourage scientific research, protect the Islamic and Arab heritage, and contribute towards Arab, Islamic and human civilization'. In such a constitutional dispensation virtually no trace of religious freedom in a liberal democratic sense can be expected to be found because 'the aim of education is to implant the Islamic Creed in the hearts of all youths'.[44] The state is entrusted with the duty to 'protect the Islamic Creed, apply the Sharia, encourage good and discourage evil, and undertake its duty regarding the Propagation of Islam'[45] and to 'protect human rights in accordance with the Sharia'.[46]

Worldview as the point of departure for dealing with religious questions is less easily recognisable in constitutional systems where religious motivations are explicitly disavowed when taking a stance on religious questions. Various versions of this category exist, usually classified as liberal democracies. Most prominent among these are the US, France, and Canada. The American approach is well-known as one of 'non-establishment' of religion by the state,[47] the French tradition is express secularism (*laïcité*) in the form of freedom *from* religion,[48] and in Canada a conscious turn towards secularism has been crafted by the Canadian Supreme Court since 1985, not particularly coherently.[49]

Rousseau famously spoke of a 'civil religion' associated with the notion of the social contract,[50] and more recently Robert Bellah strongly argued for the recognition of an American 'civil religion'.[51] The thinking of Rousseau and the influence of the American Constitution on the popularisation, especially since the second half of the 20th century of liberal democracy as an ideal, has led to global conceptual hegemony of the terminology of liberal constitutionalism. Although the idea of an American civil religion gives expression to elements of what has been describe above as religion in its extended meaning, the concept

44 Article 13 of the Basic Law.
45 Article 23 of the Basic Law.
46 Article 26 of the Basic Law.
47 The First Amendment to the Constitution of the United States of America of 1798, adopted in 1791, provides that 'Congress shall make no law respecting an establishment of religion, or prohibiting the free exercise thereof'.
48 See, e.g., Sarah Nirenberg, 'The resurgence of secularism: hostility towards religion in the United States and France' (2013) 5 *Washington University Jurisprudence Review* 131, 156.
49 See, e.g., Venter (n 16) 134–142.
50 Jean Jacques Rousseau, (1762) *The Social Contract or Principles of Political Rights* G.D.H. Cole (tr 1782), public domain, rendered into HTML and text by Jon Roland <https://www.constitution.org/2-Authors/jjr/socon.htm> accessed 25 November 2022. Book IV 8.
51 Robert Bellah, 'Civil religion in America' (1967) 96,1 *Daedalus* 1.

is not sufficiently coherent to explain the approach to neutrality and academic freedom in a liberal democracy.

Defending neutrality as the appropriate approach of the state and its organs when dealing with religion must inevitably be based on the belief that neutrality is indeed possible. Neutrality can have various meanings. One general meaning is disinterestedness, in other words, that the state eschews everything evoking religion. Such an understanding will be self-destructive because it would imply more than proscription of state support for any religious position (disestablishment): it would amount to a rejection of the social relevance of religion, meaning detachment of the state from social reality.

American disestablishment, French *laïcité*, the Canadian (and other systems') version of secularism seem to have a common (liberal) view of the nature of religion to be exclusively private, whereas the domain of the state is public, and therefore 'neutrally' elevated above the personal foibles of religious individuals and groups within the citizenry. The neutral (secular) state can therefore deal with religious affairs only by denying the relevance of the *Weltanschauung* that informs its constitutional authority. The liberal democratic worldview (religion) is rooted in a profound conviction about human nature, namely that individual dignity, freedom, and equality should motivate all public conduct. Such a view is obviously not neutral because it is sourced from convictions patently distinguishable from those based on, e.g., collectivism, socialism, and a range of other religious doctrines based upon the primacy of a deity, and, as Bryan Turner pointed out in 2012, 'The modern liberal paradox is that while a secular liberal state is committed to regarding religion as a matter of private conscience, the liberal state constantly intervenes to manage religions in the name of civil harmony and political security'.[52]

Conclusion: Can Academic Freedom, State Neutrality and Religion Be Reconciled?

For the state to be 'neutral' in any context requires a constitutional doctrine that informs the notion of neutrality. Such doctrines vary in content and in their approach to the need for and the nature of neutrality.

The doctrine or ideology upon which a constitution is founded is no superficial matter. It provides a point of departure based on the worldview of the authors and authoritative interpreters of the constitution, which correlates in ideal circumstances with the aggregate worldview of the citizenry. In some cases, such a constitutionalised worldview is expressed in religious terms in the conventional or limited understanding of religion as a structured creed involving liturgical worship of a deity practised in an institutionalised manner. However, in most cases the profound tenets of the constitutional doctrine in

52 Bryan S. Turner, 'Managing religions, citizenship and the liberal paradox' (2012) 16,8 *Citizenship Studies* 1059, 1070.

terms of which the authority of the state is justified are not associated with religion in the narrow sense even in cases where direct or indirect state support of a religious institution or institutions is prescribed or allowed for by the constitution.

Nevertheless, since every constitutional doctrine essentially relies on some foundational worldview, constitutional doctrine is rooted in religion in the comprehensive sense. Although many may consider this to be a counter-intuitive, or even misguided perspective, this is also true of 'secular' Western liberal constitutionalism. This creed of the liberal religion is founded upon the firm belief of the primacy of the free and equal human individual. It is a dogma that profoundly determines the assumed vocation of this form of constitutionalism, namely the optimal protection of the person and rights of every citizen to pursue one's conceptions of 'the good life' without, or with, minimal external interference. Deeming such a powerful ontological perspective to be capable of neutrality can be nothing other than an illusion. For the devoted adherents of liberalism, contrary views are anathema, held by enemies of sound morality. This is constantly being demonstrated in the inconsistencies and curiosities occurring in cases where liberal states are required to deal with matters of religion in the narrower sense.[53]

Since academic freedom cannot be absolute, considerations for justifiably imposing limitations on it should reveal the ideological (religious) motives behind the limitation. In constitutional orders that do not subscribe to or do not comply with liberal constitutionalism, the motives behind limitation can be expected to be obvious. Not so in the case of governments or courts of liberal democracies that claim to be secular and therefore neutral in such matters. The actual motives for limiting the freedom to teach and to research in a liberal democracy are often hidden behind broad language premised upon the assumption that liberal doctrine is self-evident. The question however remains: can such limitations be imposed neutrally?

Citing incidents like the accusation of universities by the French minister of higher education that they are promoting 'Islamo-leftism' (understood to be left-wing, anti-racist activism) and launching an investigation into the field of postcolonial studies, Liviu Matei wrote in 2021 that a 'crisis of academic freedom is looming in Europe'. He went on to provide further examples such as the drafting of bills for consideration by US state legislatures intended to prevent the teaching of 'critical race theory', and a white paper in the UK seemingly intended to 'call for radical restrictions of academic freedom in British universities'. Matei described these incidents to be 'in essence, attacks against the very notion of knowledge as a public good' and lamented the absence in Europe of a common understanding of the nature of academic freedom because, in the absence of urgent clarification, the pursuit of political

53 Venter (n 16) 129–178.

agendas allows for serious incursions on academic freedom.[54] The pursuit of political goals is the obvious cause of the limitation of academic freedom in non- or quasi-democratic states and where it occurs in liberal democracies, it also evokes essentially political responses, usually employing the tenets of liberal constitutionalism only indirectly as justification for resisting the incursions – and neutrality in politics is inconceivable.

Maintaining and protecting academic freedom requires the state to desist from imposing its religious prejudices on scholars and universities. Ironically, the notion of academic freedom as an inevitable consequence of the protection of a right not to be hampered in one's self-expression is synonymous with the liberal worldview (religion), which is a prerequisite of liberal democracy. Among the prominent liberal democracies such as the US and Canada, 'neutral' education is understood to be education devoid of religious expression, and in France the historical constitutional ideal was to be liberated *from* religion. Ironically, in such cases all religions in the narrower sense are replaced by the state's liberal religion. The end effect is that supposedly neutral limitations on academic freedom are justified on the *subjective* grounds that the scholarship and teaching concerned do not conform to the tenets of liberalism. Seen thus, there is an irresoluble tension between academic freedom, religion, and state neutrality.

All three concepts are burdened in various degrees with conceptual vagueness, the claim of state neutrality being the most obvious cause of the vagueness. If the effects of the problem are to be mitigated, the illusion of neutrality should be addressed and ideally be removed from the equation. This may be achieved by substituting supposed neutrality with deliberate *objectivity*.

The notion of neutrality is sometimes used when objectivity is intended. However, in the ordinary sense of the word, neutrality represents a subjective choice not to be engaged, involved, or drawn into matters that do not concern the neutral actor. Such is the liberal democratic argument for secular neutrality: the state must maintain a neutral stance in matters of religion because religion is a private matter between the free and equal individual citizens and should therefore in principle be of no concern to the public functions of the state. However, as soon as the constitutional religion of the state is put under pressure by individual conduct, such as the scholarly promotion of ideas inconsistent with the liberal worldview, preventative state action based on subjective considerations is deemed to be justified.

This difficulty can be alleviated without undermining the stability of the liberal democratic state by discarding the illusion of neutrality and replacing it with a demand for objectivity. Objective state conduct, ideally especially in the adjudication of disputes, requires an approach different from neutrality.

54 Liviu Matei, 'The West's crisis of academic freedom' *Project Syndicate* 29 March 2021 https://www.project-syndicate.org/commentary/academic-freedom-crisis-in-west-by-liviu-matei-2021-03 accessed 23 August 2022.

Being 'neutral' removes one from the subject matter and isolates the neutral actor from contesting views. A stance of neutrality wrongly assumes an ability not to be influenced by subjective premises. This is patently wrong because one cannot escape one's personal worldview, even if such worldview proclaims neutrality.

Objectivity, however, requires an admission and recognition of one's subjective preferences and prejudices, followed by a conscious resolution to deal fairly with others. Being objectively fair may require conduct that does not necessarily promote one's subjective preferences, but that takes into account all relevant interests, and to deal with those interests as one would wish others to deal with your interests. This is known as the 'golden rule' of reciprocity.[55]

For the democratic state to find a balance between academic freedom and religion requires a truly objective consideration of all the interests involved in scholarship and education: the legitimate interests of the state, the university, the scholars, and society.

55 Venter (n 16) 28–29 and 83.

9 Gender Equality and Religious Freedom in the Healthcare Context. Some Conflicts Involving Faith-Based Entities in United States' Law[1]

Santiago Cañamares Arribas

Introduction

Quite frequently, the doctrine of most traditional religious denominations comes into conflict with gender equality issues.[2] This reality has sparked some clashes outside the internal arena of confessional groups and has affected other entities created by religious denominations to carry out activities in the wider world, according to a particular religious ethos. For instance, faith schools have refused to teach on gender issues due to conflicts between prevailing secular principles and religious teaching. Similarly, healthcare providers with a religious ethos have refused to carry out certain medical procedures, such as abortions or gender reassignment surgeries.

At the same time, it cannot be ignored that equality laws – or equality clauses incorporated within wider legislative provisions – are being passed by numerous states in order to protect individuals from discrimination on the basis of gender identity, as well as other personal characteristics (e.g., sexuality)

1 This contribution has been financed by the research project funded by the Spanish Ministry of Science and Innovation "Gender Equality and Beliefs in the Framework of the 2030 Agenda". Reference: I+D+i PID2020 114100GB-I00. It has also been developed in the framework of the research activities carried out by REDESOC, a research group at the Universidad Complutense de Madrid. The author expresses his gratitude to Javier García Oliva (University of Manchester) and Helen Hall (Nottingham Trent University) for their invaluable assistance with the style of this contribution.

2 It has been pointed out that traditional religious doctrines are based on the existence of two sexes – male and female – that are intrinsically linked to human reproduction. In consequence, they reject those conceptions of the transgender movement that do not accept dimorphism as a key element in understanding the human species. See P. Parkinson, "Gender Identity Discrimination and Religious Freedom", *Oxford Journal of Law and Religion*, Vol. 38 (2023), pp. 12–13.

DOI: 10.4324/9781003519188-12

and the application of these may have a significant impact on the work of legal entities set up by faith groups.

Given that the concept of "gender" is relatively recent, international human rights texts, as well as domestic constitutions and legislation, do not mention it as a specific ground for protection when enshrining the right to equality. However, Western legal systems have started to protect "gender identity" under the prohibition of sex discrimination.

European Union law provides a good example of this, as the Charter of Fundamental Rights (2000) – one of the most recent supranational human rights texts – does not mention "gender identity" when prohibiting discrimination in Article 21, which quite interestingly mentions sex and sexual orientation as protected personal characteristics.[3]

EU secondary legislation does not refer either to gender identity as an object of protection against discrimination. In this respect, it is interesting to mention the EU Directive 2006/54 on equal treatment of men and women in employment and occupation, whose Explanatory Memorandum points out that in this field the

> Principle of equal treatment for men and women cannot be confined to the prohibition of discrimination based on the fact that a person is of one or other sex. In view of its purpose and the nature of the rights which it seeks to safeguard, it also applies to discrimination arising from the gender reassignment of a person.[4]

This understanding is based on the position adopted by the European Court of Justice in *P v. S and Cornwall County Council* (1996), where it affirmed that

> The scope of the directive cannot be confined simply to discrimination based on the fact that a person is of one or other sex. In view of its purpose and the nature of the rights which it seeks to safeguard, the scope of the directive is also such as to apply to discrimination arising, as in this case, from the gender reassignment of the person concerned. Such discrimination is based, essentially if not exclusively, on the sex of the person concerned. Where a person is dismissed on the ground that he or she intends to undergo, or has undergone, gender reassignment, he or she is treated unfavourably by comparison with persons of the sex to which he or she was deemed to belong before undergoing gender reassignment.

3 See also Articles 10 and 18 of the Treaty on the Functioning of the European Union, which reflect the EU's commitment to the fight against discrimination on grounds of sex and sexual orientation.

4 This is expressly stated in the Preamble of Directive 2006/54/EC of 5 July 2006 on the implementation of the principle of equal opportunities and equal treatment of men and women in matters of employment and occupation. See *Official Journal of the European Union* (OJEU) of 26 July 2006.

> To tolerate such discrimination would be tantamount, as regards such a person, to a failure to respect the dignity and freedom to which he or she is entitled, and which the Court has a duty to safeguard.[5]

Consequently, it can be affirmed that, in EU law, the protection of gender equality covers only transsexual people *stricto sensu*, that is, those who have undergone or intend to undergo sex reassignment surgery – thus not encompassing other situations which may fall under the concept of "gender identity".[6]

In the Council of Europe, the Parliamentary Assembly has tried to combat all forms of intolerance and discrimination based on sexual orientation and gender identity.[7] For the purposes of our study, its Resolution 1728 (2010) on discrimination on the basis of sexual orientation and gender identity[8] is particularly striking. On the one hand, it called on Member States to adopt relevant legislation to combat discrimination on these grounds. However, and very interestingly, this body made room for the introduction of exceptions to this regulation in favour of religious institutions and organisations, when such entities

> Are either engaging in religious activities or when legal requirements conflict with tenets of religious belief and doctrine, or would require such institutions and organizations to forfeit any portion of their religious autonomy, and if such exemptions are compatible with the European Convention on Human Rights, as interpreted by the European Court of Human Rights.[9]

5 Judgement of 30 April 1996, *P v. S and Cornwall County Council*, (Case C-13/94), para. 21–22.

6 It is widely admitted that gender identity goes beyond transgender cases as it includes those who choose other means of manifesting their gender through their personal appearance or manner of behaviour. See generally, European Union Fundamental Rights Agency/Council of Europe, *Handbook on European Non-Discrimination Law* (2018), p. 171.

7 Recommendation 1117 (1989) of 29 September 1989 on the condition of transsexuals. Text available at: https://pace.coe.int/pdf/4bc9d424b7020b3e7158849407773dfa2f6be6763925dce827ad500a048858bf/rec.%201117.pdf (Last visited, 20 April 2024). See also Recommendation 1915 (2010) of 29 April on discrimination on the basis of sexual orientation and gender identity. Text available at: https://pace.coe.int/pdf/2f7aaa53acf2d151fa4d736fb63da8d8f92a4855200795d66f775d43bc6a5ab3/rec.%201915.pdf (Last visited, 20 April 2024).

8 Resolution 1728 (2010) of 29 April on discrimination on the basis of sexual orientation and gender identity. Text available at: https://assembly.coe.int/nw/xml/XRef/Xref-XML2HTML-en.asp?fileid=17853 (Last visited, 20 April 2024).

9 See para. 17. This document invites political leaders to have spaces for dialogue with representatives of religious denominations where debates and reforms on these issues are possible. This same idea is also present in Recommendation CM/Rec(2010)5 of the Committee of Ministers to Member States on measures to combat discrimination on grounds of sexual orientation or gender identity. Text available at: https://rm.coe.int/CoERMPublicCommonSearchServices/DisplayDCTMContent?documentId=09000016804c1743 (Last visited, 20 April 2024).

On the other hand, the case law of the European Court of Human Rights has not been very explicit when protecting gender identity because it has merely stated in *Identoba v. Georgia* (2015)[10] that the prohibition of discrimination, contained in Article 14 of the Convention, covers matters related to sexual orientation and gender identity.

In sharp contrast, in the US legal system there is a clear tendency to protect gender identity under the provisions relating to the prohibition of discrimination on the basis of sex. In this respect, the decision of the US Supreme Court in Bostock (2020)[11] has been crucial since it was made clear that both sexual orientation and gender identity are protected characteristics under the prohibition of discrimination on grounds of sex contained in Title VII of the Civil Rights Act (1964), which is the main statute protecting equality and non-discrimination in employment.[12]

One of the main problems that this broad concept of sex discrimination is raising in US law has to do with its enforcement against religious entities. In fact, Justice Gorsuch affirmed when delivering the opinion of the Court in *Bostock* that compliance with these obligations may force religious denominations to violate their own doctrine.[13] Even more forcefully, Justice Alito, in his dissenting opinion, pointed out that including sexual orientation and gender identity under the concept of "sex discrimination" was irresponsible in the face of the free exercise of religion, as it could trigger an open conflict with employment practices based on religious beliefs carried out by numerous churches, synagogues, mosques, and other religious institutions. Alito agreed that "[r]eligious organizations need employees who actually live the faith", and that "compelling a religious organization to employ individuals whose conduct flouts the tenets of the organization's faith forces the group to communicate an objectionable message".[14]

It is important to remark that this broad understanding of sex discrimination is having ramifications on other federal norms. In fact, relevant conflicts are taking place in the healthcare context because the "anti-discrimination mandate"

10 *Identoba and others v. Georgia* (App. no. 73235/12) of 12 May 2015, para. 96.

11 *Bostock v. Clayton County, Georgia*, 590 U.S. ___, 140 S. Ct. 1731 (2020). On this decision, see generally R.E. Johnson, "Discrimination Because of Sexual Orientation and Gender Identity: The Necessity of the Equality Act in the Wake of Bostock v. Clayton County", *Brigham Young University Law Review*, 47(2) – (2022), pp. 685–710; J.I. Rubio López, "Un barco pirata por aguas de Scalia: Trabajo y sexo; texto e interpretación. A propósito de Bostock v. County of Clayton (2020)", *Revista General de Derecho Canónico y de Derecho Eclesiástico del Estado*, n° 54 (2020).

12 Text available at: https://www.eeoc.gov/statutes/title-vii-civil-rights-act-1964 (Last visited, 3 April 2024).

13 More specifically, the Court stated: "complying with Title VII's requirement in cases like ours may require some employers to violate their religious convictions". *Bostock v. Clayton County*, 140 S. Ct. 1731, (2020), pp. 1753–54.

14 *Bostock v. Clayton County*, 140 S. Ct. 1731, p. 1780.

of the Affordable Care Act (ACA) (2010) – also known as ObamaCare[15] – can potentially force faith-based entities to carry out gender-affirming procedures that are contrary to their religious doctrine. At the same time, this regulation has raised conflicts related to the so-called "contraceptive mandate", i.e., the employer's obligation to subscribe a health insurance for employees covering, among other things, women's access to contraceptive treatments which, in some cases, may result in abortion.

The 'Anti-Discrimination Mandate' of the ACA

Gender Equality and Religious Freedom of Healthcare Entities

The ACA contains an "anti-discrimination mandate" in Section 1557 that prohibits any healthcare entity receiving federal funds, such as hospitals and medical centres, from discriminating against patients on any of the grounds indirectly listed therein.[16]

The wording of this provision is rather confusing as it does not refer directly to any prohibited grounds of discrimination but makes a cross-reference to other federal laws. More precisely, this clause provides that no person may be subjected to discrimination on the grounds prohibited by Title VI of the Civil Rights Act (1964), Title IX of the Education Amendments Act (1972), the Age Discrimination Act (1975), and Section 794 of the Rehabilitation Act (1973).

Thus, put it simply, Section 1557 ACA provides that healthcare entities receiving federal funds may not discriminate against patients "on the basis of race, colour, or national origin" (Title VI of the Civil Rights Act), "on the basis of sex", (Title IX Education Amendments Act), "on the basis of age" (Age Discrimination Act), and "on the basis of disability" (Section 504 of the Rehabilitation Act).

15 See Patients Protection and ACA. Text available at: https://www.govinfo.gov/content/pkg/PLAW-111publ148/pdf/PLAW-111publ148.pdf (Last visited, 3 April 2024).

16 The "anti-discrimination mandate" reads as follows: "Except as otherwise provided for in this title (or an amendment made by this title), an individual shall not, on the ground prohibited under Title VI of the Civil Rights Act of 1964 (42 U.S.C. 2000d et seq.), Title IX of the Education Amendments of 1972 (20 U.S.C. 1681 et seq.), the Age Discrimination Act of 1975 (42 U.S.C. 6101 et seq.), or section 504 of the Rehabilitation Act of 1973 (29 U.S.C. 794), be excluded from participation in, be denied the benefits of, or be subjected to discrimination under, the Health Rehabilitation Act of 1973 (29 U.S.C. 794), or section 504 of the Rehabilitation Act of 1973 (29 U.S.C. 794), or section 504 of the Rehabilitation Act of 1973 (29 U.S.C. 794), be excluded from participation in, be denied the benefits of, or be subjected to discrimination under, any health program or activity, any part of which is receiving Federal financial assistance, including credits, subsidies, or contracts of insurance, or under any program or activity that is administered by an Executive Agency, or any entity established under this title (or amendments)".

Discrimination on the basis of sex is crossed referenced to Title IX of the Education Amendments Act (1972), which states that "no person shall, on the basis of sex, be subjected to discrimination under any education program or activity receiving Federal financial assistance". Quite importantly it contains an exception according to which "this section shall not apply to an educational institution which is controlled by a religious organization if its application would not be consistent with the religious tenets of such organization".

Apart from its complex wording, the incorporation of Title IX of the Education Amendments Act in the ACA's "anti-discrimination mandate" has been the source of different conflicts with religiously inspired healthcare entities. This is mainly because its regulatory developments approved by the health administration have been considered problematic from a religious freedom perspective in relation to two specific aspects. The first one is the scope of the prohibition of sex discrimination contained in Section 901 of the mentioned Title IX since the federal administration interpreted in 2016 that it included "sexual orientation" and "gender identity". The second one has to do with the application of the exception to the prohibition of sex discrimination, recognised in favour of confessional schools, to healthcare providers, disabling application of the relevant provision when it is incompatible with religious doctrine.[17]

In order to develop this "anti-discrimination mandate" of Section 1557 ACA, the Department of Health and Human Services adopted in 2016 some administrative provisions – the so-called 2016 Rules[18] – that included both "sexual orientation" (when based on sexual stereotypes)[19] and "gender identity"[20] within the concept of "sex discrimination".

This regulation was brought before the court by several faith-based healthcare providers who claimed that the health administration exceeded its powers by including gender identity as a sex discrimination issue. Additionally, they considered that its application violated the Religious Freedom Restoration Act

17 Title IX of the Education Amendments provides as follows:
"(a) Prohibition against discrimination; exceptions

> No person in the United States shall, on the basis of sex, be excluded from participation in, be denied the benefits of, or be subjected to discrimination under any education program or activity receiving Federal financial assistance, except that: … (3) Educational institutions of religious organizations with contrary religious tenets this section shall not apply to an educational institution which is controlled by a religious organization if the application of this subsection would not be consistent with the religious tenets of such organization".

18 Text available at: https://www.govinfo.gov/app/details/FR-2016-05-18/2016-11458 (Last visited, 23 April 2024).

19 Sex stereotypes were defined as follows: "stereotypical notions of gender, including expectations of how an individual represents or communicates gender to others, such as behaviour, clothing, hairstyles, activities, voice, mannerisms, or body characteristics".

20 2016 Rules understood "gender identity" as the individual's internal perception of their gender, which can be male, female, neither, or a combination of both.

(RFRA),[21] as it potentially obliged them to carry out gender-related interventions that were substantially contrary to their religious doctrine.

One of the most relevant cases is *Franciscan Alliance*, where a federal court – the District Court for the Northern District of Texas – granted preliminary injunction considering that the health administration exceeded its authority in passing the 2016 Rules. More precisely, according to the text and structure of Title IX of the Education Amendment Act, Congress only intended to prohibit discrimination between biological sexes – that is, without covering other situations based on gender identity – when it passed the prohibition of sex discrimination under the Education Amendment Act.[22]

Besides, the Court declared that the 2016 Rules were contrary to RFRA.[23] Consequently, the ruling prohibited the application of Section 1557 ACA to confessional healthcare entities in order to prevent them from being forced to carry out gender transition interventions or to perform abortions where such treatment was contrary to their religious doctrine.

Indeed, the Court found that the enforcement of the ACA's prohibition of gender discrimination – contained in Section 1557 under the prohibition of sex discrimination – to these entities was contrary to the RFRA, as it substantially burdened their religious freedom – in the form of fines or possible civil liability – without having been proven what impact the exception may have on the compelling interest pursued by this mandate – the protection of gender equality in access to the healthcare system – and whether this was the least restrictive means to achieve it.[24]

21 Article 3 of this regulation states as follows:

"Free Exercise of Religion Protected

(a) In General: Government shall not substantially burden a person's exercise of religion even if the burden results from a rule of general applicability, except as provided in subsection (b).

(b) Exception: Government may substantially burden a person's exercise of religion only if it demonstrates that application of the burden to the person (1) is in furtherance of a compelling governmental interest; and (2) is the least restrictive means of furthering that compelling governmental interest".

Text available at: https://www.congress.gov/bill/103rd-congress/house-bill/1308/text (Last visited, 25 April 2024).

22 *Franciscan Alliance, Inc. v. Burwell*, 227 F. Supp. 3d 660 (N.D. Tex. 2016), p. 669.

23 A reference should be made to the *Sisters of Mercy* case, where a Circuit Court ultimately upheld a District Court's ruling affirming that the "anti-discrimination mandate" could not be applied to the appellant entities with regard to gender reassignment interventions. See *Religious Sisters of Mercy v. Azar*, 513 F. Supp. 3d. 1113, 1122 (D.N.D. 2021), *Religious Sisters of Mercy v. Becerra*, 55 F.4th 583 (8th Cir., 2022).

24 This position was subsequently confirmed by other decisions that granted permanent injunction, affirming that the anti-discrimination mandate or any implementing regulations thereto could not be applied against Franciscan Alliance "in a manner that would require [it] to perform or insure gender-reassignment surgeries or abortions". *Franciscan All., Inc. v. Becerra*,

In 2020, the health administration passed new implementing provisions of the ACA (2020 Rules), which essentially repealed the 2016 Rules by providing that, in light of the provisions of Title IX of the Education Amendments Act, the scope of sex discrimination should be interpreted literally so that it does not include gender identity or sexual orientation.[25]

A few days after the adoption of the new Rules, the Supreme Court handed down the *Bostock* decision, which held that the prohibition of sex discrimination in employment, contained in Title VII of the Civil Rights Act also includes sexual orientation and gender identity. More specifically, the Supreme Court affirmed that firing an employee for being homosexual or transgender is unlawful discrimination that amounts to sex discrimination because "[A]n employer violates Title VII when it intentionally fires an individual employee based in part on sex".[26]

This decision had ramifications in other federal statutes. In fact, in the field of education, a federal court concluded that the prohibition of sex discrimination contained in Title IX of the Education Amendments Act should be interpreted in light of *Bostock*, that is, including sexual orientation and gender identity. More precisely, the Court of Appeal for the Fourth Circuit found in *Grimm* that a transgender student (female to male) had been discriminated against on the basis of sex because the school board initially required him to use the toilets corresponding to his biological sex and subsequently an individual toilet, without being able to use those assigned to his gender identity.[27]

Setting this case aside, the truth is that shortly after *Bostock*, several groups brought the 2020 Rules before the federal courts to broaden the scope of sex discrimination contained in Section 1557 ACA. Ultimately, they sought to invalidate the 2020 Rules and, consequently, to restore the 2016 Rules that included "sex stereotyping" and "gender identity" discrimination within sex discrimination.

In this context, a District Court decided in *Whitman-Walker Clinic, Inc. v. HHS* (2020)[28] that the federal government had failed to comply with the Administrative Procedure Act (1946)[29] when it adopted the 2020 Rules as it had arbitrarily and capriciously excluded "sex stereotyping" from sex

553 F.Supp.3d 361 (N.D. Texas 2021). This decision was upheld by the Court of Appeals in *Franciscan Alliance v. Becerra*, No. 21-11174 (5th Cir. 2022).

25 https://www.federalregister.gov/d/2020-11758/p-41 (Last visited, 20 April 2024).

26 Specifically, the Court stated: "An individual's homosexuality or transgender status is not relevant to employment decisions. That's because it is impossible to discriminate against a person for being homosexual or transgender without discriminating against that individual based on sex". *Bostock v. Clayton County*, cit. p. 9.

27 *Grimm v. Gloucester County School Bd.*, 972 F. 3d 586 – Court of Appeals, 4th Circuit 2020.

28 *Whitman-Walker Clinic, Inc. v. HHS*, 485 F.Supp.3d 1 (District Court, District of Columbia 2020).

29 The text of this federal statute is available at: https://www.justice.gov/sites/default/files/jmd/legacy/2014/05/01/act-pl79-404.pdf (Last visited, 25 April 2024).

discrimination under Section 1557 ACA. In doing so, the administration excluded discrimination on the basis of sexual orientation (when based on sex stereotyping) from the ACA's non-discrimination mandate. Interestingly, the Court found that "gender identity" had not been arbitrarily excluded from sex discrimination, bearing in mind the content of the *Franciscan Alliance* judgement delivered by a federal Court.

Similarly, the District Court of New York decided in *Walker v. Azar* (2020)[30] that the health administration adopted the 2020 Rules in an arbitrary and capricious manner – in contravention of the Administrative Procedure Act – as it did not wait for the Supreme Court's ruling in *Bostock* despite being aware that its content would have implications for the ACA. Accordingly, it decided that neither "sex stereotyping" nor "gender identity" could be excluded from the definition of sex discrimination incorporated in the "anti-discrimination mandate".

Subsequently, President Biden issued an Executive Order[31] establishing that sex discrimination must be interpreted in all federal laws in light of *Bostock*. In consequence, the health administration issued a "Notification of Interpretation and Enforcement of Section 1557 of the ACA and Title IX of the Education Amendments of 1972" providing that the prohibition of "sex discrimination" should be interpreted and applied in light of *Bostock*, which means including sexual orientation and gender identity. At the same time, it explicitly declared that in enforcing Article 1557 ACA, the health administration will respect the provisions of the RFRA and all other legal requirements.[32]

In any case, in March 2022 the federal administration started working on a new proposal of Rules implementing regulations for the "anti-discrimination mandate", which follows the same interpretative path of the 2016 Rules. That means that they include "gender identity" and "sexual orientation" under the prohibition of discrimination on the basis of sex.[33]

Exceptions in Favour of Faith-Based Healthcare Institutions

Section 1557 ACA has also raised some questions regarding the application of the exceptions embedded in Title IX of the Education Amendments Act to

30 *Walker v. Azar*, 480 F.Supp.3d 417 (E.D. New York, 2020).

31 Executive Order "Preventing and Combating Discrimination on the Basis of Gender Identity or Sexual Orientation", Exec. Order No. 13,988, 86 Fed. Reg. 7023 (20 January 2021).
Text available at: https://www.govinfo.gov/content/pkg/FR-2021-01-25/pdf/2021-01761.pdf (Last visited, 23 April 2024)

32 Text available at: https://www.govinfo.gov/content/pkg/FR-2021-05-25/pdf/2021-10477.pdf (Last visited, 20 April 2024).

33 The proposal states as follows: "The Department also proposes to address non-discrimination on the basis of sex, including gender identity and sexual orientation, consistent with *Bostock* and related case law, as well as subsequent Federal agency interpretations". The text of this proposal is accessible at: https://www.govinfo.gov/content/pkg/FR-2022-08-04/pdf/2022-16217.pdf (Last visited 20 April 2024).

healthcare providers in the same way as education institutions. In particular, this exception provides that the prohibition on sex discrimination shall not apply to an educational institution that is controlled by a religious organisation if its application would be inconsistent with the teaching of the faith group in question.

In addition, Title IX also contains an 'Abortion Neutrality provision' that reads as follows,

> [N]othing in this chapter shall be construed to require or prohibit any person, or public or private entity, to provide or pay for any benefit or service, including the use of facilities, related to an abortion. Nothing in this section shall be construed to permit a penalty to be imposed on any person or individual because such person or individual is seeking or has received any benefit or service related to a legal abortion.

The health administration acknowledged the divergence between the educational and healthcare contexts, in both the 2016 and 2020 Rules regarding the incorporation of the religious exemption and the abortion neutrality clause in the ACA's anti-discrimination mandate.

In particular, the 2016 Rules affirmed that "there are significant differences between the educational and health care contexts that warrant different approaches".[34]

First, students or parents selecting religious educational institutions typically do so as a matter of choice.

In the health care context, by contrast, individuals may have limited or no choice of providers, particularly in rural areas or where hospitals have merged with or are run by religious institutions. Moreover, the choice of providers may be even further circumscribed in emergency circumstances.

At the same time, the 2016 Rules considered that a blanket exemption could result in the denial or delay in the provision of healthcare to certain individuals and discourage them from seeking necessary care with serious and even life-threatening consequences.

Because of this lack of incorporation, the Rules included a provision making clear that "where application of this regulation would violate applicable Federal statutory protections for religious freedom and conscience, that application will not be required". Put simply, the healthcare administration considered that the free exercise of religion of faith-based entities was sufficiently protected under the RFRA, so if the prohibition of discrimination on the basis of gender identity resulted in a substantial burden of their religious freedom, it would not be applied unless it is proven to be the less restrictive means to

34 Specifically, the health administration stated: "In addition, we noted that many of Title IX's limitations and exceptions do not readily apply in a context that is grounded in health care, rather than education".

achieve the compelling interest of the government of ensuring the individual's equality rights.

With respect to the "abortion neutrality clause", the 2016 Rules stated that it was not appropriate to incorporate it into Section 1557 ACA because the specific abortion provisions embedded in this Act already provided sufficient protection for healthcare entities, in light of the prohibition against health insurers discriminating against a healthcare provider for its refusal to perform abortions.[35] Besides, in 2020, President Obama issued an Executive Order affirming that under the ACA, the federal healthcare provider conscience laws remain intact, and protections prohibit discrimination against healthcare facilities and healthcare providers based on their unwillingness to provide, pay for, provide coverage of, or refer for abortions.[36]

As previously noted, these 2016 Rules were brought before the Court and in *Franciscan Alliance v. Burwell*, a District Court in Texas stated that the failure to incorporate into the anti-discrimination mandate both the Title IX exception to the prohibition of discrimination on the basis of sex and the abortion neutrality clause was a violation of the Administrative Procedure Act (APA).[37] The District Court reasoned that the specific inclusion of the term "et seq." in the wording of ACA's cross-reference to Title IX can only mean that Congress intended to incorporate its entire statutory structure, including the religious exemptions.[38]

In light of this decision, the 2020 Rules interpreted Section 1557 ACA to incorporate Title IX's religious exemption and the abortion neutrality clause.

35 Section 1303 ACA provides, in relevant part:

> (4) No discrimination on basis of provision of abortion – No qualified health plan offered through an Exchange may discriminate against any individual health care provider or health care facility because of its unwillingness to provide, pay for, provide coverage of, or refer for abortions". See 42 U.S. Code Section 18023 – Special Rules.

36 Executive Order 13535 (24 March 2010), Patient Protection and Affordable Care Act's Consistency with Longstanding Restrictions on the Use of Federal Funds for Abortion. Text available at: https://obamawhitehouse.archives.gov/the-press-office/executive-order-patient-protection-and-affordable-care-acts-consistency-with-longst (Last visit 20 April 2024).

37 The Court noted:

> Therefore, a religious organization refusing to act inconsistent with its religious tenets on the basis of sex does not discriminate on the ground prohibited by Title IX. Failure to incorporate Title IX's religious and abortion exemptions nullifies Congress's specific direction to prohibit only the ground proscribed by Title IX. … By not including these exemptions, HHS expanded the "ground prohibited under" Title IX that Section 1557 explicitly incorporated". *Franciscan Alliance, Inc. v. Burwell*, 227 F. Supp. 3d 660, (Dist. Court, ND Texas, 2016), at 690.

38 The Court went on saying: "Failure to incorporate Title IX's religious and abortion exemptions nullifies Congress's specific direction to prohibit only the ground proscribed by Title IX. That is not permitted. Corley, 556 U.S. at 314, 129 S.Ct. 1558. By not including these exemptions, HHS expanded the 'ground prohibited under' Title IX that Section 1557 explicitly incorporated". See *Franciscan Alliance, Inc. v. Burwell*, 227 F. Supp. 3d 660, at 691.

However, as previously noted, a District Court in *Whitman-Walker* prohibited the incorporation of Title IX's religious exemption, concluding that the health administration did not provide sufficient justification for this change of position *vis-à-vis* the 2016 Rules. More precisely, the Court found that the 2020 Rules incorporated such an exemption without taking into account the consequences it could have on access to healthcare. In consequence, they were contrary to the APA, which requires the administration to take into account all relevant factors when justifying a change of approach. Furthermore, the Court noted that this exclusion did not mean that faith-based healthcare providers were deprived of protection in this field, given that they would continue to enjoy the guarantees of the RFRA.[39]

Finally, it must be recalled that the health administration is currently working on new rules of interpretation of Section 1557 ACA that embrace the same criteria contained in the 2016 Rules. That means that neither the Title IX exceptions for faith-based entities nor the abortion neutrality clause are incorporated into the mandate.

Employing virtually the same arguments as the 2016 Rules, the new proposal points out that since the Title IX exceptions specifically refer to educational institutions, their incorporation into Section 1557 ACA is inappropriate. At the same time, it affirms that the incorporation of such a religious exemption would seriously compromise Congress' primary goal of increasing access to the healthcare system. Additionally, it asserts that Section 1557 ACA, while making a cross-reference to the grounds of prohibited discrimination, expressly refers to the "enforcement mechanisms" of those federal regulations.[40] According to the health administration, that would demonstrate that if Congress had wanted to incorporate other aspects of the cross-referenced regulations – such as the exceptions to their content – it would have done so expressly.

The abortion neutrality clause is not incorporated either within the mandate. In this regard, the proposal expressly states that the Administration is not bound by the Court's decision in *Franciscan Alliance* because there are other statutory and regulatory provisions that may apply to an entity covered

39 The Court affirmed that the 2020 Rule, however, 'said almost nothing' about these important issues ... More fundamentally, nowhere did it consider the 'consequences' of such an exemption for access to care despite the fact that the 'ACA's intended purpose [is] to broaden access to health care' ... To the extent the agency even gestured at these issues, its discussion was patently insufficient to discharge its duty to provide a 'reasoned explanation' for its change in policy". See *Whitman-Walker Clinic v. US Dept. of Health*, 485 F. Supp. 3d 1 (DC, 2020), at 44–46."

40 Indeed, this provision states: "The enforcement mechanisms provided for and available under such title VI, title IX, section 504, or such Age Discrimination Act shall apply for purposes of violations of this subsection".

by Section 1557 that for religious reasons refuses to carry out abortion procedures.[41]

A Contrasting Regulation: the ACA's Contraceptive Mandate

After analysing the conflicts triggered by the application of the anti-discrimination mandate to faith-based healthcare entities, it is worth discussing the position assumed by the administration in relation to the so-called "contraceptive mandate" contained in the ACA.

In general terms, the ACA requires employers to provide their employees with a health insurance plan that covers certain basic matters without cost-sharing. The law does not specify in Section 2713 what services must be covered, it merely requires plans and insurers to cover, *inter alia*, access to certain medical benefits,[42] certain vaccines,[43] and a range of women's benefits set out in the guidelines issued by the Health Resources and Services Administration (HRSA), an agency of the HHS.[44]

Regarding the women's coverage, the HRSA approved the aforementioned guidelines in 2012 requiring health plans and insurers to cover all contraceptive methods approved by the US Food and Drug Administration – known as the "contraceptive mandate" – some of which might lead to abortion.[45] These guidelines sparked a conflict between the health administration, which considered women's access to contraception as an important public health goal, and certain employers who argued that funding these services through their health plans violated their free exercise of religion.

41 The proposal of normative development literally states as follows:

> We acknowledge that the Franciscan Alliance court vacated the challenged provisions of the 2016 rule and reasoned that the Department was required to incorporate the language of Title IX's abortion neutrality provision; however, we disagree with that decision, which does not bind this new rulemaking. The Department does note, however, that there are several other statutory and regulatory provisions related to the provision of abortions that may apply to an entity covered by Section 1557.

42 Specifically, those specified in the "A & B Recommendations" of an independent body called the US Preventive Services Task Force (USPSTF). Text available at: https://www.uspreventiveservicestaskforce.org/uspstf/recommendation-topics/uspstf-a-and-b-recommendations (Last visited, 20 April 2024).

43 Specifically, those recommended by the Advisory Committee on Immunization Practices (ACIP). Text available at: https://www.cdc.gov/vaccines/hcp/acip-recs/index.html (Last visited, 20 April 2024).

44 Text available at: https://www.hrsa.gov/womens-guidelines-2019 (Last visited, 4 August 2023).

45 https://www.hrsa.gov/womens-guidelines-2019 (Last visited, 20 April 2024).

To strike a balance between these interests, these guidelines exempted religious denominations[46] from this obligation. Later versions of these regulations went further by providing that non-profit religious organisations (confessional schools, faith-based universities) could be subject to these obligations only in so far as was compatible with the requirements of their ethos or religious doctrine. Basically, this accommodation allowed such entities to avoid paying directly for the coverage because it shifted the responsibility for providing it to the employer's insurance company and therefore does not place any direct or indirect cost on the religious organisation or its employees.

However, "for-profit employers" were initially excluded from this exemption regardless of whether their business activity was inspired by religious principles. This situation changed when the US Supreme Court decided on *Hobby Lobby* (2014),[47] upholding an appeal brought by the owners of a company who alleged that the obligation to provide contraceptive coverage for their female employees amounted to an infringement of their religious freedom because some of the financed treatments might result in an abortion.

The Supreme Court found that these guidelines violated the RFRA, which protects the free exercise of religion of both natural and legal persons, regardless of whether they are for profit or not.[48] In addition, when carrying out the strict scrutiny imposed by this Act the Court affirmed that the regulations approved by the health administration entailed a burden on the free exercise of religion, since providing coverage for contraception would violate sincerely held religious beliefs as it might cause the death of an human embryo. The Court agreed that the burden was substantial as the contraceptive mandate would force these closely held corporations to violate their religious beliefs or to face severe economic penalties.

The Court also accepted that contraceptive coverage for working women amounted to a compelling state interest in guaranteeing cost-free access to the challenged contraceptive methods. However, it concluded that it had not been proved that forcing closely-held corporations to finance this coverage

46 More precisely, these guidelines referred to religious employers, which means "entities whose primary purpose is to inculcate religious values; which primarily employ and serve people who share the same religious principles; and which are not for profit".

47 *Burwell v. Hobby Lobby Stores, Inc.*, 573 U.S. 682 (2014). On this judgement see generally C. Ciocchetti, "Religious Freedom and Closely Held Corporations: the Hobby Lobby Case and Its Ethical Implications", in *Oregon Law Review*, Vol. 93, no. 2 (2014), pp. 259–354; A.M. Ruiz González, "Repensando los derechos constitucionales de la persona jurídica a la luz del Obamacare", *Revista de estudios políticos*, no. 181, (2018), pp. 187–216; J. Kříž, "Religious Autonomy of Business Corporations: on the Hobby Lobby Judgment", in *Revista General de Derecho Canónico y Derecho Eclesiástico del Estado* 48 (2018).

48 The Supreme Court held that a corporation was a "person" covered by the RFRAct, as it can exercise religion through business practices that are compelled or limited by the tenets of a religious doctrine. See *Hobby Lobby*, 573 U.S. at 701–719. S.G. Wood, B.G. Scharffs, "Applicability of Human Rights Standards to Private Corporations: an American Perspective", in *The American Journal of Comparative Law*, Vol. 50, (2002), pp. 531–566.

was the least restrictive means of achieving this objective, considering that the health administration could apply the same accommodation standard to for-profit entities, already granted to non-profit organisations with a religious character.

Finally, in light of *Hobby Lobby*, the administration approved new guidelines in 2015 that extended the accommodation regime provided for religious non-profit organisations to closely-held corporations, which means for-profit entities that are not publicly traded and are majority owned by a small number of individuals.[49]

However, this was not the end of the conflict between the free exercise of religion and the contraceptive mandate. Some religious non-profit organisations argued that the accommodation procedure which, as noted above, consisted of shifting the obligation to finance contraceptive benefits from the employer to the insurance companies still affected their collective religious freedom because it required an active participation from religious organisations and such collusion would make them morally complicit in the destruction of human life.

These claims were unsuccessful in federal courts. In fact, in *Little Sisters of the Poor* (2015) the Court of Appeals noted that

> [P]laintiffs do not find their rights violated because their task is minimal and purely administrative in nature. All opt-out mechanisms require some act to release objectors from the obligations they face. Logic demands, then, that those objectors who wish to assert their claims do so themselves, without delegating their obligations to other actors.[50]

These clashes were ultimately decided by the Supreme Court in *Zubik v. Burwell* (2016)[51] when resolving an appeal filed by several religious entities claiming that the accommodation provided for in the guidelines approved by the health administration infringed their religious freedom, as it obliged them to take active steps –making a declaration of incompatibility – to be exempt from the contraceptive mandate. In other words, these organisations were opposed not only to direct financing of contraceptive coverage, but also to carry out any other action that would indirectly facilitate or make them complicit in the financing of contraceptive treatment.

In *Zubik*, the Supreme Court did not decide the case on the merits since it did not discuss whether the accommodation procedure entailed a substantial

49 Coverage of Certain Preventive Services Under the ACA, 80 Fed. Reg. 41,318, 41,324 (14 July 2015). Text available at https://www.govinfo.gov/content/pkg/FR-2015-07-14/pdf/2015-17076.pdf (Last visited, 30 April 2024).

50 *Little Sisters of the Poor Home for the Aged, Denver, Colo. v. Burwell*, US Court of Appeals, 794 F.3d 1151 (10th Cir., 2015), p. 1192.

51 *Zubik v. Burwell*, 578 U.S. ___ (2016).

burden of the free exercise of religious non-profit organisations. Equally, it did not make any reference to whether the challenged procedure constituted the least restrictive means to achieve the underlying compelling interest. On the contrary, the Court provided only that the parties would have to agree with the health administration to find an alternative procedure that would not trigger objections from the affected entities.[52]

In consequence of this decision, the health administration published two Interim Final Rules in 2017. The first one extended the automatic religious exemption, which was initially expected to cover only religious entities in favour of any non-governmental employer (including non-closely held corporations) refusing to fund contraception on religious grounds.[53] The second one extended the grounds to the objections of a moral nature ("moral exception"), a different criterion from establishing that the objection to funding was rooted in religious convictions. However, this exception only applied to "closely-held corporations".[54]

These Interim Final Rules were challenged before the Court by Pennsylvania and New Jersey alleging that they were substantively unlawful because the Departments lacked statutory authority under either the ACA or RFRA to promulgate the exemptions at stake. However, their validity was confirmed by the Supreme Court in *Little Sisters of the Poor* (2020)[55] concluding, *inter alia*, that the ACA authorised the administration to establish religious exemptions to the contraceptive mandate and that they were introduced in accordance with the APA.

More precisely, the Supreme Court affirmed that the ACA provides a basis for these exceptions and consequently, there was no need to decide whether RFRA independently compelled a satisfactory solution from the health administration. However, the Court warned that the health administration must take RFRA into account when developing the guidelines in question. However, Justice Alito in his concurring opinion – which Justice Gorsuch joined – affirmed that the Supreme Court should have gone further and stated that "I would hold not only that it was appropriate for the Departments to consider

52 On this issue, see S. Isaacson, "Derechos Establecidos y Nuevos Desafíos que Enfrenta la Objeción de Conciencia en los Estados Unidos" en *Revista General de Derecho Canónico y Derecho Eclesiástico del Estado*, N°. 42, (2016).

53 Interim Final Rules "Religious Exemptions and Accommodations for Coverage of Certain Preventive Services Under the Affordable Care Act", Federal Register / Vol. 82, No. 197 / Friday, 13 October 2017 / Rules and Regulations. Text available at: https://www.govinfo.gov/content/pkg/FR-2017-10-13/pdf/2017-21851.pdf (Last visited, 23 April 2024).

54 Interim Final Rules "Moral Exemptions and Accommodations for Coverage of Certain Preventive Services Under the Affordable Care Act", Federal Register / Vol. 82, No. 197 / Friday, 13 October 2017 / Rules and Regulations. Text available at: https://www.govinfo.gov/content/pkg/FR-2017-10-13/pdf/2017-21852.pdf (Last visited, 20 April 2024).

55 *Little Sisters of the Poor Saints Peter & Paul Home v. Pennsylvania*, 591 U.S. _ (2020).

RFRA, but also that the Departments were required by RFRA to create the religious exemption (or something very close to it)".[56]

Final Remarks

One of the most difficult tasks faced by Western legal systems is harmonising the right to equality and non-discrimination, with the free exercise of religion of both religious denominations and faith-based entities.

Such difficulties are evident in the healthcare context of the US particularly with regard to the application of the "anti-discrimination mandate" and the "contraceptive mandate" contained in the ACA.

It is important to note that the differences between the protection of religious freedom provided by healthcare administration under these mandates are quite striking. With regard to the "contraceptive mandate" many entities have been exempted from its compliance while no exceptions at all have been recognised to the "anti-discrimination mandate" in favour of healthcare institutions with a religious ethos. Therefore, in these latter cases the protection of the free exercise of religion of the concerned entities depends entirely on the application of the strict scrutiny that is embedded in the RFRA.

However, a close reading of the most recent case law of the US Supreme Court reveals that it is far from clear whether this statute will be applied in every case where a faith-based entity considers that the enforcement of the anti-discrimination mandate is infringing its free exercise of religion.

At this point, it is worth mentioning that the Supreme Court in *Fulton v. City of Philadelphia*[57] (2021) did not apply RFRA to resolve a conflict between, on the one hand, the equality provisions contained in both the foster care contract and the Ordinances of the City of Philadelphia and, on the other hand, the free exercise of religion of a Catholic foster care agency that, based on its religious ethos, refused to treat same-sex couples as eligible foster parents. In this case, the Supreme Court decided to apply the Smith test – that is, the rational basis test[58] – because it considered that the local prohibition of discrimination on the basis of sexual orientation did not substantially burden the free exercise of the Catholic foster care agency.[59]

56 *Little Sisters of the Poor v. Pennsylvania*, Alito J. Concurring opinion, p. 19.

57 *Fulton v. City of Philadelphia*, 593 U.S. ___ , 141 S. Ct. 1868 210 L. Ed. 2d 137.

58 *Employment Division Dept. of Human Resources of Oregon v. Smith*, 494 US 872 (1990).

59 However, the Supreme Court considered that this case fell outside *Smith* because the City had burdened the Catholic agency's religious exercise through policies that did not satisfy the threshold requirement of being neutral and generally applicable. More precisely, the non-discrimination requirement of the City's fostercare contract was not generally applicable, since Section 3.21 permitted exceptions at the "sole discretion" of the Commissioner. In consequence the Court concluded that the inclusion of a mechanism for entirely discretionary exceptions renders the non-discrimination provision not generally applicable.

Thus, if we cast this doctrine over the potential conflicts that the ACA's "anti-discrimination mandate" may raise against the free exercise of faith-based healthcare entities, it is highly probable that courts might consider the prohibition of gender discrimination as a neutral and generally applicable rule that does not substantially burden the religious exercise of these entities.

Although there is a growing criticism over the Smith test, it still remains in force, signifying that clarification of its crucial elements by the US Supreme Court is much needed. In particular, the more challenging questions are what does "neutral or generally applicable rule" mean[60] and when does a regulation impose a substantial burden on the free exercise of religion?

However, the protection of religious freedom could be even more compromised in US law if the Equality Act is passed by the Senate in the terms that it has been approved by the House of Representatives.[61] This Bill as drafted accords the right to equality priority over free exercise of other liberties. This would mean that affirming the RFRA of 1993 would not provide a claim concerning, or a defence to a claim under, a covered title, or provide a basis for challenging the application or enforcement of a covered title.[62]

It remains uncertain whether the Bill will be approved by the Senate and also whether it will be considered constitutional by the Supreme Court insofar as it declares inapplicable a super statute – as Gorsuch put it in *Bostock* – when the free exercise of religion collides with the right to equality and non-discrimination. As can be easily understood, this provision goes much further than Smith when protecting religious freedom in the US.

60 It is interesting to recall that the Supreme Court made it clear in *Masterpiece Cakeshop* (2018) that the government does not act neutrally when it acts in a manner that is intolerant to religious beliefs. *Masterpiece Cakeshop v. Colorado Civil Rights Commission*, 584 U.S. ___ (2018); 138 S. Ct. 1719; 201 L. Ed. 2d 35.

61 According to its title, this Act is aimed "To prohibit discrimination on the basis of sex, gender identity, and sexual orientation, and for other purposes". H.R.5 – 117th Congress (2021–2022). The text of this Bill (passed by the House of Representatives) is available at: https://www.congress.gov/bill/117th-congress/house-bill/5 (Last visited, 20 April 2024). In relevant part, the Bill states as follows:

> SEC. 1107. CLAIMS. The Religious Freedom Restoration Act of 1993 (42 U.S.C. 2000bb et seq.) shall not provide a claim concerning, or a defense to a claim under, a covered title, or provide a basis for challenging the application or enforcement of a covered title.

62 See K. Colby, "The Equality Act's Direct Assault on All Americans' Religious Freedom", *Christian Lawyer* 17, no. 1 (Spring 2021), pp. 29–35.

Index

FSC
www.fsc.org
MIX
Papier | Fördert gute Waldnutzung
FSC® C083411

Kolibri 360 GmbH
Ferdinand-Jühlke-Straße 7
99095 Erfurt, Deutschland
produktsicherheit@kolibri360.de